GEOGRAPHY AND SOCIAL MOVEMENTS

Social Movements, Protest, and Contention

Series Editor: Bert Klandermans, Free University, Amsterdam

Associate Editors: Sidney Tarrow, Cornell University
Verta A. Taylor, The Ohio State University
Ron R. Aminzade, University of Minnesota

GEOGRAPHY AND SOCIAL MOVEMENTS

Comparing Antinuclear Activism in the Boston Area

Byron A. Miller

Social Movements, Protest, and Contention
Volume 12

University of Minnesota Press
Minneapolis • London

Portions of this book were previously published in "Collective Action and Rational Choice: Place, Community, and the Limits to Individual Self-Interest," *Economic Geography* 68, no. 1 (1992): 22–42; in "Political Empowerment, Local-Central State Relations, and Geographically Shifting Political Opportunity Structures," *Political Geography* 13, no. 5 (1994): 393–406; and in "Political Action and the Geography of Defense Investment: Geographical Scale and the Representation of the Massachusetts Miracle," *Political Geography* 16, no. 2 (1997): 171–85 (Elsevier Science Ltd.). Reprinted with permission.

Published by the University of Minnesota Press
111 Third Avenue South, Suite 290
Minneapolis, MN 55401-2520
http://www.upress.umn.edu

Library of Congress Cataloging-in-Publication Data

Miller, Byron A., 1957–
Geography and social movements : comparing antinuclear activism in the Boston area / Byron A. Miller.
    p.   cm. — (Social movements, protest, and contention ; v. 12)
Includes bibliographical references and index.
ISBN 0-8166-2950-1 (hc : acid-free) — ISBN 0-8166-2951-X (pb : acid-free)
1. Antinuclear movement—Massachusetts—Boston.   2. Social movements.
3. Social movements—Massachusetts—Boston.   4. Social change.   I. Title.
II. Series.
HD9698.M43 M55 2000
303.48'4—dc21   00-008303

Printed in the United States of America on acid-free paper

The University of Minnesota is an equal-opportunity educator and employer.

11 10 09 08 07 06 05 04 03 02 01 00   10 9 8 7 6 5 4 3 2 1

In memory of
Mary Heath Miller (1930–95),
who worked for peace
and in hope for
a more just and peaceful world
for generations to come

Contents

Acknowledgments

This book could not have come to fruition without the cooperation, help, patience, and support of a great many people. It began as my doctoral research and was originally conceived as a modestly modified version of my dissertation. But things rarely go as planned. In the course of writing this book, the intended ratio of three-quarters dissertation material to one-quarter new material ended up being roughly reversed and the project took on a life of its own (a warning to others pursuing similar projects!). It goes without saying that I have racked up numerous debts of gratitude to many people along the way.

Short of naming several hundred people, it would be impossible to thank all those in the Boston-area peace movement who made the empirical portion of this research possible by granting interviews, filling out questionnaires, and providing access to files and other sources of information. A special debt of gratitude is due key contacts in each of the four Boston-area peace organizations I studied: Olivia Abelson of Cambridge SANE/Freeze; Rachel Rosenblum of the Lexington Committee for a Nuclear Weapons Freeze; Dee Kricker of Waltham Concerned Citizens; and Tony Palomba of Boston Mobilization for Survival. Rob Leavitt of the Institute for Defense and Disarmament Studies also provided considerable assistance in the early stages of this project. Each of these people was more helpful than any researcher could dare hope. They, of course, bear no responsibility for any shortcomings of this project.

Several people at the University of Minnesota provided support in a variety of ways. Eric Sheppard and Helga Leitner were the mentors every young scholar hopes for but few are lucky enough to find. Ron Aminzade and Barbara Laslett provided helpful guidance in the design of this research, and John Adams inspired me to formulate my ideas in a manner that will, hopefully, be persuasive to a broad audience. Will Craig of the University of Minnesota's Center for Urban and Regional Affairs provided helpful suggestions on survey design and the University of Minnesota Graduate School helped defray survey research expenses with a Doctoral Dissertation Special Grant. My good friends Bruce Baum and Jodi Burmeister-May have been good critical sounding boards and important sources of moral support. Deborah Martin, whose own research also deals with the geography of social movements, came to my rescue when I was running out of gas. She collaborated with me on the first chapter of this book and an article manuscript, reenergizing me for the final stretch of this project.

Friends and colleagues at the University of Cincinnati, especially Howard Stafford and Michael Romanos, have been very supportive of my work and have helped me to develop it as a springboard for new research projects on state restructuring and sustainable development in Thailand and Greece. They have patiently waited to see the final version of this project. Your patience has finally paid off: here it is.

Thanks also go to the publishers of *Economic Geography* and *Political Geography* for granting me permission to incorporate reworked portions of three previously published articles into this book.

My greatest debt of gratitude is to my family. My wife, Kristin Miller von Ranson, was the happiest surprise of this project. We met on the first day of my 1990 research trip to Boston and have been together ever since. She has helped me with everything from the mundane to the ethereal and has been a constant source of love and support. Finally, but by no means least, I owe a great deal to my parents, Gus and Mary Miller. My parents raised me to think about the moral and political dimensions of everyday life and my mother's own work in the peace movement likely planted the seed for this research. Her arrest with Carl Sagan and other notable scientists at the Nevada nuclear testing site made clear to me that science and politics are rarely neatly separable and that we, as scientists, must always consider the interests that our work serves. It is to her memory that this book is dedicated.

Introduction

Perspective is at the source of all knowledge. What we see depends on where we stand. . . .

From a car, the intimacy of each bend in the road is reassuring. You can stop and take the measure of the place, revel in its particulars. Each letter or syllable of the topography stands alone, its relation to others not very clear. From the air, the patterns of nature and works of man mingle to make sentences, phrases, pages. . . .

To see from the air is to see philosophically because you see the patterns. But what is the correct height from which to see America? How high do you have to be to see the nation? What is the height of being able to see not just geographically but politically, socially, morally? (Codrescu 1996, 6–10)

Andrei Codrescu, more lyrically than any other author I know, captures the essence of geography. How we see things, and how things fit together, is the essence of geography. One can never stand outside geography. On the contrary, each and every actor, each and every institution, is constituted through it. This is not a trivial matter. Changing the location of things changes how they interact. Changing our own location changes what we see and how we understand. To view the world from a distance allows us to see broadscale interactions, but may also leave us too far removed to see small things that are no less important. To view the world from up close provides an intimacy and experiential richness that is crucial to understanding human actors, but may blind us to the powerful institutional and structural forces in which they act. Clearly, a balanced view of the world requires a variety of geographic lenses.

"Geography," "place," and "space" have received quite a bit of attention in recent years. There has been considerable talk of a "geographic turn" in the social sciences as social scientists have increasingly come to realize that objects of study have no innate essence. Put simply, context matters. How things are constituted in time and space affects how objects act and how processes play out. Yet the extent to which these insights have been incorporated into theory and research has been spotty at best. In this book, I strive to show how the geographic structuring of a social movement has important implications for its mobilization and demobilization, successes and failures. Moreover, I attempt to show that attention to the geography of social movements enriches our understanding of social movements beyond what is possible through aspatial analyses.

I deliberately title this book *Geography and Social Movements* because it is really not about one particular movement, but about the importance of geography in any social movement. The book focuses on space, place, and scale because these are three key geographic concepts that call our attention to the different ways in which geography matters. All social movement processes involve interaction over space, place-specific milieus give rise to synergistic effects and particular circumstances, and scale defines the extent of relevant processes. Geography, however, not only defines the constitution of social movement processes, it is also an "object" of struggle. Altering geography can alter power relations, and so social movements frequently struggle over the construction of geographies. The struggles over, and uses of, space, place, and scale are overlooked in most treatments of social movements.

Of course, human geography never exists separately from social processes, so it is crucial to specify the social theories and categories whose geography will be examined. In chapter 1 I review the major bodies of social movements theory: resource mobilization theory, political process models, and new social movements theory. Special attention is paid to the missing, implicit, and sometimes explicit geographic dimensions of these theories. In chapter 2 I propose a geographic model of social movement mobilization that synthesizes major social movements theories, taking an explicitly geographical perspective. Drawing heavily from Jürgen Habermas's *Theory of Communicative Action*, I look at the geographic constitution of the system (the economy and the state) and the lifeworld (the realm of cultural reproduction). More accurately, I look at systems and lifeworlds, economies, states, and cultures (all plural). Acknowledging a highly differentiated, geographically structured world yields a considerably different understanding of social movement processes than if one simply, and unrealistically, assumes one system and one lifeworld. To flesh out my geographic reconceptualization of Habermas's work, I turn to Henri Lefebvre's conceptualizations of abstract space and social space, which have clear parallels to Habermas's notions of system and lifeworld. Lefebvre's work continues to be an important influence in efforts to rethink aspatial social theories. Within a geographically sensitized metatheory, I then turn to a variety of mid-level theorists who help us to understand the geographies of economies, states, and lifeworlds.

In chapters 3 through 6, I analyze the geographic structuring of one particular social movement—the nuclear arms race–focused branch of the peace movement that captured the attention of the nation and much of the world from the late 1970s to the mid-1980s. It is to better understand the importance of geography in the genesis and unfolding of social movements, generally, that I have chosen to study this movement. The peace movement was, by many accounts, the most visible and successful social movement in the United States in the 1980s. It was, and is today, a very complex phenomenon, overdetermined in several respects.

The peace movement represents conflict over economic interests, state power, and cultural values. This is not the common conceptualization of the peace movement. Much has been written about the peace movement as a "new social movement," primarily a cultural movement that represents a new form of politics or even an antipolitics. Such a conceptualization, I argue, is wrong. It *is* correct to characterize the peace movement as a cultural movement. But it is also a movement that usually draws its following from a particular class base, advocates policies that have particular class effects, strives for state power, and is very geographically uneven.

The peace movement, as with virtually all social movements, represents the articulation of several processes operating at different geographic scales. The massive defense buildup under the Carter and Reagan administrations played a significant role in restructuring the U.S. economy. The effects of this restructuring were unevenly distributed, with some regions benefiting tremendously and others experiencing relative or absolute economic decline. This uneven distribution of economic stimulus affected the mix of interests represented in the political arena as defense industries came to play more significant roles in the economies of many cities and states. Depending on the political efficacy of defense-dependent class fractions, some cities and states competed and lobbied for further defense expenditures. At the same time, the geographic differentiation of defense industry buildups made these very same localities primary targets in the event of nuclear war, a fact not lost on many local peace activists.

The central state was crucial not only for its defense-based economic impact; it was also the political realm in which the decisions that drove the arms race were made. However, given the conservative makeup of the federal government and the strength of the defense industries at this level of the state, the peace movement had little hope of directly affecting central state military policy. Instead, the peace movement stressed local organizing during the early 1980s. Many local peace movement organizations attempted to use local states as platforms from which to challenge central state military policy. The success of these efforts varied greatly, depending in part on local organizational resources and the political structures of local states.

The decisions and actions of local peace movement organizations themselves played a central role in the movement's successes and failures. Different local organizations had to respond to the characteristics of different places. Although the peace movement is generally characterized as a white, middle-class movement, the support of this constituency could not be taken for granted. Moreover, some organizations varied substantially from the norm. Issues of class, race, and gender surfaced to varying degrees in different places. The sociospatial recruitment strategies pursued by different peace movement organizations greatly shaped the alliances that were built across different axes of social identity. These alliances had much to do with the successes of the movement; at the same time, the movement's failure to build some key alliances led to its defeat in some crucial battles.

The most recent "cycle" of peace activism was very complex and provides many potential research foci. After a period of relative inactivity, the movement saw a tremendous resurgence during the late 1970s and early 1980s. The Nuclear Freeze campaign, resistance to Federal Emergency Management Administration (FEMA) nuclear war evacuation planning, and the Nuclear Free Zone movement represented a level of mobilization not seen in the peace movement since the Vietnam War era. Mobilization, however, was not manifest in the same way in all places. Levels, as well as the type of mobilization, varied significantly from place to place.

My intent is to demonstrate the importance of geographic structuring in the mobilization of the peace movement. It is not to provide a comprehensive overview of the last major cycle of peace activism—that has already been accomplished in a number of excellent volumes.[1] To date, there have been relatively few explicitly geographical studies of social movement mobilization, and none that examine space, place, and scale. Cutter, Holcomb, and Shatin (1986) appear to be alone among geographers in examining spatial patterns of support for the Freeze campaign. Although they provide a good "first cut" at explaining the spatial variation of the

Freeze, their reliance on regression analysis and statewide data (examining only one scale) precludes sensitivity to crucial place-specific characteristics and the interaction of sociospatial processes operating at a variety of scales. There are also a number of cross-national comparative studies of the peace movement (e.g., Kitschelt 1986; Kriesi et al. 1995b), but again these studies presume that mobilization can be understood and explained by examining only one scale.

What is sorely lacking in the existing literature is an analysis of local mobilizing efforts and their interactions with broader-scale processes. This is not to argue for a research agenda that addresses only those processes that can be locally circumscribed. Rather, the interaction of spatial processes operating at different scales, as they articulate in place-specific contexts, needs to be examined.

It is with this lacuna in the existing literature in mind that I examine peace movement mobilization in Cambridge, Lexington, and Waltham, Massachusetts, from the late 1970s to the mid-1980s. Why pick these three Boston metropolitan-area municipalities? Because successful social movement mobilization is the focus of this research, a region well known as a center of peace movement activism is most appropriate. Two metropolitan regions have been especially prominent during the most recent cycle of peace protest: Boston and San Francisco. Of the two, the Boston metropolitan area was the center of the principal campaign of the most recent cycle of peace activism: the Nuclear Freeze campaign. The Boston area also spurred a successful campaign (originating in Cambridge) against FEMA's nuclear war evacuation planning directive as well as a highly contentious campaign to ban local nuclear weapons research and development and production activities in Cambridge. The Boston metropolitan area, moreover, is an older metropolitan area with very distinct municipalities, in terms of both class structure and identity. It also has local states with vastly different formal and informal political opportunity structures. For these reasons I have chosen to select cases from within the Boston metropolitan area.

Cambridge, Lexington, and Waltham, Massachusetts (figure 1), are similar in several regards: all share a basic regional history and culture; the high-tech defense industry comprises a significant portion of their local economies (exemplified by Draper Laboratory in Cambridge and Raytheon in both Lexington and Waltham), "bringing home" the war as well as the economic issues of defense contracting; all three are subject to the same general swings in the regional economy; all three are recognized for their distinct and cohesive communities reflecting class and ethnic structures (multiple communities in the cases of Cambridge and Waltham); and peace movement organizations,

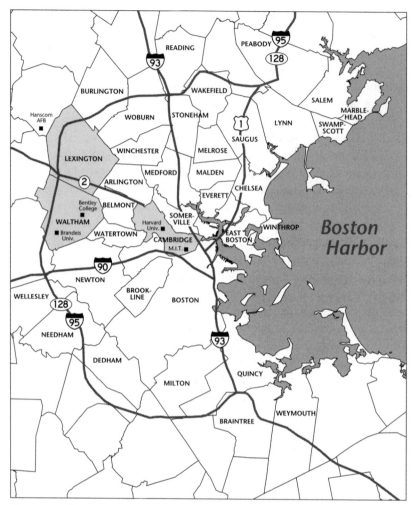

Figure 1. The Boston metropolitan area.

all with decentralized, participatory structures, have been active (albeit to varying degrees) in all three cities.

There are, however, crucial differences in the social geography, history, and political opportunity structures of these municipalities. Cambridge has an extremely heterogeneous class structure and a long history as a center of both learning and industry. Harvard University and the Massachusetts Institute of Technology (MIT) are located in Cambridge; Cambridge boasts a prominent academic/student population, a large working class, and a significant number of professionals working in high-tech (often defense) industries.

Cambridge also has a very open local state: of greatest significance is Cambridge's proportional representation electoral system, which ensures the representation of minority political groups on the city council.

Lexington has a much more homogeneous class structure and a relatively short history as a large town, having grown largely as a result of the high-technology boom around Route 128 since the early 1970s, although it has existed as a small town since pre-Revolutionary War days. Its residents are largely professionals who work in high-technology (often defense) industries. Lexington has no institutions of higher learning and no student or working-class populations to speak of. It does, however, have an extremely open local state based on a town meeting structure of government.

Although Waltham experienced high-tech industrial growth (much of it defense-related) and a concomitant expansion of the middle class in the early 1980s, it has a long history as a working-class city (it is considered a prototypical working-class city by many scholars) and is still predominantly working-class. It is also home to two prominent academic institutions—Brandeis University and Bentley College—although these institutions play a comparatively minor role in the life of the city. The Waltham local state presents a relatively unfavorable political opportunity structure to the peace movement: some councilpersons are elected at large (which is inimical to minority representation) and some by wards, and the political complexion of the city council is generally conservative.

The peace movement has been active in all three municipalities. Peace movement organizations typically exhibit decentralized, participatory structures in all three municipalities. Activism levels during the most recent cycle of protest, however, were very high in Cambridge and Lexington, while a more moderate level of activism was to be found in Waltham (which is in no way to imply that the core activists in Waltham have been less active or devoted than those in other cities). The highest level of activism was to be found in Cambridge; it was, arguably, the center of the national peace movement. Both the middle-class reformist wing (exemplified by SANE/Freeze) and the radical wing (represented by Mobilization for Survival) of the peace movement have been strongly represented in Cambridge.

The peace movement was also strong in Lexington. A sizable proportion of Lexington households (roughly 10 percent through the late 1980s) were members in the very active local Freeze chapter. The radical wing of the peace movement, however, has been virtually nonexistent in Lexington.

The peace movement in Waltham is most difficult to characterize. There was no local chapter of SANE/Freeze, and Mobilization for Survival had few members; there is, however, a very active multi-issue organization, Waltham

Table 1. Case selection following Mill's method of difference

	Cases of agreement		Differing case
	Cambridge	Lexington	Waltham
Overall similarities			
Activism level	extremely high	very high	moderate
Regional economy	New England	New England	New England
Regional culture	New England	New England	New England
Significant nuclear weapons industries	yes Draper Lab/ MIT	yes Raytheon/ Lincoln Lab	yes Raytheon
Sense of local community	strong multiple class/ethnic	strong upper-middle class	strong working-class/ethnic
Structure of peace movement organizations	decentralized participatory	decentralized participatory	decentralized participatory
Crucial differences			
Class structure	working-class/ professional	professional	working-class
Political opportunity structure	very favorable	favorable	unfavorable
Institutions of higher learning	yes Harvard/ MIT	no	yes Brandeis/ Bentley

Concerned Citizens, that has addressed peace as well as local housing and environmental issues.

In sum, the selection of these three municipalities as case studies allows for comparative study following the logic of John Stuart Mill's indirect method of difference.[2]

The Cambridge and Lexington cases are similar in that they exhibit high levels of peace activism, while Waltham, with a more moderate level of activism, provides a contrasting example. All three cases share a number of important similarities: presence of nuclear weapons industries, strong sense(s) of local community, location within the same regional economy and culture, and similarly structured peace movement organizations. There are crucial differences, however, which should help to explain differing levels of activism: political opportunity structures, class structures, and presence of institutions of higher learning. The pattern of differences, with the exception of the presence of institutions of higher learning, differentiates Cambridge and Lexington (with characteristics that are generally recognized as favoring activism) from Waltham. This is in accord with the logic of Mill's indirect method of difference. The one exception to this logic is the presence of institutions of higher learning in Waltham and their absence in Lexington. This departure from the strict logic of Mill's method, however, provides an opportunity to more clearly differentiate the effects of class and political opportunity structures from those of institutions of higher learning in a way that would not be possible were all three characteristics favorable to activism in Lexington and unfavorable in Waltham.

Data for this research come from a variety of sources. Extensive archival records were made available to me by all four organizations. Key organizers were kind enough to grant in-depth interviews. All organizations allowed me to attend board meetings and other gatherings. Newspaper accounts, Census and Department of Defense data, city records, and other secondary sources were invaluable. Also crucial were survey data collected through a questionnaire mailed to members of all four organizations during the summer of 1990.[3] In return for their generous assistance, I incorporated questions of interest to the organizations and provided all four organizations summaries of all the data I collected.

Response rates to the survey were generally high: 73.3 percent of the 120 active members of the Lexington Committee for a Nuclear Weapons Freeze responded (N = 88); 66 percent of the 159 active members of Waltham Concerned Citizens responded (N = 105); 63.5 percent of the 260 active Cambridge members of Boston Mobilization for Survival responded (N = 165); and 47 percent of the active members of Cambridge SANE/Freeze responded (N = 70).[4] Although the response rate for Cambridge SANE/ Freeze members was lower than that of the other organizations, follow-up telephone calls to a sample of nonrespondents failed to reveal any consistent pattern of response bias. By established survey research standards, the response rates suggest that the data collected are very representative of the survey populations (the four organizations).[5] Analysis of these and other data, then, should provide considerable insight into peace mobilization in Cambridge, Lexington, and Waltham.

It should be stressed that although the peace mobilization activities of the four organizations examined here were extremely important and ultimately influenced peace mobilization on a national scale, they do not represent the full spectrum of U.S. peace movement activities from the late 1970s through the mid-1980s. The peace movement, broadly defined, addressed many issues in addition to the nuclear arms race—ending U.S. intervention in Central America and dismantling the apartheid regime in South Africa being foremost among these.[6] Moreover, the four organizations of this study do not represent the full spectrum of the nuclear arms race branch of the peace movement. The Lexington Committee for a Nuclear Weapons Freeze, Waltham Concerned Citizens, the Cambridge contingent of Boston Mobilization for Survival, and Cambridge SANE/Freeze all engaged in electoral politics; for example, they promoted Freeze-related referenda and, in the case of the Cambridge contingent of Boston Mobilization for Survival, a binding referendum that would have halted all nuclear-weapons-related activities within the city of Cambridge. Because of their involvement in electoral politics, these organizations tried to cobble together coalitions that would represent a majority of voters in their municipalities. A majoritarian orientation, at least at election time, meant that identity politics were not strongly emphasized, although such politics did play a role—which varied geographically. In other peace campaigns not addressed here, identity politics played a much more prominent role, the Greenham Commons Women's Peace Camp perhaps being the most well known example (for an excellent account, see Cresswell 1996).

In Cambridge, Lexington, and Waltham, as elsewhere, geographically uneven economic, political, and cultural processes interacted to shape the material circumstances of the lives of potential social movements participants. Material circumstances, in turn, provided the context in which individuals and groups constructed and reconstructed the social identities, meanings, and understandings that would guide their lives. These geographically constituted processes are central to virtually all types of social movement mobilization and alliance building. By coming to better understand the geographic structuring of peace mobilization in Cambridge, Lexington, and Waltham, we will gain insight into the ways in which space, place, and scale matter in social movement mobilization more generally.[7]

1

Missing Geography: Social Movements on the Head of a Pin?

(with Deborah G. Martin)

Geography and Social Movements

Social movements, like all social relations, are geographically constituted[1] (Giddens 1984; Gregory and Urry 1985; Lefebvre 1991). Geographic constitution is fundamental to all processes affecting social movements. Not surprisingly, geographers have been concerned with social movements and other forms of collective action for some time, studying them in a variety of contexts as well as from a variety of theoretical perspectives. Early work by geographers includes that of Sharp (1973) on the diffusion of postal strikes, Demko et al. (1973) on geographic variation in campus unrest, and Adams (1973) on place-based characteristics fostering urban protests. In the 1980s, geographers increasingly turned their attention to urban social movements. Notable studies include those of Cox (1984, 1986, 1988, 1989), Harvey (1985), Cox and Mair (1988), Fincher (1987a), and Harris (1987, 1988). Toward the end of the 1980s, geographic social movements research became increasingly diverse, with considerable attention paid to issues of gender (e.g., Cooke 1985; Fincher and McQuillen 1989; Laws 1994; Staeheli and Cope 1994; Cresswell 1996), labor (e.g., Bennett and Earle 1983; Hudson and Sadler 1986; Herod 1991, 1997; Ellis 1995; Earle 1993), environmental justice (e.g., Pulido 1994, 1996; Heiman 1996), citizenship (e.g., Staeheli 1994; Brown 1997b), peace (e.g., Cutter, Holcomb, and Shatin 1986, 1987; Cutter 1988; Miller 1994, 1997), collective identity construction (e.g., Rogers 1990; Keith and Pile 1993; Marden 1997; Pile and Keith 1997), and the rootedness of social movements in place-specific contexts (e.g., Barnes and Sheppard 1992; Miller 1992; Clark 1993; Routledge 1993, 1994, 1997). This brief survey is by no means exhaustive, nor does it illustrate the diverse array of theoretical perspectives from which geographers have drawn in social movements research.

The early social movements research (and some later research) of geographers was rooted in a positivist epistemology and relied heavily, if usually implicitly, on the theoretical assumptions of the *homo economicus* model of human behavior. Relying on quantitative measures, this research sought general, if not universal, explanations of geographic variation in social movements. The 1980s brought an epistemological and theoretical sea change to human geography, including social movements research. Political economy approaches, rooted in historical materialism and critical realism, became dominant. Class analysis and analysis of the state—both central and local— came to the fore as geographers de-emphasized the search for general, context-independent explanations and instead focused on social struggle in particular geographic contexts. By the late 1980s advances in feminist and poststructuralist theory led to further shifts in geographic research. Recognition of the social construction of social categories, as well as multiple axes of social struggle, resulted in a tremendous broadening of research agendas with attention devoted to a wide array of new social movements and place-specific mobilization processes.

Within the broader and much more extensive sociological and political science literature, there also exist several distinct theoretical and substantive branches of social movements research. Scholars in the United States, for example, have focused their efforts refining resource mobilization theory (RMT), which addresses internal organizational characteristics and argues that money, expertise, networks, and incentives for participation are crucial to movement mobilization (McCarthy and Zald 1977; Jenkins 1983; Kitschelt 1991; Morris and Mueller 1992). Also significant in the United States in recent years has been political process research (Tilly 1978; McAdam 1982; Tarrow 1983, 1989; Jenkins and Klandermans 1995; McAdam, McCarthy, and Zald 1996), which focuses on the ways in which the political environments in which organizations operate—political opportunity structures— shape their capacity to mobilize and achieve goals. European scholars, in contrast, have emphasized the study of new social movements (NSMs), focusing on broad structural changes in Western societies and attendant changes in lifestyles, collective identities, and political demands (Habermas 1984, 1987; Offe 1985; Eder 1985; Melucci 1985, 1989; Touraine 1985; in the United States, Johnston, Laraña, and Gusfield 1994).

A growing number of edited collections indicate that social movements researchers are realizing the need to work across theoretical boundaries (Klandermans, Kriesi, and Tarrow 1988; Rucht 1991; Morris and McClurg Mueller 1992; Johnston, Laraña, and Gusfield 1994; Jenkins and Klandermans 1995; McAdam, McCarthy, and Zald 1996). Increasingly, sociologists and political scientists working in the RMT, political process, and NSM traditions are recognizing the complementarity of their approaches and developing theoretically integrated, synthetic models. Despite these advances, however, there are still significant gaps in the debates and discussion among researchers of social movements. One significant gap is the absence of attention to the geographic structuring of social movements. Although some significant contributions have come from sociology and political science, such research remains largely confined within disciplinary boundaries of geography. One can make a strong case that such disciplinary isolation has been to the detriment of social movements research conducted on all sides of the disciplinary divides. A more geographically sensitive conceptualization of social movements is necessary if social movements are to be understood in their full complexity and variability.

To call for a more geographically sensitive understanding of social movement mobilization is not simply a matter of disciplinary assertion or insecurity. Increasingly, scholars across the social sciences have recognized the central importance of context—both geographical and historical—in shaping social processes. As noted sociologist Anthony Giddens observed in the early 1980s:

> Most social analysts treat time and space as mere environments of action and accept unthinkingly the conception of time, as measurable clock time, characteristic of modern Western culture. With the exception of the recent works of geographers . . . social scientists have failed to construct their thinking around the modes in which social systems are constituted in time-space . . . [I]nvestigation of this issue is one main task imposed by the "problem of order" . . . It is not a specific type or "area" of social science that can be pursued or discarded at will. It is at the very heart of social theory . . . and should hence also be regarded as of very considerable importance for the conduct of empirical research in the social sciences.
>
> Fortunately, we do not need to tackle these issues *de novo*. Over the past few years there has taken place a remarkable convergence between geography and the other social sciences, as a result of which geographers, drawing upon the various established traditions of social theory, have made contributions to social thought of some significance. Most such writings, I think it would be true to say, remain unknown to the majority

of those working in the rest of the social sciences, although they contain ideas of very general application. (1984, 110–11)

With the publication and favorable reception of edited volumes such as Gregory and Urry's (1985) *Social Relations and Spatial Structures,* and the founding of interdisciplinary journals such as *Environment and Planning D: Society and Space,* it appeared that the old Kantian dualism separating "the social" from "the spatial" was beginning to break down and a new era of cross-fertilization between geography and other social sciences was beginning to emerge. This cross-fertilization, however, appears to be primarily a British phenomenon; it has occurred to only a very limited extent in the United States and the rest of the non-British Western world.

Indeed, within the social movements literature there is increasing recognition of the need to pay close attention to context, but in most studies this is largely taken to mean historical context. A case in point is Tarrow's (1983, 1989) illuminating concept of "cycles of protest." Tarrow quite correctly calls our attention to historical fluctuations in social movement mobilization that need to be understood in light of complex "interactions between external political opportunity structure and the mobilization of internal resources" (1983, 34). These interactions need to be examined as they unfold and build upon each other, over time. Tellingly, there is no parallel attention to "spaces of protest" or "places of protest" that would direct the social movements scholar to look at geographic variations in resources, political opportunities, place-specific characteristics, and spatial interactions effecting social movement mobilization.

Geographic concepts are not completely absent from the sociological and political science literature. Tarrow, as early as 1983, briefly discusses the importance of the diffusion of social conflict. He mentions diffusion again in 1989 and in 1996 discusses the role of social networks in the diffusion of national social movements. Hedstrom (1994) also examines diffusion, looking at the contagious spread of trade unionism in Sweden. Katznelson's (1981) classic work, *City Trenches,* can be interpreted as a place-sensitive analysis of workplace and community politics, as can Savage's (1987) brilliant but underappreciated *The Dynamics of Working-Class Politics.* Charlesworth's (1983) edited volume on rural protest in Britain may well be the most thorough mapping of a particular form of social protest to be found in any discipline. Other social movements scholars also make reference to geographic concerns, but by and large, these are the exception. For the most part, geographic structuring is ignored or, at best, treated as a minor side issue. If geography is considered at all, it is typically *(a)* reduced to a separate distance variable to be included among a variety of independent social variables, thereby maintaining the old dualism of "the social" and "the spatial," or *(b)* limited to examination of national-level differences in movement characteristics, thereby incorrectly implying national homogeneity in mobilization processes.[2] Although attention to distance and national differentiation can indeed be illuminating, such emphases represent an extremely truncated version of contemporary geographic conceptualizations.

For all his many insightful and instructive observations, Jenkins (1995) illustrates the aspatiality of most social movements research well. In the second chapter of *The Politics of Social Protest,* "Social Movements, Political Representation, and the State: An Agenda and Comparative Framework," he poses the critical question for social movements research: "How should we proceed?" (33). Jenkins summarizes four suggestions that the contributors to his coedited volume make:

> First, our inquiries should be broadly comparative. *States constitute distinct systems,* making it necessary to treat states as units of observation as well as contexts for study. . . .
>
> Second, *studies of social movements and the state need to be sensitive to temporal processes.* Although cross-sectional studies are useful so long as the analyst is aware of their limitations, the development of movements and their impact is a process that occurs over time. . . .
>
> Third, *the study of social movements needs to address the international aspects of protest.* Past conceptualization has treated movements as prisoners of their states, but there is growing evidence that international components are central . . . Just as "societies" are not always congruent with the boundaries of their "states," so social movements span conventional boundaries, operating at local as well as regional and international levels. As we move toward an increasingly globalized society, social movements become increasingly global. . . .
>
> Fourth, these *studies need to draw on ideas developed in other fields.* Students of the state, for example, have developed a rich conceptual understanding of *the nature of the state and political processes* . . . Similar gains might also come from drawing on *ecological studies of organizations* . . . Discussions of movement identities and ideologies can also gain from *cultural studies.* (33–34; emphasis added)

These are all valuable suggestions that clearly recognize the need to study social movements in context, as well as the potential contributions of a variety of disciplines to the understanding of social movements. Nonetheless, they also betray a conceptualization of the world that barely recognizes the geographic constitution of social processes. National-level states, for instance, may indeed be distinct systems, but they are also internally differentiated with substantial variations among local and regional-level state units that can substantially affect social movement mobilization. Jenkins is correct to argue for attention to temporal processes—diachronic causation cannot be identified otherwise—but similarly, synchronic causation cannot be identified without attention to space. His call to address the international aspects of protest and acknowledgment that social movements operate "at local as well as regional and international levels" represents recognition of geographic differentiation, but still only in a descriptive sense. For the most part, space is viewed as little more than a container for aspatial social processes; there is no recognition that the spatial constitution of mobilization processes affects their operation. Finally, his call to draw on ideas from other fields is welcome, but surprisingly absent is reference to geography, a field centrally concerned with contextualized understanding of social processes.

It is difficult to understand why geography has been overlooked in an era when context is increasingly stressed and numerous prominent social theorists (e.g., Giddens 1981, 1984; Castells 1983; de Certeau 1984; Jameson 1984; Harvey 1989, 1996; Soja 1989; Lefebvre 1991; Mouffe 1995) emphasize its centrality. Certainly, there has been a dramatic rise in the use of spatial metaphors such as "spaces," "fields," "boundaries," "places," "margins" when discussing social processes, but these rarely carry over into analyses of material spatial relations. Smith and Katz (1993) and Silber (1995) have argued that spatial metaphors destabilize positivist and universalist constructs that are increasingly viewed as obsolete, as well as lead readers to think relationally. Smith and Katz (1993) contend, however, such metaphors ultimately appeal to a naturalized, fixed notion of space, providing a false sense of analytic certainty and material grounding, while doing little to illuminate the spatiality of social processes. In interdisciplinary journals such as *Environment and Planning D: Society and Space,* and in cultural studies generally, there has been much discussion of a "geographic turn," but such a turn seems to have much more to do with the advent of postmodernism and poststructuralism—and their frequent employment of spatial metaphors—than with explicit attention to geography. Indeed, Agnew (1995, 380) notes that "the absence of any explicit spatial or contextual referencing in such a major recent compendium of disputes in social thought as Seidman and Wagner (1992) [mentioned by Sheppard (1994)] could lead to the conclusion that there is a *lack* of explicit attention to geography in most contemporary currents of social thought rather than any kind of widespread interest in it." In sum, the absence of geographic analysis within the social movements literature is by no means unique within the social sciences. Why this is so is not entirely clear. It may, in part, have to do with a very problematic understanding of geographic concepts, not only among the general public, but also among social scientists, including geographers! Indeed, human geographers have been debating and altering their concepts virtually continuously since at least the 1930s, and many concepts commonly employed within particular geographic "schools of thought" are frequently ignored within others. In contemporary human geography, space is widely (but by no means universally) seen as socially constructed, just as society is seen as inherently spatially constituted. But there are competing understandings of spatiality and, indeed, different notions of space have dominated geography at different times. A second reason for the dearth of geographic analysis in the social movements literature may be geographers' somewhat spotty attention to the social movements theories of sociology and political science. Recently, geographers have paid a great deal of attention to the new social movements literature, some attention to the resource mobilization literature, and very little attention to the political process literature. Geographers' limited bridge building is compounded by the fact that even when geographers do draw from the major bodies of social movements theory, they tend not to use the term *social movements* in the titles of books and journal articles. Instead, *resistance* increasingly turns up in geographic titles, making it difficult for sociologists and political scientists to readily identify relevant geographic analyses. (It should be noted that *resistance* is a broader term than *social movements*.) A third major reason may have to do with institutional forces maintaining disciplinary boundaries within academia. Frequently, academics are not rewarded for publishing in journals outside their discipline. Moreover, disciplinary communities are harder to build and maintain if the importation of "foreign" ideas is not limited. Undoubtedly the relative absence of geographic analysis within the broad social movements literature can be traced to some combination of these reasons. To suggest that social movements research would benefit from explicit attention to the geographic structuring of social movements requires, in any case, clarification of what it is that geographers mean by their core concept: "space."

Evolving Notions of Space

Not only is space generally not considered to be static and "fixed" in contemporary human geography, but spatial concepts are themselves far from fixed. Widely accepted popular understandings of geography date back to the "old" regional geography last widely practiced in the 1950s. This regional geography was highly empiricist and atheoretical, aiming at the classification and description of regions. Although few geographers today work in this tradition, concepts from this era still show up in game-show "geography" questions, some grade-school geography courses, and occasionally in popular geography magazines.

In the late 1950s and 1960s, geography underwent dual positivist and quantitative revolutions that aimed to put the discipline on a scientific footing. Scientific geography, in its positivist incarnation, aimed at the discovery and construction of laws of human spatial behavior. This new "spatial-analytic" geography became centrally concerned with variations on the question "Why are spatial distributions structured the way they are?" (Abler, Adams, and Gould 1971, 59). To answer this question geographers increasingly turned to large quantitative data sets, statistical analysis, and models borrowed from neoclassical economics and physics that promoted and facilitated a search for spatial order. Two spatial concepts are central to this school: absolute space and relative space. Absolute space is defined by locations on a mathematical grid such as latitude and longitude. "Such locations are absolute in the sense that once a locational description of this kind has been adopted, it does not change over time" (ibid.). Relative space is defined with respect to the relations between a variety of locations. Relative space is expressed in terms of dimensions indicating the relative ease or difficulty of spatial interaction, such as travel time or travel cost. Both forms of space, nonetheless, represent a very narrow conceptualization of space based on various distance-related metrics that facilitate quantification and statistical generalization.

Although spatial-analytic geography represented a switch to generalization and law building, it remained heavily empiricist. Spatial data were taken as a "reflection" of "reality." Indeed, Peter Haggett, one of the major contemporary practitioners of the spatial-analytic school, speaks of "maps as [geographical] mirrors" (1990, 5), borrowing a metaphor from Barbara Tuchman's book on the fourteenth century, *A Distant Mirror.* Tellingly, Haggett approvingly relates physicist Freeman Dyson's use of the same metaphor as well as Dyson's view of the world: "Dyson goes on to argue for a scientific vision of the universe as a harmonious whole in which time past and time future have no absolute existence. For him, as for Einstein, the distinction between past, present and future is only a 'stubbornly persistent illusion'" (ibid., 3). Two points from this quote are particularly salient. One is that the universe is presented as a *whole,* implying the existence of universal laws that operate independently of space and time. Such a view may be defensible in applied physics, but in the social sciences the spatial and temporal variation of open human societies would be difficult to dismiss as an "illusion." The underlying belief structure of positivist scientific geography, with its goal of universal law discovery, consistently downplays the varying and potentially ungeneralizable effects of geographic context. Second is that the universe is a *harmonious* whole. The supposed laws and structures of positivist science are presumed to operate harmoniously; social conflict plays no role. Indeed, social conflict is absent from virtually all explanations put forward by the spatial-analytic school; implicitly, spatial laws are believed to operate in isolation from social forces.

The spatial-analytic school, its concepts of space, and its conceptualization (or lack thereof) of the relationship between society and space began to come under attack in the late 1960s. Sack (1974) criticized the school for its "spatial separatism," the notion that purely spatial explanation and prediction was possible and appropriate. Similar attacks came under the guise of a critique of "spatial fetishism"—an obsession with spatial structure accompanied by a profound neglect of social process. Sack argued that models of spatial structure are appropriate as descriptive devices but that explanation required an understanding of human decision making, which could not be reduced to empirical spatial patterns.

Geography underwent another series of revolutions in the wake of the critique of spatial fetishism and, perhaps more importantly, the social unrest of the late 1960s and early 1970s. As many geographers came to seriously question notions of harmonious, social-context-free spatial systems, adoption of political economy and humanistic approaches became widespread. With these new approaches came dramatically new conceptions of space. Early Marxian-based political economy studies gave explanatory priority to social relations, seeing spatial patterns as the outcome of social struggle. Lipietz's (1977) early work is a good example of this prioritization of the social. Lipietz defined the spatial in terms of a "correspondence between 'presence-absence' in space and 'participation-exclusion' in . . . particular system[s] of social practice" (Gregory 1994b, 583). Based on this formulation, Lipietz identified three social structures of the capitalist mode of production: economic, political-juridical, and ideological—each with its own spaces/topologies, simultaneously existing in the same physical space. Lipietz's work represented a radical departure from prior spatial separatist conceptualizations. Humanistic geography, drawing on existentialism and phenomenology, took a different tack, stressing the understanding, meaning, and value of space and place. Like the emerging political economy approach, humanistic geography (e.g., Entrikin 1976; Tuan 1976; Ley 1978; Buttimer 1979) emphasized the social construction of space and place, but did so putting human agents rather than social structures at the fore.

By the mid-1980s, however, geographers began to come to a consensus that the early political economy and humanistic approaches to geography had their own shortcomings. As Massey put it:

> Essentially, only one half the argument had been followed through. It had been agreed that the spatial is a social construct. But the corollary, that social processes necessarily take place over space, had not been taken on board . . . [Most social scientists] continued to function, by and large, *as though the world operated, and society existed, on the head of a pin, in a spaceless, geographically undifferentiated world.* . . . For "space" was seen as only an outcome; geographical distributions as only the *results* of social processes.
>
> But there is more to it than that. *Spatial distributions and geographical differentiation* may be the result of social processes, but they also *affect how those processes work. "The spatial" is not just an outcome; it is also part of the explanation.* It is not just important for geographers to recognize the social causes of the spatial configurations that they study; it is also important for those in other social sciences to take on board the fact that the processes they study are constructed, reproduced and changed in a way which necessarily involves distance, movement and spatial differentiation. (1984a, 4; emphasis added)

Massey's notion of "the social" and "the spatial" as being mutually constituting is widely accepted among social-theoretically inclined geographers (and many other social scientists) today. This consensus, nonetheless, does not constitute a definition of "space." Indeed, contemporary definitions of "space" contain many components. In an early formulation that still stands up fairly well today, Massey wrote that

> the full meaning of the term "spatial" includes a whole range of aspects of the social world. It includes distance, and differences in the measurement, connotations and appreciation of distance. It includes movement. It includes geographical differentiation, the notion of place and specificity, and of differences between places. And it includes the symbolism and meaning which in different societies, and in different parts of given societies, attach to all of these things. (Ibid., 5)

A definitive contemporary definition of "space" is virtually impossible to provide. Geographers have produced numerous book-length treatments of space and society; most are in broad agreement with Massey's formulation (e.g., Sack 1980, 1986; Gregory and Urry 1985; Pred 1986; Harvey 1989, 1996; Soja 1989; Entrikin 1991; Johnston 1991; Bird et al. 1993; Duncan and Ley 1993; Jones, Natter, and Schatzki 1993; Keith and Pile 1993; Gregory

1994a; Massey 1994; Benko and Strohmayer 1997). It is also important to note that several sociologists have given serious attention to "the spatial" (e.g., Giddens 1981, 1984; Gottdiener 1985; Shields 1991; Friedland and Boden 1994). And one would be remiss not to mention the extremely important work of French social theorist Henri Lefebvre, whose magnum opus, *La production de l'espace* (1974), was published in English in 1991. Lefebvre's writing on "the production of space" has been a powerful influence on some of the most influential social theorists in geography, including David Harvey, Edward Soja, and Derek Gregory. A brief excursus into Lefebvre's conceptualization of space—and its elaboration by David Harvey—followed by consideration of the related concepts of place and scale—should provide a general, although definitely incomplete, outline of contemporary spatial ideas.

Lefebvre's Conception of Space

Henri Lefebvre (1991) argued that to understand the production of space one must examine both its materiality and its representations. Working in a humanistic vein of historical materialism, Lefebvre eschewed both idealist and crudely materialist conceptualizations of space. Instead, he proposed a "spatiality" that included both a "mental space" of perceptions, ideology, and imagination and a "material space" of economic activity, state regulation, and physical infrastructure. For him, the "essential spatial contradiction of society is the confrontation between *abstract space*, or the externalization of economic and political practices originating with the capitalist class and the state, and *social space* [also called concrete space], or the space of use values produced by the complex interaction of all classes in the pursuit of everyday life" (1979, 241). Although Lefebvre saw systematic conflict at the center of modern capitalist societies, he was concerned not only with class conflict, but also with the expansion of capitalist social relations and the gendering of space.

Gregory (1994a) provides a succinct overview of the twin processes producing abstract space (figure 2). Abstract space is produced, first, through "an intensified *commodification of space*, which imposes a geometric grid of property relations and markets on the earth, and an intensified *commodification through space*, which involves the installation of economic grids of capital circulation by means of which abstract space inscribes abstract labor and the commodity form," and second, by "a heightened *bureaucratization of space*, whereby each administrative system 'maps out its own territory, stakes it out and signposts it,' and a heightened *bureaucratization through space*, which involves the installation of juridico-political grids by means of which social life is subject to systematic surveillance and regulation by the state" (1994a, 401).

Abstract space, in other words, is the commercialized, commodified space constructed through capitalist social relations, and the territorialized space constructed through the exercise of state military and police power. It stands in stark contrast to what Lefebvre calls social (or concrete) space. Social space is the space of everyday life rooted in noncommodified and nonbureaucratized spatialities. It is "a space of 'subjects' rather than of calculations" (Lefebvre 1991, 362), of unalienated being-in-the-world.

Many readers will recognize a clear parallel between the core ideas of Lefebvre and those of German social theorist Jürgen Habermas (1984, 1987), who has been a major figure in the development of new social movements theory (discussed later in this chapter and in chapter 2). In particular, Lefebvre's concepts of abstract space and social space are very close to Habermas's notions of the system and the lifeworld. And Lefebvre's treatment of the commodification and bureaucratization of the social spaces of everyday life is virtually identical to Habermas's discussion of the "colonization of the lifeworld." But, as Gregory (1994a) argues, Habermas's failure to discuss the spatial constitution of commodification and bureaucratization represents a major difference between the two theorists. One could argue that the highly abstract character of Habermas's work is directly related to his neglect of space, which is, in turn, related to the difficulty many have had in bringing it to bear on a variety of everyday lived experiences, each with its own spatial constitution and expression.

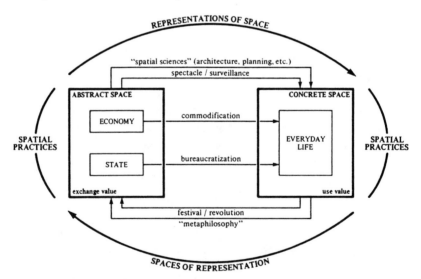

Figure 2. The commodification and bureaucratization of space. Source: Gregory 1994a.

In contrast, Lefebvre provides a nuanced account of spatial practices affecting "the colonization of everyday life [through] the superimposition and hyperextension of abstract space" (Gregory 1994a, 403). As Harvey observes:

> Spatial and temporal practices, in any society, abound in subtleties and complexities. Since they are so closely implicated in processes of reproduction and transformation of social relations, some way has to be found to depict them and generalize about their use. The history of social change is in part captured by the history of the conceptions of space and time, and the ideological uses to which those conceptions might be put. Furthermore, any project to transform society must grasp the complex nettle of the transformation of spatial and temporal conceptions and practices. (1989, 218)

Not surprisingly, Harvey (1989) has drawn extensively from Lefebvre's understanding of the spatial practices shaping modern societies. In particular, he focuses on three forms of spatial practice: "material spatial practices," "representations of space," and "spaces of representation." Drawing from Lefebvre (1991), Harvey summarizes them in a nutshell as "the experienced, the perceived, and the imagined" (1989, 219). He also provides more detailed definitions:

> *Material spatial practices* refer to the physical and material flows, transfers, and interactions that occur in and across space in such a way as to assure production and social reproduction.
>
> *Representations of space* encompass all of the signs and significations, codes and knowledge, that allow such material practices to be talked about and understood, no matter whether in terms of everyday common-sense or through the sometimes arcane jargon of the academic disciplines that deal with spatial practices (engineering, architecture, geography, planning, social ecology, and the like).
>
> *Spaces of representation* are mental inventions (codes, signs, "spatial discourses," utopian plans, imaginary landscapes, and even material constructs such as symbolic spaces, particular built environments, paintings, museums, and the like) that imagine new meanings or possibilities for spatial practices. (1989, 218)

Harvey goes beyond Lefebvre, however, in distinguishing four geographical dimensions of Lefebvre's spatial practices:

> *Accessibility and distanciation* speak to the role of "friction of distance" in human affairs. Distance is both a barrier to, and a defense against, human

interaction. It imposes transaction costs upon any system of production and reproduction. . . .

The *appropriation of space* examines the way in which space is occupied by objects (houses, factories, streets, etc.), activities (land uses), individuals, classes, or other social groupings. Systematized and institutionalized appropriation may entail the production of territorially bounded forms of social solidarity.

The *domination of space* reflects how individuals or powerful groups dominate the organization and production of space through legal or extralegal means. . . .

The *production of space* examines how new systems (actual or imagined) of land use, transport and communications, territorial organization, etc. are produced, and how new modes of representation . . . arise. (Ibid., 219–22)

Based on this 3 by 4 "grid of spatial practices" (table 2), Harvey is able to begin a more detailed discussion of the ways in which social and spatial practices are mutually constituted. Yet the recurring theme of Harvey's work is time-space compression—the restructuring and effective shrinking of space as capital becomes increasingly mobile, whereas Lefebvre's is the colonization of social space—two processes that substantially differ (Gregory 1994a, 398–414). Both, nonetheless, have bearing on the changing nature of particular places. Understanding the dynamics of "place" is crucial to the analysis of social movement mobilization, not only because it directs us to geographically specific social relations, but also because place can be a powerful basis for collective identity construction—a crucial component of virtually all forms of collective action.

Evolving Notions of Place

Many geographers (e.g., Agnew 1987; Entrikin 1991; Johnston 1991) have argued that the concept of "place" is at the very center of contemporary geography. Place, however, like space, has taken on many meanings. The importance of place, and the related experiential concept "sense of place," were emphasized by humanistic geographers in the 1970s as part of the reaction against positivist geography. As such the concept took on a highly subjective, experiential connotation related to humanistic geography's grounding in existentialism and phenomenology. The concept was broadened in the 1980s as economic geographers working from a political economy perspective began examining the ways in which general economic restructuring processes are shaped and altered by place-specific conditions, as well as how places are produced through those general processes (Massey 1984b; Massey and Allen 1984).

Table 2. Grid of spatial practices

	Accessibility and distanciation	Appropriation and use of space	Domination and control of space	Production of space
Material spatial practices (experience)	flows of goods, money, people labor power, information, etc.; transport and communications systems; market and urban hierarchies; agglomeration	land uses and built environments; social spaces and other "turf" designations; social networks of communication and mutual aid	private property in land; state and administrative divisions of space; exclusive communities and neighborhoods; exclusionary zoning and other forms of social control (policing and surveillance)	production of physical infrastructures (transport and communications; built environments; land clearance, etc.); territorial organization of social infrastructures (formal and informal)
Representations of space (perception)	social, psychological, and physical measures of distance; map-making; theories of the "friction of distance" (principle of least effort, social physics, range of a good, central place, and other forms of location theory)	personal space; mental maps of occupied space; spatial hierarchies; symbolic representation of spaces; spatial "discourses"	forbidden spaces; "territorial imperatives"; community; regional culture; nationalism; geopolitics; hierarchies	new systems of mapping, visual representation, communication, etc.; new artistic and architectural "discourses"; semiotics
Spaces of representation (imagination)	attraction/repulsion; distance/ desire; access/denial; transcendence; "medium is the message"	familiarity; hearth and home; open places; places of popular spectacle (streets, squares, markets); iconography and graffiti; advertising	unfamiliarity; spaces of fear; property and possession; monumentality and constructed spaces of ritual; symbolic barriers and symbolic capital; construction of "tradition"; spaces of repression	utopian plans; imaginary landscapes; science-fiction ontologies and space; artists' sketches; mythologies of space and place; poetics of space; spaces of desire

Source: Harvey 1989.

Today, "place" is generally understood as a multidimensional concept. Agnew's (1987, 28) definition probably best captures the general usage of the term by geographers today:

> Interwoven in the concept of place . . . are three major elements: *locale,* the settings in which social relations are constituted (these can be informal or institutional); *location,* the geographical area encompassing the settings for social interaction as defined by social and economic processes operating at a wider scale; and *sense of place,* the local "structure of feeling." Or, by way of example, home, work, school, church, and so on form nodes around which human activities circulate and which *in toto* can create a sense of place, both geographically and socially. Place, therefore, refers to discrete if "elastic" areas in which settings for the constitution of social relations are located and with which people can identify. The "paths" and "projects" of everyday life, to use the language of [Pred's (1984)] time-geography, provide the practical "glue" for place in these three senses.

Place, then, refers to the ways in which social activity and thought are geographically constituted in discrete settings, and how this constitution affects that activity and thought. It includes not only processes of material reproduction, but also the meaningful shaping of lifeworlds.

Place is a crucial concept, above all, because it calls our attention to the spatial or contextual "situatedness" (Agnew 1996) of all human action and institutions. Agnew (1996, 130) notes that most social scientists who take note of context do so in an extremely limited way, usually reducing it either to national territory and its implied cultural significance, or to more localized social group membership and its presumed relationship to individual attitudes and behavior. In both cases space is seen as an incidental outcome of nonspatial social processes. A notion of context rooted in place, in contrast, views human action

> as threading out from the here and now of face-to-face social interaction into more extensive fields of mediated interaction managed by institutions and organizations . . . [In such a view], rather than adding together the categorical traits of an abstracted individual, explanation is better served by establishing the configuration or juxtaposition of stimuli to behavior within a relevant space-time matrix. (Ibid., 131)

In this conceptualization, space cannot be reduced to the elements found within it. Nor can it be reduced to a spatial variable to be added to an otherwise aspatial analysis.

Places are shaped through a variety of processes. Agnew (ibid., 132–33) identifies six particularly important characteristics shaping political activity in particular places: (1) the spatial division of labor effecting class structure, social structure, and community affiliations; (2) communications technology and patterns of accessibility to it; (3) characteristics of local and central states; (4) class, gender, and ethnic divisions and the ways in which they are expressed through local culture, work authority, and history; (5) predominant local bases for collective identity formation, including class, ethnic, and gender divisions as well as place-based identities oriented to the local, regional, or national level; (6) the microgeography of everyday life (e.g., work, residence, school) through which patterns of social interaction are spatially structured.

Apparent in Agnew's list is that "place" is not to be equated with "local." Rather, place is based on a notion of context that incorporates the

> hierarchical (and non-hierarchical) "funneling" of stimuli *across geographical scales* or levels to produce effects on politics and political behavior. These effects can be thought of as coming together in *places* where micro (localized) and macro (wide-ranging) processes of social structuration are jointly mediated. As a result, politics can be mapped not simply as the geographical outcome of non-spatial processes of political choice, but as a spatialized process of political influence and choice. (Ibid., 132; emphasis added)

Place-based contextual effects, then, are not reducible to localized neighborhood effects. They represent the interaction of multiple processes operating at a variety of geographic scales. Such a conceptualization serves to de-emphasize the individual actor as the bearer of clearly defined and stable traits and instead moves the social-geographic context to the fore in the analysis of meanings and causes.

Evolving Notions of Scale

The concept of place clearly carries within it issues of geographic scale. Geographic scale has commonly been thought of "simply as different levels of analysis (from global to local) in which the investigation of political processes is set" (Delaney and Leitner 1997, 93). In recent years, however, many geographers have come to reject the notion of scale as pregiven and unproblematic. Drawing on the framework of Lefebvre and Harvey, one can examine not only the scales at which economic and political material processes operate, but also how they are represented, especially through the rhetoric of political actors. In both respects, scale is taken not as "simply an external fact awaiting discovery but a way of framing conceptions of reality" (ibid., 94–95), which are part and parcel of political struggle. Various social groups and individual actors are "placed in very distinct ways in relation to [the] flows and interconnections [of sociospatial processes]," creating what Massey (1992, 61) calls a "power-geometry."

One way of altering one's position of power with respect to these flows and interconnections is to alter their scale—what Smith (1993, 90) refers to as "jumping scales." Scale, then, is not given, but constructed.

> The construction of scale is not simply a spatial solidification of contested social forces and processes; the corollary also holds. Scale is an active progenitor of specific social processes. In a literal as much as metaphorical way, scale both contains social activity and at the same time provides an already partitioned geography within which social activity takes place. Scale demarcates the sites of social contest, the object as well as the resolution of contest. (Ibid., 101)

Some actors will try to shift the scale of struggle to gain advantage, while others, favored by an extant scale, will attempt to lock it in. The "scale of struggle and the struggle over scale are two sides of the same coin" (Smith 1992, 74). Altering the scale of material processes, such as shifting from regional to national-scale labor bargaining (Herod 1997) or expanding corporate operations overseas, is one means of dramatically changing power relations. Altering scales of representation can have similar effects: "If workers can be persuaded, for example, that space is an open field of play for capital but a closed terrain for themselves, then a crucial advantage accrues to the capitalists . . . power in the realms of representation may end up being as important as power over the materiality of spatial organization itself" (Harvey 1989, 233).

Scale issues are clearly inherent in the strategies of social movements. Scale variations in political opportunity structures, for instance, may cause movements to emphasize decentralized struggle within local states or to focus on the central state. Likewise, contested framings of the appropriate geographic scale at which to address particular social issues may dramatically affect the legitimacy of a movement.

Clearly, the geographic constitution of processes effecting social movement mobilization shapes the operation of those processes. In the following sections, an attempt is made to sketch out some of the geographic research that has direct bearing on the understanding of social movement mobilization. Although much of this research has been conducted by geographers, some very good geographic work has been conducted by nongeographers, and this is incorporated as well. Particular emphasis is placed on the ways in which attention to space, place, and scale might help to provide more powerful formulations of the main bodies of social movements theory: resource mobilization theory, political process models, and new social movements theory.

Geography and Resource Mobilization Theory

Resource mobilization theory (RMT) provided the dominant framework for American social movements research from the mid-1960s through the mid-1980s, and remains important today, although it is increasingly merged with political process and new social movements (NSMs) perspectives. Asserting that the primary determinant of collective action is the availability of resources for protest, RMT has focused on the internal characteristics of social movement organizations. It has paid special attention to the influence of money, leaders, social networks, and organizational form in social movement mobilization (McCarthy and Zald 1973; Jenkins 1983; Gamson 1990 [1975]; Oliver and Marwell 1992). The ability of organizations to mobilize resources, rather than variations in grievances, is considered of central importance. Most of RMT explicitly or implicitly adopts a rational choice framework; the expected benefits to the individual presumably explain the individual's participation in social movements.

As with the spatial-analytic tradition in geography, the influence of neoclassical economic theory is apparent in RMT. Mancur Olson's *The Logic of Collective Action* (1965) was the chief avenue through which neoclassical economic concepts were imported into social movements research, in particular the conceptualization of social movement participants as rational, self-interested, purposive actors who participate in collective action when benefits outweigh costs. Free-ridership is Olson's central dilemma: why would individuals participate in collective action when they benefit regardless of whether they participate? His answer is that selective incentives are required for participation. Empirical evidence, however, shows a great deal of participation without selective incentives. Much of RMT research attempts to explain why many individuals participate in collective action even when selective benefits are not offered.

Many theorists have stressed the importance of shared values and group or community belonging as rational bases for movement participation (Fireman and Gamson 1979; Jenkins 1983; Calhoun 1988). In general, there has been a shift among RMT theorists away from the notion of individual identity as the sole basis from which to theorize social movement mobilization. Jenkins (1983) captures this shift well:

Group solidarity and purposive incentives are collective in that they entail the fusion of personal and collective interests. Movement supporters, like all socialized actors, act in terms of internalized values and sentiments as well as calculations of self-interest. The major task in mobilization, then, is to generate solidarity and moral commitments to the broad collectivities in whose name movements act. (537–38)

Similarly, Morris and Mueller (1992) argue for a broader conception of the rational actor as socially embedded; calculations of costs and benefits need to be seen as socially constructed. Ferree (1992), likewise, argues that the rational actor has too long been considered an isolated, social automaton with no gender, class, or ethnic understanding of his or her identity. Benford (1993b) goes a step further, concluding that RMT alone is insufficient as a framework for examining the complex process of collective identity formation in a social movement. He suggests that analysis of the framing of collective action is crucial, and that this requires a theoretical merging of social-constructionist and RMT approaches. A central issue is that frames of efficacious beliefs vary across time, social movement organizations (SMOs), and movement actors. Unfortunately, Benford's otherwise exemplary analysis does not acknowledge that beliefs—as well as values and collective identity—vary across space and are geographically constituted.

Explicit attention to the geographical dimensions of core RMT issues may prove helpful. In their geographical critique of the rational actor model, Barnes and Sheppard (1992) argue that rational choice theory, on which RMT relies, errs in

assuming a single, essential motive for human action, thereby eliminating other influences by assumption. The solution is to include the [place-based] communities within which people live and work as an integral element in the theoretical analysis of the formation of consciousness, rather than treating them as a contingent modifying factor. . . . Research examining the geographical and historical contexts within which class consciousness arises shows that space and place are deeply implicated in class formation. (14–15)

Geographical context plays a crucial role in the constitution of rational action in part because place-based communities can dramatically and in place-specific ways affect the monitoring of individual behavior, in turn affecting strategic calculation (Miller 1992). Even more significant may be the geographically specific ways in which place-based identities are formed (Thrift and Williams 1987; Miller 1992). Place-based identity construction has been analyzed by numerous geographers (e.g., Tuan 1977; Pred 1986; Agnew 1987, 1989; Keith and Pile 1993; Routledge 1993; Cresswell 1996). Rebecca Smith (1984, 1985), for example, points to the role of place identity in her examination of neighborhood activism in Minneapolis. She argues that participation in a neighborhood organization is tied not only to high levels of home ownership, education, and income, but also to a strong sense of place, as measured through recognition of boundaries and use of the neighborhood name. She found that activists in a neighborhood organization focused many of their activities on increasing a sense of place among residents through social activities and physical improvements.

The spatial structuring of social interaction results in a variety of geographically specific conceptions of class, work, gender, ethnicity, and race (Thrift 1983; Thrift and Williams 1987; Routledge 1993; Gregory 1994b; Cope 1996), as well as place-based identities. Geographically specific constructions of collective identity—whether place-based or not—have implications for the bases on which particular social movement organizations are built, including the possible avenues for and barriers to alliance formation. As Gregory puts it, "the formation of social movements depends upon the ability of their members (whatever their social location) to make sense of what is happening around them and to formulate their views discursively . . . a major task . . . must be to map what Thrift calls, more generally, 'geographies of social knowing and unknowing'" (1989b, 199–200).

One important branch of RMT has been concerned with the networks, groups, and structures through which social movement organizations recruit members. Individuals may join or discover a social movement organization through their existing networks and relationships, thereby sharing a set of attitudes, commitments, and rules for behavior that provide incentives to participate (Friedman and McAdam 1992). Organization is crucial in the recruitment of participants (Oberschall 1973, 1980) and most theorists agree that it enhances the chances for success (e.g., Gamson 1975; cf. Piven and Cloward 1979). Explicitly or implicitly, all organizations employ geographic recruitment strategies with important implications for the organizations' social and resource base, yet accounts of how differing geographies of recruitment affect resource mobilization are relatively rare.

A good illustration of the geography of movement support is evident in Harvey's (1985a) analysis of the class and gender politics of Paris from 1850 to 1870. His discussion of the city's social geography and maps of public meeting places and electoral patterns provide a clear sense of the geography of recruitment and support for the workers' movement. Castells (1983, 146) offers another, albeit brief, example of place-specific recruitment in his discussion of the role of gay bars, social gathering places, businesses, stores, and professional offices in the construction of the San Francisco gay community. Kriesi (1988) also provides a very interesting account of local mobilizing efforts through the case of the Dutch peace movement. Stressing the distinction "between the *national* and the *local/regional level* of structuration" (45), he offers a clear account of how preexisting countercultural network structures vary among six different places, and how those place-specific differences alter recruitment.

In his discussion of the Orcasitas, Madrid, citizens' movement Castells (1983) provides perhaps the most explicit example of the spatial structuring of social interaction and how social networks can be constructed through place building:

> Orcasitas, in common with most shantytowns in Madrid and elsewhere, was a fragmented, hostile, and alienated world, made up of individuals fighting each other for survival. One of the first initiatives of the association was to break down these inner social walls and to establish a cultural bond (for instance, an annual religious parade was organized to honour a Saint who, the leaders said, was going to protect Orcasitas . . .). A major element in this strategy was the building of the association's public hall in the centre of the neighbourhood . . . The hall became the centre of a new communal life, a place where you could take a warm shower, drink beer at a reduced price, play cards, attend meetings, hold discussions with neighbours, and make friends . . . This way a new social world evolved for the neighbourhood with celebrations, picnics, and in shared mobilizations. (1983, 246)

In Orcasitas, citizens created places that would serve as centers of social and cultural bonding, what hooks (1990) calls "homeplaces." Regardless of whether new places and spaces are created, or existing ones utilized, there is clearly a geography to organizational recruitment. Geographic patterns of social, cultural, and economic characteristics give rise to a variety of forms of segregation, spatial inequality, and place-specific patterns of social interaction that establish the baseline conditions for mobilization. Where organizations distribute leaflets, march in parades, circulate petitions, canvass, protest, run advertisements, and participate in community events directly influences which audiences will and will not hear the organizations' message, in turn affecting who is likely to join, and consequently the resources that will be at the organizations' disposal.

Of course, the geography of recruitment activity does not alone determine an organization's membership and resources. Also critical are the ways in which issues are framed and how these frames resonate with various populations; to this there is also a geography.

A rapidly expanding literature on framing has developed out of the RMT and NSMs literatures (e.g., Feree and Miller 1985; Snow et al. 1986; Klandermans 1988; Snow and Benford 1988, 1992; Benford 1993a, 1993b; Gamson and Meyer 1996). This literature examines the "politics of signification," or, in other words, how social movements "frame, or assign meaning to and interpret, relevant events and conditions in ways that are intended to mobilize potential adherents and constituents, to garner bystander support, and to demobilize antagonists" (Snow and Benford 1988, 198). A central issue is whether the "framing strike[s] a responsive chord with those individuals for whom it is intended" (207). An affirmative answer depends on the *empirical credibility* (fit with events), *experiential commensurability* (personal experience of the target populations), and *narrative fidelity* (resonance with cultural stories, myths) of the framing (ibid., 208). Events, experiences, and cultural narratives exhibit substantial geographic differentiation. Accordingly, one should not expect the same framing to be equally efficacious everywhere. Indeed, a framing that may be highly effective in one place may be completely ineffective in other places (e.g., Brown 1997a). Snow and Benford suggest the importance of geographic differentiation in their discussion of differences in the experiential commensurability of American, Japanese, and Western European peace movement framings. Their discussion, however, only recognizes geographic differentiation at the national scale. Yet geographic differentiation occurs at all scales and national scale differences are not always the most significant.

Cresswell (1996) provides a unique and compelling analysis of the construction and interpretation of meaning at the scale of every day lifeworlds, with important implications for the resonance of social movement frames. He shows that

> spatial structures and the system of places provide historically contingent but durable "schemes of perception" that have an ideological dimension. In particular, the place of an act is an active participant in our understanding of what is good, just, and appropriate. (16)

> "Normality" is defined, to a significant degree, geographically, and deviance from this normality is also shot through with geographical assumptions concerning what and who belong where. (27)

Cresswell convincingly illustrates his argument through three case studies, including one of the Greenham Common women's peace camp. The women's peace camp attracted a great deal of attention in substantial measure because the women transgressed place-specific norms of appropriate behavior. Acting in a carnivalesque manner that was "out of place" (both literally and metaphorically), they "denaturalized the dominant order [and] showed people that what seemed natural, could, in fact, be otherwise" (125). The women's peace camp members deliberately framed their message to challenge the dominant norms of "proper" place-based behavior.

Analysis of the geographic constitution of resource mobilization, then, can hardly be confined to recognition of national-scale differences. Social movement mobilization is geographically constituted at a variety of scales, operates in place-specific contexts, draws on place-based and place-structured identities, and employs spatial strategies. Not infrequently social movement organizations strive to create their own places and spaces as part of the mobilization process. But it would be insufficient to stop at the analysis of social movement organizations. Organizations operate in broader, geographically constituted, political contexts.

Geography and Political Process Models

Political process models have their roots in Eisinger's influential article "The Conditions of Protest Behavior in American Cities" (1973). In contrast to the sociological literature of the time, Eisinger argued that it was reasonable to assume that "the incidence of protest . . . is related to the nature of the [political] opportunity structure" (12). This he defined in terms of the relative openness or closure of municipal government structures in U.S. cities. Eisinger's rather narrow definition has since been expanded by other social movement theorists (Tilly 1978, 1984; McAdam 1982, 1996; Tarrow 1983, 1989, 1996), but all conceptualizations stress the importance of the relationship between internal organizational characteristics and the external political environment. As Tilly (1978) puts it, the actions of social movement organizations and their outcomes "result from an *interaction* between challengers and other groups . . . they result from the interplay of interests, organization, and mobilization, on the one side, and of repression/facilitation, power, and opportunity/threat, on the other" (138).

Analytically, political process models represent a shift away from a virtually exclusive focus on actors—individual or collective—toward attention to the political context of action. Although various authors differ on the specific aspects of political context that count most, there seems to be a broad consensus that both the formal institutional structures and the informal constellation of power relations in a political system are important. Surveying the literature, McAdam (1996, 27) finds a high degree of consensus on the key dimensions of political opportunity:

1. The relative openness or closure of the institutionalized political system.
2. The stability or instability of that broad set of elite alignments that typically undergird a polity.
3. The presence or absence of elite allies.
4. The state's capacity and propensity for repression.

These dimensions very closely resemble Tarrow's (1983, 1989) definition of political opportunity structures. Tarrow's conceptualization is not meant to be static, however. He observes that there are times in which constraints are relaxed and resources are mobilized so as to produce "periods of general mobilization in whole social systems" giving rise to "cycles of protest." During given historic periods, cycles of protest will arise across social and economic sectors as "a climate of optimism brought about by the delegitimation of old elites" produces new waves of mass support for change and emboldens leaders to "seize historic opportunities" (Tarrow 1983, 37).

Yet political opportunities are as much geographic as they are historic. All four dimensions of political opportunity clearly exhibit geographic variation. Political systems are more open in particular places and at particular scales; elite alignments are rarely stable everywhere; the presence or absence of elite allies varies from place to place; the state's capacity and propensity for repression vary not only among states but also among regions and highly localized geographic areas within states.

Early political process models grew out of a strong sense that protest activity needed to be understood in *historic and geographic context*. No clearer statement of this need can be found than Lipsky's 1970 call for social scientists to redirect their analyses

> away from system characterizations presumably true for all times and all places. . . . Should it not at least be an open question as to whether the American political system experiences . . . stages and fluctuations? Similarly, is it not sensible to assume that the system will be more or less open to specific groups at *different times* and at *different places?* (Lipsky 1970, 14; emphasis added)

It is surprising, then, to find no notion of "spaces of protest," "places of protest," or "landscapes of protest" in the political process literature. Social movements obviously start some*where*—most likely in *places* where political opportunities are ample, and diffuse across *space* to other *places*—most likely to where political opportunities are also relatively favorable. In the broad political process literature, the geographic constitution of political opportunity remains severely underdeveloped, and any notion of geographically uneven political opportunity is vague and indirect at best.

To the extent that the literature does address geographic variation in political opportunity, it does so almost exclusively at the national level. Kitschelt's (1986) well-known study of the political structure of four democratic states (France, Sweden, West Germany, and the United States) investigates the ability and willingness of governments to respond to grassroots challenges, and to incorporate those challenges into public policy. This work explicitly recognizes geographical differences in political frameworks and public policies, but, as with numerous other studies (e.g., Kriesi 1995; Opp et al. 1995; Dalton 1995; Nollert 1995; Wallace and Jenkins 1995; Rucht 1996), only at the national level.

Likewise, diffusion studies found in sociology and political science focus almost exclusively on the cross-national spread of social movements (e.g., McAdam and Rucht 1993; Kriesi et al. 1995a) and, with rare exceptions (e.g., Hedstrom 1994), ignore the diffusion literature found in geography. This lack of disciplinary cross-fertilization is quite surprising, given that diffusion has been a major research focus in geography since the 1960s and most geographic studies have examined diffusion at a variety of subnational scales (e.g., Hagerstrand 1968, 1970, 1975, 1982; Yapa 1977; Blaikie 1978; Carlstein, Parkes, and Thrift 1978; Gregory 1985). Review of the intense debates that have taken place in the geographic literature is beyond the scope of this book, but it should be stressed that contemporary models of geographic diffusion stress the centrality of the structural arrangements that constitute interaction matrices, resistances, barriers, and so forth. Although these models generally have not been applied to the diffusion of social movements (cf. Earle 1993; Hedstrom 1994), it should be noted that they could be adapted to do so, incorporating a notion of political opportunity structures that vary by scale and place.

There are some exceptions to the typical national-level focus of the political opportunity literature. Charlesworth's (1983) atlas of rural protest in Britain connects the spatial patterning of collective protest to repressive measures taken by the authorities, but the theoretical implications of this observation remain underdeveloped. McAdam (1988), in an illuminating analysis of Freedom Summer, briefly discusses the "geographic context" of Mississippi, specifically its social and economic conditions, as well as aspects of state repression. Nonetheless, geographic variations in political opportunity receive no systematic treatment. Tarrow (1988), on the other hand, provides a detailed analysis of a cycle of religious protest that seeks to explain, through example, why "social movements appear only in some sites and not in others" (283). Tarrow's analysis includes a nuanced account of differing resources, conflicts, and political opportunities within the city and region of Florence, the Isolotto neighborhood of Florence, as well as the Florentine church.

In an edited volume that otherwise addresses only national political opportunity structures, Kriesi (1995) provides a very interesting analysis of the political opportunity structures of new social movements. He argues:

> The degree of formal access to the state is, first, a function of the degree of its (territorial) centralization. The greater the degree of decentralization, the greater is the degree of formal access. Decentralization implies multiple points of access. In a federal system, such as those of Germany, Switzerland, and the United States, there are *multiple points of relevant access on the national, regional, and local levels.* (171; emphasis added)

Kriesi also discusses other factors affecting formal access to the state: the functional concentration of state power, coherence of public administration, and the degree to which direct democratic procedures, such as popular initiatives and referenda, are institutionalized. An important theme of his analysis is that states are internally (geographically) differentiated, that political opportunities differ at different levels of the state, and that this differentiation affects social movement mobilization and success. However, with the exception of the Swiss case, his general argument is "restricted to the national POS level." He starts "from the general idea that the national POS level . . . constitutes the major point of reference" (193), but nonetheless concludes that "we have to allow for the fact that in some instances, the sub- or supra-national opportunity structure is at least as relevant for the mobilization of a specific conjunctural movement as the national one" (ibid.).

One could easily make the case that subnational opportunity structures are highly relevant in all three of the federal states to which Kriesi refers. McAdam (1996, 49–50), for instance, argues that "the federal American state produced movements that were more often couched at the state and local levels" and that "intranational variations" are an important aspect of social movement dynamics—although the latter argument is primarily posed in terms of aspatially conceived social sectors rather than social and political geography.

Broadbent (1988) provides one of the few analyses found in the sociological literature addressing the relationship between political opportunity and shifting geographic scales of governmental control. He examines "how two local governments within the same area [of Japan], the Oita prefectural government and the Oita City government, responded differently to similar demands" (134) for increased public participation. Broadbent's account shows how shifting party control and interest group alliances at the urban and regional scales affected the openness of the political system. "In one case, a city government backed by the Japan Socialist Party allowed thorough participation. In the other, the prefectural government backed by the Liberal Democratic Party located in the same city allowed only superficial participation" (132). Broadbent attributes these differences to different "structural contexts," but his analysis makes clear how important the shifting geographic scale of "structural context" is.

In contrast to the national focus of the sociological and political science literature, a large literature within geography focuses on the local state (e.g., Clark and Dear 1984; Duncan and Goodwin 1988; Duncan, Goodwin, and Halford 1988; Peck and Tickell 1992; Goodwin, Duncan, and Halford 1993; Bakshi et al. 1995). Although a comprehensive review of this literature is beyond the present purview, it should be noted that most accounts in this literature grant the local state some degree of autonomy from the central state. In other words, the local state is seen as a forum of real social struggle and its institutions can be instruments for real social change—both emancipatory and repressive. The local state is not seen as a simple reflection of the central state. Although it derives its powers from the central state, it has its own formal structures. Local governments, moreover, have their own constellations of political alliances. In short, local states exhibit structures of political opportunity that may differ substantially from each other as well as from the central state.

These geographic differences have important implications for the spatial strategies of social movements. If movements mobilize more readily where political opportunity structures are favorable, either decentralized or centralized mobilization strategies may be appropriate, depending on the opportunities present at the central versus local states. Many major American social movements began, in fact, as highly decentralized locally oriented movements that that aimed at capturing power and effecting change locally. Only after successfully mobilizing public opinion through a decentralized strategy did they switch their focus to the scale of the central state.

There is a significant and rapidly growing literature on the politics of scale in the contemporary geographical literature. A number of studies examine how political movements struggle to shift the scale of political contests to take advantage of more favorable political conditions (e.g., Herod 1991, 1997; Massey 1992; Smith 1992; Miller 1994). Likewise, political movements will try to legitimize their own demands and delegitimize their opponents through scale-specific representations that raise questions about the appropriateness of claims and actions (e.g., Harvey 1989; Herod 1991, 1997; Jonas 1994; Miller 1994, 1997). Virtually all of this literature, moreover, recognizes scale as socially constructed. Scale is not pregiven, but is itself an "object" of struggle with political consequences (Massey 1992; Smith 1992, 1993; Agnew 1993, 1996; Jonas 1994; Delaney and Leitner 1997; Herod 1997; Leitner 1997; Miller 1997). Acknowledgment of the social construction of scale suggests broader questions regarding the social construction of the collective identities and political alliances that lie at the core of social movement mobilization—issues that are taken up most directly in the new social movements (NSM) literature.

Geography and New Social Movements

Most scholars argue that NSMs are less interested in class-based concerns than they are in issues such as the environment, peace, religion, sexuality, or women's emancipation (Habermas 1981; Melucci 1988; Buechler 1995). NSMs are generally understood to be about creating or defending certain collective identities and forms of life against the intrusion of the state or the economy. Many theorists consider NSMs to be nonclass movements (e.g., Touraine 1985; Klandermans and Tarrow 1988), although that characterization is increasingly questioned. Core NSM issues do not directly concern economic redistribution and thus are not explicitly class-oriented, but the social base of NSMs is often class-specific. Offe (1985) argues that NSMs are in fact more middle-class movements than classless movements. Other analysts have used the term *new class* to indicate the middle-class and professional base of most NSMs (Ehrenreich and Ehrenreich 1977; Gouldner 1979; Eder 1993; Wallace and Jenkins 1995). The new class literature argues that people with the education, income, and time flexibility needed to protest or defend their cultural identities are, by and large, those of the middle classes. Others have explicitly argued that the class/culture dichotomy set up in much of the NSM literature is a red herring. Plotke (1990) expresses this last position well: "proponents of new social movement discourse are right to insist that contemporary collective action really is about culture, not merely about cultural expression of class elements. But this is not very new. In the US class conflict has always existed alongside cultural, ethnic, and racial struggle, never as a pure form" (89). In sum, while cultural and class grievances differ substantially, all social actors simultaneously occupy both cultural and class positions. Mobilization around issues in one realm is bound to be affected by, and have repercussions in, the other.

Although there have been a great many influences on new social movements theory (e.g., Melucci 1980, 1985, 1988; Habermas 1981, 1984, 1987;

Touraine 1981, 1985, 1992; Castells 1983; Cohen 1985; Laclau and Mouffe 1985; Offe 1985), most conceptualizations are, in broad outline, Habermasian (see also Hannigan 1985; Rucht 1988; Buechler 1995). In *The Theory of Communicative Action* (1984, 1987), Habermas identifies two separate but interdependent spheres within society—the system and the lifeworld. The lifeworld is a symbolic space of collectively shared background convictions within which cultural traditions, social integration, values, and institutions are reproduced and modified through ongoing interpretive processes. These processes are rooted in communicative action, a form of rational, noncoercive, communicative exchange aimed at understanding rather than instrumental or strategic manipulation. The system, in contrast, is the sphere of the economy and the state. Action in the economy and the state is coordinated through instrumentally and strategically rational action that is oriented toward success, rather than understanding. Through the media of money and power, more and more of daily life becomes commodified and bureaucratized. This "colonization of the lifeworld" by the system is, according to Habermas, the central dilemma of modernity and the impetus giving rise to NSMs that seek to defend, restore, or create new spaces for a communicatively based lifeworld. Habermas's schema has strong parallels to the spatially sensitive work of Lefebvre, but lacking a sensitivity to spatial differentiation, Habermas's work has proven vulnerable to a number of critiques.

Habermas's analysis has been critiqued from a variety of perspectives. Embodying the spirit of communicative action, Habermas has offered thoughtful replies to many of his critics in several edited books (e.g., Thompson and Held 1982; Bernstein 1985; Dews 1986; Honneth and Joas 1991) and in the process revised his own thinking. He remains resistant, however, to the most fundamental critiques of his work—those deriving from poststructuralism.

Rejecting rationalism, the Enlightenment, universalism, and essentialism, poststructuralists criticize

> the idea of a universal human nature, of a universal canon of rationality through which that nature could be known, as well as the possibility of a universal truth. Such a critique of rationalism and universalism, which is sometimes referred to as "postmodern" [or poststructuralist], is seen by authors like Jürgen Habermas as a threat to the modern democratic ideal. They affirm that there is a necessary link between the democratic project of the Enlightenment and its epistemological approach and that, as a consequence, to find fault with rationalism and universalism means under-

mining the very basis of democracy. This explains the hostility of Habermas and his followers towards the different forms of post-Marxism, poststructuralism, and postmodernism. (Mouffe 1995, 259)

Habermas's earlier formulations, including those of his magnum opus, *The Theory of Communicative Action,* did indeed contain universalistic overtones, little theoretical attention to difference, and a defense of modernity, albeit in terms quite different from most such defenses. In contrast, poststructuralists have emphasized the free play of signifiers, incommensurable language games, antirationalism, antiuniversalism, and explicit attention to difference—often linked to geographic differentiation. It is not surprising, then, that many recent treatments of NSMs have drawn heavily from poststructuralism (e.g., Laclau and Mouffe 1985; Young 1990; Escobar and Alvarez 1992; Mouffe 1993; Cresswell 1996; Probyn 1996), and many identity-oriented NSMs implicitly make poststructuralist arguments.

Yet in many respects, the differences between Mouffe, on the one hand, and Habermas, on the other, seem overdrawn. Both owe a substantial intellectual debt to historical materialism, while recognizing the need to substantially revise it. Both have stressed the roles of ideology and conscious human action in social movements. And both are, ultimately, committed to radical democratic politics. Although Habermas's dichotomy of system and lifeworld—instead of emphasizing systems and lifeworlds—is highly problematic, his position does not imply the assimilation or reduction of differences into one universal lifeworld perspective, as poststructuralists often claim. His notion of communicative rationality, on the contrary, presumes the expression of difference that is respected and altered only by mutual, noncoercive consent. As Dews (1986, 24) summarizes: "Habermas's theory of consensus has nothing to do with the homogenization of language-games, or with the establishment of the supremacy of one language-game, but rather with the condition of possibility of plurality." As Habermas (interviewed in Dews 1986, 107) has himself asserted, "Modern lifeworlds are differentiated and should remain so in order that the reflexivity of traditions, the individuation of the social subject, and the universalistic foundations of justice and morality do not all go to hell."

These "universalistic foundations of justice and morality" lie not in universal outcomes but in universal conditions of respect, noncoercion, and mutuality under which communicatively rational dialogue can occur. Nonetheless, Habermas's neglect of geographic differentiation—and the variety of identities and lifeworlds it implies—has led him to substantially underestimate the difficulties of negotiating and resolving grievances across lifeworlds (Young 1990; Mouffe 1995).

Mouffe stresses that identities are contingent, differentiated, and relational, and thus pose dilemmas for consensus building. But she, sounding very much like Habermas discussing communicative rationality, argues that "an 'adversary' [should be regarded as] somebody with whose ideas we are going to struggle, but whose right to defend those ideas we will not put into question" (1995, 263). How, then, to find ground for a common emancipatory politics in a world of differentiation? She argues that social movements must locate "hegemonic nodal points" (264). These nodal points, as Jones and Moss (1995, 255) explain, are "temporary fixations around which identities—and politics—are sutured." Mouffe (1995, 264) explicitly recognizes that "not only are there no 'natural' and 'original' identities, since every identity is the result of a constituting process, but that this process itself must be seen as one of permanent hybridization and nomadization. Identity is, in effect, the result of a multitude of interactions which take place inside a space, the outlines of which are not clearly defined."

Although Mouffe and Habermas both seek a basis on which to build a radical democratic politics, they do so from diametrically opposed sociospatial perspectives. Habermas, on the one hand, virtually ignores sociospatial dialectics and thus underestimates sociospatial differentiation and many of the attendant dilemmas it poses for building a consensual basis for emancipatory politics. Mouffe, on the other hand, foregrounds, albeit in a vague way, sociospatial differentiation and the geographic constitution of identity formation. She emphasizes the impermanence of nodal points of common ground, ongoing processes of differentiation, and the "nomadic" existence of social actors.

One could easily argue that both perspectives are too extreme. Habermas's work has an obvious shortcoming: theorizing social processes as if they took place on the head of a pin. Mouffe—and poststructuralists generally—overemphasize the flux and ephemerality of sociospatial formations. In fact, the geographic structuring of society produces not only difference, but also commonality. Sociospatial formations exhibit not only flux, but also a degree of fixity. Ultimately, however, questions of flux and fixity in the construction of identities, lifeworld values, systemic characteristics, and the bases for political alliances are empirical questions—empirical questions that cannot be adequately addressed without taking into account the geographic constitution and differentiation of social processes.

The geographic constitution of systems and lifeworlds—or abstract spaces and social spaces, to use Lefebvre's spatial terminology—is manifest in a variety of ways. The territories that some collectivities build and defend are not just metaphorical but also real places, such as neighborhoods, residential developments, schools, community centers, places of worship, and parks. The abstract spaces of the economy and state include workplaces, transportation facilities, day care centers, hospitals, clinics, and other formal institutions with tangible geographic manifestations in people's lives. Geographic scale is crucial to identity construction, not only in terms of material patterns of spatial interaction, but also in terms of how people conceptualize and represent the geography of their lives. People may identify the local scale of home and community as the main site of interpersonal contact, values, and belonging, yet may also have a strong sense of "imagined community" (Anderson 1983) at the regional, national, or even international scale. Disjunctures in the geographic scales of articulating processes may also have important implications for social movement mobilization. Place-based social interaction may provide the strongest basis for lifeworld construction, but its destabilization and colonization may be traceable to processes of commodification, bureaucratization, and capital mobility operating at broader, even global, scales (Miller 1992).

Alberto Melucci (1988, 1989, 1994) and Manuel Castells (1983) are among the few NSM theorists to explicitly acknowledge the importance of spatial structuring in NSM mobilization. Melucci has focused on the creation of collective cultural identities as both a necessary prerequisite for collective action, and as a form of resistance, in and of itself. He observes that

> Individually and socially produced identity must constantly cope with the uncertainty created by the ceaseless flow of information, by the fact that individuals belong simultaneously to a plurality of systems, by the variety of their spatiotemporal frames of reference. Identity must be forever reestablished and renegotiated. The search for identity becomes a remedy against the opacity of the system. (1994, 114)

Melucci recognizes not only the spatiotemporal framing of identity construction, but also that social actors are constituted and in a field of crosscutting social processes operating at a variety of geographic scales. The actions of social movements, accordingly, reverberate across geographic scales.

Melucci's conceptualization points toward the significance of geographic structuring in the formation and mobilization of NSMs, yet few NSM theorists have explored its concrete implications through geographically sensitive empirical research. Stoecker's (1995) work on collective identity is a significant contribution in this regard. Stoecker clearly presents the spatial constraints on the neighborhood organizations he studies, and the importance of place in identity construction. Addressing different forms of organizing in different parts of East Toledo, he emphasizes the "incursions of the state into personal life" and "contradictions and incursions . . . experienced at the community level" (1995, 124). The relationships and experiences of the communities, organizations, and movements of East Toledo differ depending on location and the degree to which place attachments are shared. Stoecker shows how the interrelations occurring in place continually develop and re-constitute the identities of individuals and groups within places, and how the ways in which people articulate and define their place shift with changes in the local economic and social structure. Stoecker's equation of the geo-graphic structuring of identities with the production of explicitly place- or territory-based identities is highly problematic, however. He asks, "what do we do with 'communities of interest' . . . based in gender, sexual, health, racial, or other identities, which may not be rooted in geographic space at all, but instead in collective identity?" (125). Numerous studies show that collective identities are constructed through spatial interaction, whether those identities become place-based or not. "The social" and "the spatial" are not so neatly separated.

A substantial geographical literature explicitly links spatial processes to social-theoretical work on identity (Marston 1988; Wolch and Dear 1989; Keith and Pile 1993; Rose 1993; Clark 1994; Laws 1994; Massey 1994, 1995; Staeheli 1994; Staeheli and Cope 1994; Cope 1996; Cresswell 1996; Ruddick 1996; Pile and Keith 1997). Many of these studies demonstrate how common identities, experiences, understandings, and power relations are constructed in and through the spaces and places of interaction. As Rose (1993, 37) argues, "everyday space is not only not self-evidently innocent, but also bound into various and diverse social and psychic dynamics of sub-jectivity and power." Similarly, Ruddick (1996, 135) shows that "public spaces serve not simply to *surface* particular pregiven behaviors, but become an active medium through which new identities are created or contested . . . new social identities and new meanings of public space are seen to be con-structed together."

Indeed, there are innumerable examples of the ways in which sexual, gender, "racial," class, and ethnic identities are constructed through, and ob-tain their meaning in, space. Marston (1988, 196), for instance, found that among the Irish of nineteenth-century Lowell, Massachusetts, "ethnic resi-dential segregation gave a decisive advantage to the rise of ethnic solidarity over class solidarity, which is much more abstracted from the realities of everyday social life." In other words, patterns of spatial interaction were more important to developing a strong collective identity than was an aspa-tial "objective" social position. Gender constructions are also clearly spatial-ized, as norms of gender-appropriate behavior vary by location and the spaces of daily life are conventionally structured in terms of a female private/ domestic sphere and a male public/political/economic sphere. Many of the efforts and aims of the women's movement can be interpreted in terms of challenging the spatial order of gender relations. The development of "racial" identity is clearly spatialized as well, as "racial" identities and interpretations are suffused with spatial connotations such as the ghetto, the "wrong side of the tracks," and so on that influence not only how majority groups view minority groups in particular places, but how minority groups think of themselves in those places. Transgressing sociospatial norms of appropriate place-based behavior is frequently central to social movement resistance strategies (Cresswell 1996) as evidenced by the feminist slogan "a woman's place is in the . . . ," the emphasis of the civil rights movement on desegregation, the significance of gay and lesbian "coming out"—demanding to be accepted in public spaces, and in a host of other ways. Indeed, Melucci (1980, 219) recognizes the innate spatiality of NSMs, fighting for the "reappropriation of time, of space, and of relationships in the individual's daily experience."

Although many analysts attempt to divide NSMs into either cultural/ identity-oriented movements or political movements (see Cohen 1985; Eder 1985; Offe 1985; Buechler 1995), a quick survey of NSMs reveals that the most significant NSMs—the women's, environmental, civil rights, gay and lesbian, and peace movements—have been at the forefront of political as well as cultural change. Castells, whose work is sometimes assigned to the political NSM category, actually provides good examples of the links between both the cultural and the political, as well as the social and the spatial. His 1983 analysis of several urban social movements shows how people may organize themselves according to their shared residential locations, rather than around their workplaces or class position. When people organize in their neighborhoods, they often articulate demands related to collective consumption, for example, housing, education, garbage collection, street maintenance, and recreational space. Such demands cannot be reduced to simple issues of class, politics, or culture. On the contrary, urban social movements seek to defend or improve residential spaces against the processes of commodification and bureaucratization, while striving to expand or protect political autonomy and cultural identity.

Geographers increasingly emphasize the interaction between spaces of production and reproduction, as well as between civil society and the state (Laws 1994; Staeheli 1994; Staeheli and Cope 1994; Cope 1996; Brown 1997a, 1997b). In his study of Act Up in Vancouver, Brown (1997a, 165), for example, found that "ACT UP's political geography neglected the contemporary webbing of . . . two spheres of life [civil society and the state]"; he warns "against merely dichotomizing 'old' state-centered locations of politics and 'new' ones in civil society" (ibid.). Similarly, in her study of the relationships among identity, space, and power in nineteenth-century Lawrence, Massachusetts, Cope (1996, 202) observes that

> [there are] many [relevant] spaces . . . rang[ing] from homes to neighborhood social halls to the mills to the streets and common spaces. Actions and identities intersect these spaces, creating a rich complexity in which simple divisions of public/private are no more appropriate than a binary distinction between work/community, class/ethnicity, or powerful/powerless. The power geometry of an individual, creating a sense of identity-in-place through a web of interactions and spaces, disallows the separation of public and private and reaffirms their mutual constitution.

In short, geographically informed studies of identity construction and politics make clear the multiplicity of identities and roles social actors hold, how those are constituted in a variety of place-specific contexts, and how the spatial constitution of daily life-paths shapes the ways in which identities articulate, merge, modify, and transform. These malleable identities and the political alliances they give rise to affect a variety of forms of politics at the same time that they are shaped in geographically constituted political contexts.

Summary and Implications

In recent years, many social movements theorists have attempted to develop synthetic models of social movement mobilization that integrate the insights of resource mobilization theory, political process models, and new social movements theory. Although these synthetic models have different emphases, all attempt to provide a framework for understanding how social movements and social movement organizations are shaped in a broader societal context. Political processes, socioeconomic restructuring, collective identity construction, issue framing, and the mobilization of resources are examined in interaction and, increasingly, in their historical context. The interaction of processes is recognized to unfold over time; the past clearly shapes the possibilities of the present and future. Unfortunately, the geographic constitution of social movements—and its role in shaping mobilization processes and their interaction—has received little attention, although there are some notable exceptions. Geographic concepts of space, place, and scale remain underdeveloped in social movements theory despite an increased emphasis on context and discussion of a "geographic turn" in the social sciences and humanities.

Specifically, social movements research could address the geographic constitution of social movement mobilization processes in several ways. Resource mobilization research could examine the spatial distribution of resources among different SMOs and the communities they attempt to mobilize. Research on framing could address the geographic targeting of frames and whether they match place-specific cultural constructions. Political process research could explore the geographic differentiation of the state across places and scales, and how that differentiation affects social movement strategies, successes, and failures. New social movements research could examine how the spatial structuring of people's daily lives affects the construction of their identities, as well as how place attachments relate to identity and behavior. And of course all of these processes—and others—interact and modify each other. How that occurs and plays out is very much a function of geography.

Routledge (1993, 1994, 1997) provides one example of how one might go about incorporating geography in the analysis of social movements. His studies draw explicitly from Agnew's (1987) conception of place as location, locale, and sense of place. Beginning with a nuanced conception of place, Routledge attempts to explain differential strategies among environmental movements in India (1993) and why unrest in Nepal was most evident in the area around the capital city (1994). He demonstrates that "each locale produces its own set of circumstances, constraints, and opportunities for social action" (1993, 140). Routledge advocates a rich, place-based understanding of social movements for three reasons:

> First, the concept of place informs us about why social movements occur where they do and the context within which movement agency interpellates the social structure. Second, the concept of place informs us about the nature of specific movements. . . . Finally, . . . place provides the means of understanding the spirit of movement agency, that which inspires and motivates people, the articulation of the experiences of everyday life. (Ibid., 21)

Routledge integrates his understanding of place with both resource mobilization theory and new social movements theory. His work has received attention from geographers (e.g., Reynolds 1994; Ó Tuathail 1995; Herbert 1996; Pile and Keith 1997), yet a book review (Crist 1994) in *Contemporary Sociology* may represent the sole opportunity most social movement scholars have to encounter his work, outside perusing geographical journals and books. Crist's (1994) review embodies some of the difficulties involved in communicating the relevance of geographic concepts to social movements research (see also Lobao 1994). Crist agrees with "Routledge's justifiable criticism of the general absence of place as an organizing concept within movement analyses" (544), but then equates place with "the fact that each [movement] mobilized to defend a locality" (545), ignoring the other dimensions of place Routledge explores in his extensive analysis. Crist also believes that attention to place "limits . . . generalizability to other movements" (ibid). Although attention to place may reveal some place-specific qualities of a particular mobilization, the inclusion of space, place, and scale in social movement research ought to enhance theory and lead to more reliable empirical analyses.[3] Generalizability is, ultimately, an empirical issue. Indeed, there is fluidity as well as fixity in the real, geographically constituted world that cannot be adequately understood through aspatial analyses. But this does not preclude generalization. One cannot make meaningful claims to generalization without first understanding an object of study in its geographic and historic diversity. Acknowledging the geographic constitution of human action does not limit insights gained from studying it, but instead, like historical analysis, enhances our understanding.

Hopefully, this examination of the literature builds a persuasive case for explicitly considering the geographic constitution of social movements. Over the last three decades geographers have profitably borrowed from sociology and political science; likewise, sociologists and political scientists have borrowed from geography. Nonetheless, disciplinary barriers remain strong. There are many academic institutional and cultural forces inhibiting interdisciplinary exchange. The real world, however, is not as neatly compartmentalized as the academy. A more powerful, dynamic understanding of social movements would greatly benefit from redoubled efforts toward interdisciplinary synthesis. In the following chapter, one such synthesis is proposed.

2

A Geographic Model of Social Movement Mobilization

> In the field of social movements, sociology inherits a legacy of dualism . . . Collective action has always been treated either as an effect of structural crises and contradictions or as an expression of shared beliefs and orientations. (Melucci 1985, 790)

> To speak of place-specific constraints and enabling conditions that are based on resources, rules, and norms is to speak of constraints and enabling conditions that are based on geographically and historically specific power relations between individuals, collectivities, and institutions. (Pred 1984, 286)

The dualistic formulations of traditional sociological treatments of social movements are, quite fortunately, falling by the wayside. Increasingly, sociologists and others conducting social movements research are attempting to integrate diverse perspectives. Numerous recent treatments make important strides toward developing integrated, synthetic approaches to the understanding of social movement mobilization that transcend traditional oppositions of structure and agency, socioeconomic context and ideology. These approaches increasingly emphasize the relationship between social movement actors and the contexts within which they operate. Unfortunately, the new developments in social movements theory still tend to neglect the geographic dimension through which both social movement actors and their contexts of action are structured.

The newer models of social movement mobilization recognize that the major bodies of social movements theory—resource mobilization theory, political process models, and new social movements theory—are complementary rather than contradictory. Broadly conceived, resource mobilization theory has focused on internal organizational considerations and attempted to explain social movement mobilization in terms of the resources available to organizations, for example, money, skills, leaders, and social networks. Political process models, in contrast, have focused on conditions external to social movement organizations, in particular changes in the structures of political opportunity. New social movements theory takes a third tack, emphasizing social and economic structural change that gives rise to new grievances and collective interests, values, and identities. For each of these bodies of theory there are corresponding geographies. Organizations have particular geographic constitutions, as do the communities within which they operate. The mobilization of resources is very much a function of where resources are available, how types of resources vary among places, and the spatiality of organizational recruitment strategies. Political opportunities, likewise, have their own geographies. Formal structures of political opportunity, as well as the landscape of political alliances, vary from place to place, as well as by geographic scale. The processes addressed by new social movements theory have distinct geographies too. Social and economic restructuring has differential effects across nations, regions, cities, and neighborhoods. Collective identity construction is dramatically shaped through patterns of spatial interaction, and some forms of collective identity are explicitly place-based.

Neglect of the geographic structuring of articulating social processes is evident in attempts to integrate diverse social movements theories. Rucht (1988, 325), for instance, hints at geographic structuring when he calls for a bridging of macro- and microstructural analysis by focusing on intervening variables "such as national opportunity structures, the environment and specific issues of various movements, endogenous parameters of the latter, precipitating incidents, etc."—but the importance of space and place in bridging "the macro" and "the micro" remains unexplored.

Klandermans and Tarrow (1988, 10–12) suggest that mobilization is best studied "broken down into its constituent phases: the formation of mobilization potentials, the formation and activation of recruitment networks, the arousal of the motivation to participate, and the removal of barriers to participation." Yet spaces and places of mobilization are overlooked.

Kriesi (1988, 364–65), in contrast to Klandermans and Tarrow, emphasizes the broader systemic processes in which social movements are intertwined:

> we cannot simply discard the insight of the classical "breakdown" theories
> that mobilization processes originate from crisis situations and that these

situations are to some extent structurally determined by long-term developments not under the control of the political actors involved . . . Changes in size and make-up of mobilization potentials, changes in the political opportunity structure and in political culture should, I believe, be linked to large-scale processes of social change to account for the development of critical situations providing the catalytic movement at the origin of social movements.

But the large-scale processes Kriesi emphasizes are clearly geographically differentiated. Economic restructuring, to take one well-known example, produces regional, metropolitan, and even neighborhood winners and losers—with implications for a geographically differentiated pattern of "crisis situations" that may give rise to mobilization.

In one of the most recent formulations, McAdam, McCarthy, and Zald (1996, 2) observe that there is an emerging synthesis of social movements theory that involves

the same three broad sets of factors in analyzing the emergence and development of social movements/revolutions. These three factors are (1) the structure of political opportunities and constraints confronting the movement; (2) the forms of organization (informal as well as formal) available to insurgents; and (3) the collective processes of interpretation, attribution, and social construction that mediate between opportunity and action.

McAdam, McCarthy, and Zald (1996) indirectly suggest the significance of geographic differentiation in shaping the interaction of factors affecting social movement mobilization. Mentioned are Tilly's (1975, 1978) work "documenting the critical role of various grassroots settings—work and neighborhood, in particular—facilitating and structuring collective action" (4) and the "growing awareness among movement scholars of the diversity of collective settings in which movements develop" (ibid.). Unfortunately, the geographic structuring and diversity of mobilization processes is given little more than passing comment.

To adequately remedy the dualisms of traditional social movements theory one must think in terms of conjunctures of a variety of processes that articulate in different ways in different places. As Melucci (1994, 108) argues:

a theoretical question of major importance is whether one can conceive of a dominant logic that does not necessarily manifest itself in a global and overarching form, but which instead distributes itself among various areas of the system to produce a wide variety of arenas and actors of conflict.

This is a logic to be identified not just in the . . . workings of great apparatuses but . . . in daily interaction.

Melucci's formulation resonates extremely well with an explicitly geographic analysis of social movements. To understand the differential effects of
"great apparatuses" as well as patterns of "daily interaction," one must begin
with a recognition of the geographic constitution of all social institutions.

An appropriate starting point from which to address the geographic
constitution of processes effecting social movements is that of French social
theorist Henri Lefebvre. As discussed in chapter 1, Lefebvre (1979, 241) argues that the essential line of conflict in society is "the confrontation between *abstract space,* or the externalization of economic and political practices originating with the capitalist class and the state, and *social space* . . . the
space produced by the complex interaction of all classes in the pursuit of
everyday life." Lefebvre, in other words, is directly concerned with the spatiality of both the "great apparatuses" and "daily interaction," as well as with
the different logics they follow. Drawing on Lefebvre, Gottdiener (1985,
127) observes that "in modern society, abstract space—a homogeneous,
fragmented, hierarchical space—has come to dominate social space, or the
integrated space of social communion." According to Lefebvre, the expansion of abstract space, rooted in ever-increasing commodification and bureaucratization, gives rise to social movements seeking to reclaim, defend, or
expand social space. Such a conceptualization can form a basis for understanding not only the differentiation of processes affecting social movements
across space, but also how they may interact in specific places, giving rise to
different types and forms of movements in different places. Moreover, it
makes clear that the "transformation of everyday life must proceed with the
radical transformation of space because the one is bound up with the other"
(Gottdiener 1985, 150).

Lefebvre and Habermas (1984, 1987) share a similar set of theoretical
precepts, although Habermas pitches his analysis at a highly abstract level
that ignores the spatial constitution and differentiation of society. More so
than Lefebvre, however, Habermas analyzes in detail the systemic processes—
commodification and bureaucratization—that drive the production of abstract space, and the lifeworld processes, rooted in communication, through
which social space is produced. Habermas also addresses interactions between the system and the lifeworld in considerable detail. Consequently,
Habermas's work probably represents a better starting point for the construction of a broad framework for the analysis of social movement mobilization, but his work needs to be modified—with Lefebvre in mind—to

foreground the *differentiated systemic and lifeworld spaces within which mobilization takes place, and over which struggle occurs.*

A geographic model of social movement mobilization must begin with the recognition of the different forms systems and lifeworlds can take in different places, the variety of processes operating at diverse scales that affect them, and the variety of ways they can articulate in particular places. In many respects, a geographic model of social movement mobilization has to be more of a sociospatial ontology—guiding the researcher toward crucial processes on which to focus—than a formal theory of how social movements evolve over space and time. Indeed, the movement of the social sciences toward greater acknowledgment of context and the constructed nature of social reality means the abandonment of universalist foolproof methods, theories, and findings—and recognition that different processes may play out in different ways in different places. This does not mean, however, that all theories or frameworks for the analysis of social movements can be equally valid, or that one cannot make qualified generalizations.

Habermas's work has proven to be a powerful, if overly abstract, framework for addressing the key processes that McAdam, McCarthy, and Zald (1996), Rucht (1988), Kriesi (1988), Melucci (1988), and others identify as central to social movement mobilization. Reformulated in light of the geographic constitution and differentiation of the processes it addresses, Habermas's work can provide a more dynamic, accurate, and nuanced understanding of the mobilization of social movements. Before this can be done, however, the key propositions and shortcomings of Habermas's work must first be sketched out.

The Habermasian Model of Social Movement Mobilization

In *The Theory of Communicative Action* (1984, 1987), Habermas identifies two distinct but interdependent spheres of society: the system and the lifeworld. These closely correspond to what Melucci (1985) refers to as systemic fields and action systems, respectively. Habermas defines the system as the primary sphere of material reproduction (coordinated through strategic and instrumental action) and the lifeworld as the primary sphere of symbolic reproduction (coordinated through communicative action). In his schema, society is "steered by imperatives issuing from problems of self-maintenance, that is, problems of materially reproducing [through the system, the basis of] the lifeworld" (1984, 148). It is from the imperatives of self-maintenance, and the threats to it, that social movements arise.

Habermas takes a "materialist approach to disturbances in the symbolic reproduction of the lifeworld" (ibid.) that recognizes the interaction of the

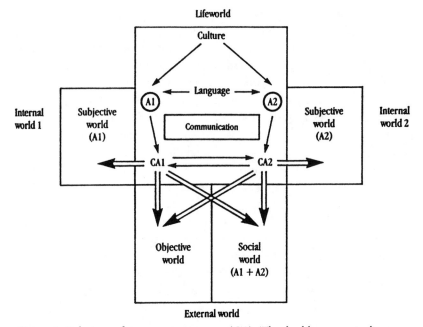

Figure 3. Relations of communicative acts (CA). The double arrows indicate the world-relations that actors (A) establish with their utterances (CA). Source: Habermas 1987.

system and lifeworld. This interaction produces objective (material), social (interpersonal), and subjective (personal) worlds within which social actors are located. Together, social actors must come to terms with these simultaneous worlds. According to Habermas (1984, 120),

> Communicative action relies on a cooperative process of interpretation in which participants relate simultaneously to something in the objective, the social, and the subjective worlds, even when they thematically stress only one of the three components in their utterances. Speaker and hearer use the reference system of the three worlds as an interpretive framework within which they work out their common situation definitions.

Accordingly, Habermas sees the genesis of social movements as the result of interacting material systemic processes and interpretive lifeworld processes. Considering social movements in this way not only provides insight into the ways in which intertwining material and symbolic reproduction shape social movements; it also suggests that the analyst adopt two different and equally valid perspectives on social movements: the "internal" subjective

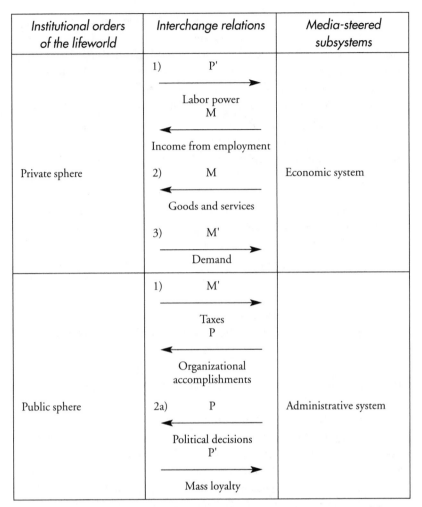

Institutional orders of the lifeworld	Interchange relations	Media-steered subsystems
Private sphere	1) P' → Labor power M ← Income from employment 2) M ← Goods and services 3) M' → Demand	Economic system
Public sphere	1) M' → Taxes P ← Organizational accomplishments 2a) P ← Political decisions P' → Mass loyalty	Administrative system

Figure 4. Relations between system and lifeworld from the perspective of the system. M=money medium; P=power medium. Source: Habermas 1987.

perspective of the lifeworld and the "external" objective perspective of the system.

Habermas divides the system into two subsystems: the economy and the state, affecting the private sphere and the public sphere of the lifeworld, respectively. As Habermas would have it, the public and private spheres form complementary realms of social integration.

The private sphere of the lifeworld (primarily nuclear families) receives income and goods and services from the economy in order to maintain and reproduce itself materially; in return the economy receives labor power and demand for goods and services. The public sphere of the lifeworld (comprised of communicative networks operating through cultural institutions, the press, and the mass media) is chartered and enabled by the state; in return the state receives tax revenue and political legitimation.

Habermas's schema is a simplification in several respects. The nuclear family is obviously not the only domestic arrangement within the private sphere, and there are important interactions between the economic and state subsystems, between the private and public spheres, between the private sphere and the state, and between the public sphere and the economy. Fraser (1987) provides a particularly compelling critique of Habermas's neglect of women's unpaid labor in the private sphere and its significance to the functioning of the formal economy. Moreover, individual subjects usually operate across these spheres rather than exclusively or primarily within them. Yet Habermas's overly simplified schema does provide a starting point from which to understand how the "mediatization [through money and state power] of the lifeworld turns into its colonization" (318).

Mediatization entails the supplanting of lifeworld-based communicative processes by the media of the economy and state: money and state power. As mediatization occurs, traditional forms of life within the private and public spheres die out as they are "split off from symbolic structures of the lifeworld through the monetary redefinition of goals, relations and services, life-spaces and life-times, and through the bureaucratization of decisions, duties and rights, responsibilities and dependencies" (322). This process can proceed quite far when limited to economic and political functions, but the steering media of the system "fail to work in domains of cultural reproduction, social integration, and socialization; they cannot replace the action-coordinating mechanism of mutual understanding in these functions. Unlike the material reproduction of the lifeworld, its symbolic reproduction cannot be transposed onto foundations of system integration without pathological side effects" (322–33). The pathological side effects of this "colonization of the lifeworld" provoke lifeworld-based reactions in the form of new social movements.

Of course, an individual's participation in a social movement is predicated on the strength of his or her identification with that movement. The theory of communicative action provides insight into the construction of identities by calling attention to the central lifeworld functions of cultural reproduction, social integration, and socialization. Habermas argues that identities are rooted in shared *culture* that gives meaning to daily life; *social integration* entails the development of semistructured bases for interpersonal relations that stabilize group identities; and *socialization* allows actors to connect themselves with the past and the future thus providing a sense continuity and collective purpose. In short, when cultural reproduction, social integration, and socialization processes operate effectively, individuals develop a sense of *meaning, identity,* and *security* in the world. However, when colonization leads to a breakdown of lifeworld functions, social movements may mobilize around grievances rooted in issues of meaning, identity, and security. New social movements strive to address these grievances through efforts to create new bases of meaning, identity, and security. Conversely, "old" social movements address issues of economic redistribution while building support rooted in existing forms of meaning, identity, and security.

By conceptualizing new social movements in this manner, Habermas clearly points to the cultural focus of new social movements, at the same time stressing their connection to developments in the system. Similarly, "old" social movements may primarily focus on systemic issues of economic redistribution, but clearly retain an important cultural dimension. Habermas's work provides a clear and far-reaching framework for the analysis of social movements, both new and old. The theory of communicative action addresses systemic processes of material reproduction (in both the economy and the state), lifeworld processes of symbolic reproduction, some aspects of these processes' interaction, the formation of individual and collective identities, and the generation of conflicts that give rise to social movements.

Nonetheless, the theory of communicative action, like most theories of social movements, no more than nominally considers the geographic constitution of social processes. Although Habermas's work provides a very good starting point for the analysis of social movements, his failure to consider the geographic constitution of critical processes leads to a number of significant oversights. It is to the missing geographic dimension of Habermas's work that we now turn.

Geography and the Theory of Communicative Action (1): The Economy

Because he views society without regard to its geographic constitution, Habermas only detects the undermining of the lifeworld through its colonization by the economy and the state. Overlooked is the ever-increasing mobility of capital and its equally destructive impact on lifeworld functions. Both colonization and capital hypermobility derive from the expansionary logic of capitalism, but the increasing spatial mobility of capital does not in itself represent an expansion of systemic forms of action coordination. Capitalist decision making has always been based in strategic and instrumental rationality. Changes in the nature of production processes and financing, however, have allowed capital to relocate more readily. This relocation, in turn, can destabilize or destroy the lifeworld institutions that depend on capital.

Since the breakdown of the Fordist regime of accumulation in the early 1970s, capital has increasingly turned to spatial fixes to counteract declining rates of profit (Harvey 1982, 1989; Swyngedouw 1989; Amin 1994). The relative spatial stability of Fordism has been replaced by accelerated spatial restructuring as firms search the globe for places favorable to capital accumulation. Diminished transportation costs, improved communications technology, and the dominance of highly mobile finance capital have facilitated this search.

The communities that often form the basis for collective political action can be significantly affected and even destroyed by capital hypermobility. Deindustrialization, lack of capital investment, and declining governmental funding can harm or reshape many of the institutions of everyday social interaction, produce or accentuate conflicts among community members, force people to move elsewhere in search of a livelihood, and otherwise break down or preclude the formation of the collective identities that are prerequisites for collective action.

Understanding the geography of collective action requires an understanding of the different ways in which capital hypermobility affects places. Markusen (1987, 1989) provides what is perhaps the most detailed and systematic analysis of the impact of industrial restructuring on place-based politics. She argues that "the map of the United States is densely dotted with 'economic enclaves'—industry-specific production units that dominate the economic lives of the surrounding communities" (1989, 115). The "disparate industrial structures, growth dynamics, and inherited management-labor relations" (ibid.) of these enclaves represent the primary material forces shaping regional and place-based politics.

Drawing on the product/profit cycle model of industrial change, Markusen identifies three industrial stages that are likely to shape regional politics: "an innovative stage of superprofits, a competitive stage of 'normal profits,' and a hypercompetitive stage of profit squeeze" (116). These stages are not to be viewed as a "natural" progression but rather as ideal types that may or may not occur in sequence. Particularly important in this argument are the implications each stage has for spatial restructuring. New innovative industries, in monopoly or oligopoly positions, can extract superprofits. Because they depend on highly specialized labor pools, require close links with supporting industries, and experience very little competitive pressure that would spur them to relocate to lower-cost sites, these industries tend to cluster in a small number of nodes. Mature industries that have developed standard processes for large-scale production focus on market penetration. In such industries, innovation becomes less important and the need to be near the original agglomeration declines. Instead, as competition increases and super-profits disappear, mature industries relocate old plants and site new plants at lower-cost locations and near untapped markets. In the hypercompetitive stage, profits drop to below-average levels and substitutes begin to replace the industry's products. Older plants in older regions are shut down to reduce costs.

Regions or "economic enclaves" can be characterized by the stage of their industries: "those booming from indigenous expansion of new, innovative superprofit sectors; those expanding with an influx of older, mature profit-squeezed sectors; and those contracting from the exit of those same profit-squeezed sectors" (115). Each type of economy has a tendency to develop a particular type of politics:

> [L]ocalities and regions enjoying a superprofit boom will develop a regional politics pivoting on internal conflicts over land use, infrastructure, and environmental issues. Similarly, regional economies on the receiving end of migrating profit-squeezed sectors will evolve internally conflictual politics, but the substantive issues will revolve around preserving the business climate—low wages, absence of unions, a low social wage—which is the basis for their newfound prosperity. In contrast, regional economies besieged with the loss of traditionally strong sectors will tend to develop an externally oriented politics that levies claims upon the federal state for redistribution and redress. (Ibid.)

Industrial stages also have implications for the type of labor force that is likely to be developed in or recruited to a region. New, highly innovative industries require a highly skilled professional/technical labor force. Expansion and standardized production processes tend to encourage unionization (where labor laws are favorable) and the development of a dual (or multiply differentiated) labor force. Industries in contraction also have a bifurcated labor force, although one that is more likely to exhibit a high degree of spatial segregation.

Massey (1984b) develops an argument similar to Markusen's, although Massey emphasizes changes in the spatial division of labor rather than industry or sector-wide growth and decline. Massey, for instance, makes clear that it was the corporate concentration of managerial, finance, and other control activities (rather than particular industries), aided by the encouragement of the state, that led to the concentration of "high-status people" in southeast

England. The growth and decline of particular industries is part of the story, but this cannot be equated with shifts in the spatial division of labor.

Bennett and Earle (1983) and Earle (1993) make an argument that includes elements of both Markusen's and Massey's work. Within the uneven geography of nineteenth- and early-twentieth-century U.S. industrialization, Bennett and Earle show that there was also a significant division of labor, particularly as it relates to skill and wage differentials. Where wage and skill differentiation was significant, socialist politics were undermined.

All of these analyses provide materialist frameworks for understanding the effects of economic and spatial restructuring on regional politics. According to Markusen, the stage of a region's industries substantially influences the issues that dominate its politics and the geographic scale at which political struggle is likely to be manifest. The spatial division of labor determines, in large measure, the economic groupings that are likely to engage in struggle in a particular place, the types of coalitions that can be formed, and the skills and resources available to political causes. As Jonas (1993, 285) observes, "national and international restructurings do not simply impact upon localities . . . but rather how local people (e.g. councilors, public officials, trades unions, chambers of commerce, and community groups) organize (or are already organized) and act collectively [to] shape the local forms and effects of restructuring."

Markusen's framework, while reasonable, is perhaps too closely tied to the regional scale. Many of her generalizations could, for instance, be applied to metropolitan areas, cities, or even large neighborhoods with equal validity. Moreover, the material interests outlined in Markusen's model have broader implications. The politics of systemic maintenance (primarily, economic growth) are likely to be of overriding significance in places of industrial exit, while the politics of lifeworld disruption (environmental degradation, congestion, housing affordability, etc.) are more likely in places where industry is expanding. In other words, the nature of struggles over the articulating spaces of systems and lifeworlds will vary geographically. Moreover, interactions between abstract systemic spaces and social lifeworld spaces should not be conceptualized in a static or undifferentiated manner. Actions in each sphere impact the other; in the "real world" there is no rigid separation between systemic and lifeworld processes. Indeed, in some cases systemic and lifeworld activities may occur in one and the same physical space. Markusen's model provides a good preliminary indication of how the geography of economic restructuring may relate to the geography of social movements, but her model is by no means comprehensive.

Markusen downplays the roles of the state and culture in politics,

Table 3. Regional coalition membership, issues, and unity levels associated with profit cycle stages

Sages	Coalition members and opponents	Major issues	Level of government most involved	Degree of internal unity within region
Superprofit boom region	Incoming corporations, pro-growth coalition versus residentialists, traditional sectors, business interests linked to traditional sectors	Land use, infrastructure; environment	1. Local 2. State 3. National	Low
Region of entry	Regional businesses, business	Maintenance of low wages, low taxes; growth management; unionization	1. State 2. Local 3. National	High
Region of exit	Workers, local business versus transregional corporations, other regions	Reinvestment, capital controls, compensation, adjustment aid	1. National 2. State 3. Local	High

Source: Markusen 1989.

although she does acknowledge their importance as "mediating factors." Although economic processes may provide material impetus for many political struggles, the state and culture are crucial to the manifestation of what might otherwise be latent conflict. As political process theorists make clear, the state, as the "other half" of the system, structures the opportunities for and constraints to political action. Political process models provide insight into the state's structuring of political action, but they, like the theory of communicative action, neglect its geographic constitution.

Geography and the Theory of Communicative Action (2): The State

In the theory of communicative action, Habermas stresses the role of the state, as well as the economy, in mediatizing and colonizing lifeworld functions. These processes produce grievances around which new social movements mobilize. But the state is not only a source of grievances; it is also a forum of political struggle. In the discussion of political process models in chapter 1, strong connections were drawn between state structures of political opportunity and social movement mobilization. Although such models complement and extend Habermas's analysis, they suffer from a common aspatiality.

By recognizing a geographically differentiated state system and the analytic distinction between grievances and political opportunity structures, we can begin to understand the shifting geographies of social movement mobilization. Political mobilization need not necessarily be aimed at the state(s) (central or local) whose actions produce grievances. Rather, if political opportunity structures differ significantly among central and local states, political mobilization may be directed at the state(s) with the most open structures of political opportunity.

Capture of local states can be an effective means to pursue a political agenda, even when grievances lie with the central state. Local states exhibit a degree of autonomy from the central state and from the imperatives of capital accumulation (Cooke 1983; Duncan and Goodwin 1988; Duncan, Goodwin, and Halford 1988; Cox 1993; Goodwin, Duncan, and Halford 1993) that can make them an effective platform from which to challenge central state actions and policies. There are clearly constitutional and economic limits to this autonomy (Cockburn 1977; Clark and Dear 1984; Harvey 1985b; Duncan and Goodwin 1988; Cox 1993) stemming from local states' charters, fiscal dependency on higher level states, and a need to maintain the economic growth that produces tax revenue. Nonetheless, within limits, local states can serve as sites of resistance and political experimentation. In the American context, social movements have been particu-

larly effective at the local level. The environmental, women's, gay and lesbian, civil rights, labor, and peace movements have all, to varying degrees,
mobilized, fought battles, and effected policy change at the local level. Many
broad national movements have been built on the successes of decentralized
local campaigns. The local state's relative autonomy provides a structural
arena for potentially meaningful change as well as a platform from which to
promote alternative geographic framings of social issues.

The geographic scale of the processes that give rise to grievances is often
far from self-evident. Many groups and institutions have well-defined scales
of material operation—for example, multinational corporations, nation-
states, urban growth coalitions, and neighborhood associations—but these
scales of operation are established through conflict and negotiation; their
scales are not natural or pregiven. Representations of scale, moreover, play
an important role in social struggle. Scales that provide opponents more political opportunity can be portrayed as illegitimate; scales that provide opponents the fewest political opportunities may be portrayed as "appropriate."
As discussed in chapter 1, attempts to shift the balance of power frequently
entail shifts in the scale of both material practice and representation.
Shifting geographic scale is integral to social and political struggle as contestants seek to shape spatial relations to their advantage. Scale struggles become
especially significant in a geographically differentiated state system in which
local states maintain a degree of autonomy.

The complex interplay of grievances, political opportunity structures,
and political mobilization at different geographic scales is portrayed in figure 5. By focusing on these relationships we can come to better understand
the geographic dynamics of social movements. As Tarrow (1983, 1989) asserts, clear and significant grievances (usually stemming from the state or the
economy), as well as political opportunity, are required for the mobilization
of social movements. These prerequisites, however, are geographically differentiated. The focus of mobilization—directed at the local state or the central
state—may be determined as much by the structures of political opportunity as by the origins of grievances. When political opportunity structures
channel protest to the local state, the local state can serve as a platform for
expressing opposition to central state policy and diffusing protest to other
localities. However, when protest moves beyond the symbolic realm and begins to threaten the economic interests of particular fractions of capital,
these fractions will likely attempt to discipline their opponents through capital strikes and other measures (Harvey 1985b). At this point the limits to
state autonomy—both central and local—become apparent.

By examining the manner in which state structures affect the strategies of

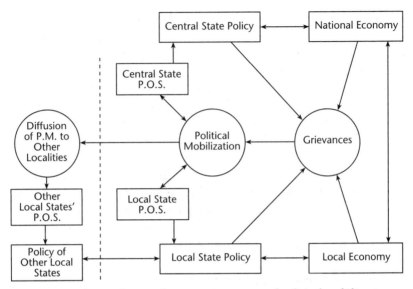

Figure 5. Local-central state relations, grievances, and political mobilization.

social movement organizations and economic restructuring shapes material interests, we gain a systems view of social movement mobilization. Understanding social movement mobilization from the perspective of the lifeworld, in contrast, must begin with the construction of the identities of social movement participants in the spaces and places where they live. Collective identities and consciousness are key links to individuals' participation in social movements.

Geography and the Theory of Communicative Action (3): The Lifeworld, Identity Construction, and Collective Action

Habermas's attention to the processes of cultural reproduction, social integration, and socialization provides important insights into the construction of individuals' identities as well as the problems that may arise when these processes are disturbed by the encroachment of the system. Habermas, however, fails to consider the geographic structuring of identity construction and the crucial role it plays in enabling collective action.

Several studies have directly linked collective identity formation to communicative interaction and the solving of the free-rider problem—why it is that individuals participate in collective action when they could choose not to and still reap benefits that are public and free (Calhoun 1988; Dawes, van de Kragt, and Orbell 1990; Mansbridge 1990). Like Habermas, many communitarian and feminist theorists argue that collective identities are formed through communication. Consensually formed common under-standings provide the basis for a morally valued way of life and the construc-tion of collective identities that transcend the individual. Such identities represent "communities" of one sort or another and have value in and of themselves. Calhoun (1988, 161) argues that community is "not necessarily an additional good to be valued beyond other selfish interests, but in many cases a condition of continuous selfhood for [its] members." The fact that we may identify with people other than ourselves provides a basis for un-selfish forms of behavior; we may "incorporate [others'] interests into our subjective welfare function, so that their interests become our own" (Jencks 1979, 54). Under such conditions, free-ridership ceases to be an issue. Jencks terms this consideration of others' interests "communitarian unselfishness." It involves

> identification with a collectivity rather than with specific individuals. This collectivity can take virtually any form, but the most common examples in modern societies are probably the family, the work group, the nation-state, and the species. In each case we redefine our "selfish" interest so that it in-cludes our subjective understanding of the interests of a larger collectivity of which we are a part. In large complex societies we usually identify at least partially with more than one such collectivity.

Other communitarian theorists such as Unger (1975), Sandel (1982), Balbus (1983), and Charles Taylor (1989) put "collective attributes at the core of in-dividual identity," and point out that "the self must always be 'situated' and 'encumbered'" (Mansbridge 1990, 20). Geography is central to the "situated-ness" of the self, as I will argue. Feminist theorists especially have stressed the importance of relationships, mutuality, and community in collective action (Gilligan 1981; Boyte and Evans 1984; Benhabib 1986; Young 1986), and some prominent feminists have pointed directly to the significance of place in shaping and maintaining community identity (e.g., Young 1990; Taylor and Whittier 1992).

Although numerous theorists of collective action look to community to solve the free-rider problem, not all of them link community to nonself-interested communicative processes. The work of Michael Taylor perhaps best exemplifies the approach of rational choice theorists who look to notions of place-based community (Calhoun 1988; Elster 1989; M. Taylor 1988, 1990) or place-specific social interaction (e.g., Axelrod 1984; Coleman 1990) to influence the strategic calculations of individuals in collective action.[1]

In analyzing peasant revolutions, Taylor argues that "pre-existing rural *community* [makes] it [strategically] rational for the individual peasant to participate in . . . collective action" (1988, 77). Community is important in Taylor's analysis because it means that "individual behavior can more easily be monitored" and because "a strong community has at its disposal an array of powerful, positive and negative social sanctions which [are] highly effective in maintaining social order" (ibid., 67). In Taylor's scheme, individuals always act strategically and "cooperate" only for reasons of individual self-interest; they engage in what Elster (1989) terms "selfishly rational cooperative behavior." Axelrod (1984, 100) elaborates: "The basic idea is that an individual must not be able to get away with defecting without the other individuals being able to retaliate effectively. The response requires that the defecting individual not be lost in a sea of anonymous others." The time-space continuity of community clearly plays a central role in shaping individuals' decisions. The effectiveness of social sanctions, the knowledge that others are engaged in conditional cooperation, and the experience of conditional cooperation itself "all derive from the fact that the participants in [collective action] are members of a pre-existing community and will continue to be members of the same community after the rebellion" (M. Taylor 1988, 69).

Community, then, is fundamental to Taylor's solution to the free-rider problem. But Taylor uses a very specific notion of community. For him, community is not primarily a set of moral relations rooted in communicative understanding, but rather a collection of people who interact with each other in a common territory. Taylor uses the term *community* to emphasize that the common occupancy of a particular place influences individuals' strategic actions.

Although the significance of place-based community in collective action is widely recognized (e.g., Webber 1964; Tilly 1973; Hudson and Sadler 1986; Calhoun 1988; M. Taylor 1988; Agnew 1989; Epstein 1990), confusion over the nature of community and its relationship to place is widespread. The frequent conflation of the terms *community* and *place* derives from the strong relationship between the construction of communal bonds and place-based social interaction. Nonetheless, community and place are not equivalent and affect collective action in very different ways. Accordingly, it is imperative that they be separated analytically.

Community has an especially ambiguous meaning. Its two distinct connotations are (1) "a morally valued way of life" and (2) "social relations in a discrete geographical setting" (Agnew 1989, 13). *Place* also has multiple definitions. It is most commonly understood in terms of (1) a "sense of place," affective bonds developed toward territory through living in it, and (2) locale, or "the settings for everyday routine social interaction provided in a place" (Agnew and Duncan 1989, 2).

The source of confusion over the terms *community* and *place* is clear: the second definitions of both terms are, for all practical purposes, the same. If, however, we recognize two different forms of social interaction, based on Habermas's distinction between communicative and strategic action, as well as the fact that social relations are constituted both in discrete places and stretched across space, a more sensible distinction between community and place can be made.

Community, understood in the sense of a "morally valued way of life" rooted in communicative action, strongly parallels Habermas's concept of lifeworld. Community can be place-specific (in the sense of being constituted in a discrete geographical setting) or geographically extensive (shared by dispersed populations). Systems, rooted in strategic and instrumental action, can also be place-specific—as in the actions of a local state or the institutions that reproduce a local labor pool—but often are more geographically extensive and involve flows of commodities or the projection of instrumental power across space. The notions of community and place under this formulation are analytically distinct, which is not to deny that strong communities are usually rooted in specific places.

Sense of place, in this formulation, represents a bridge between the concepts of community and place. Sense of place can be considered a "structure of feeling" or consciousness that people develop through experiences in a place. These experiences can be of a personal or shared nature, but, as Habermas reminds us, even personal experiences are never completely divorced from shared social context. Sense of place, Cosgrove (1986, 425) argues, involves "'insidedness,' existential belonging where location and human life are fused into centres of human meaning, and are counterposed to 'outsidedness,' where one does not belong because of either personal or cultural separateness from the meanings incorporated in the place or because of 'placelessness.'" Sense of place, in other words, is rooted in place-based community. The meanings, understandings, and sense of "existential belonging" developed in a place-based community are rooted in communicative action; this in turn can have implications for political action. There is a "widely observed tendency of people to cleave to their own place, to identify with and [politically] defend their region . . . there is an entire sphere of human practice, organized outside the workplace, which has strong territorial aspects to it" (Markusen 1989, 42).

The identities and bonds formed in this "sphere of human practice, organized outside the workplace"—that is, the social spaces of the lifeworld—provide a critical avenue for people to come together and act collectively.

Nonetheless, it is extremely important that our understanding of the significance of place-based interactions not be reduced to the formation of place-based identities. As will be detailed in the next section, the place-specific structuring of interaction affects all forms of identity construction, whether the identities formed are overtly place-focused or not. Notions of race, ethnicity, gender, and so on are constructed in place-specific interaction with others and vary geographically as well as historically. Patterns of interaction are difficult to understand exclusively from a lifeworld perspective. The communicative processes of lifeworlds always occur simultaneously with the workings of systems. The identities and consciousness of individuals are formed in the concrete nexus of systems and lifeworlds.

Geography and the Theory of Communicative Action (4): Interactions of Economies, States, and Lifeworlds

> Where . . . can we locate the action of contemporary movements? Through an ever-growing interlacement of economic structures, complex societies produce apparatuses of political regulation and cultural agencies. . . . Conflicts move from the economic-industrial system to the cultural sphere. They focus on personal identity, the time and space of life, and the motivation and codes of daily behavior. (Melucci 1994, 109)

When considering the effects of systems on individual and group identity construction, a central, although frequently overlooked, consideration is the role of economic processes. The geographically uneven nature of capitalist development assures that different industries and economic complexes structure daily life in a fashion that often varies radically from place to place. Geographic variations in employment opportunities carry with them different skill requirements (met either by training or by recruitment), levels of development, income profiles, class mixes, and work scheduling. The geography of employment opportunities is further shaped through place-specific constructions of gender, class, and race.

Savage (1987), for example, shows how gender relations took dramatically different forms in different places in late-nineteenth- and early-twentieth-century Britain. In some places, women were virtually banned from paid employment; in other places, women were relegated to segregated and subservient roles; and, in yet other places, gender relations were "remarkably egalitarian." Geographic variations in gender relations greatly shaped gender solidarity and the gendering of local politics. In a similar fashion, Young (1996) argues that gender should not be thought of in essential terms. It is, rather, a seriality, that is, a social collective whose members are passively united by their roles in society, but who do not necessarily self-identify based on those roles. Gender, as the self-conscious grouping of women with common objectives, is something that ebbs and flows over time, Young argues. Her argument has an obvious parallel: gender (and other constructed forms of collective identity, such as race) should not only be viewed as seriality, but also as spatiality. Groups that organize based on collective identities and common objectives vary geographically as well as historically.

Numerous geographers and sociologists have pointed out that identity and consciousness are constituted through place-specific social practices (Giddens 1981, 1984; Thrift 1983, 1985; Pred 1984, 1986; Rustin 1987; Thrift and Williams 1987; Agnew 1989; Kirby 1989; Gregory 1989b; Staeheli and Cope 1994; Cope 1996). As Thrift and Williams (1987, 16) explain:

> Particular practices, encapsulating social relations, are generated by institutions which provide people with other people to intermix with through the course of their lives; home, work, school, shop and so on. These practices impart accounts of the world, drawing upon particular institutional stocks of knowledge in doing so. Since institutions both produce and are produced by social divides like class it follows that different persons will be constituted differently by them. There is a "political economy of [consciousness] development opportunities."

Such practices are clearly routinized in time and space. Hagerstrand's well-known conceptualization of daily time-space paths can be viewed as representing the material structuring of identity construction in place (figure 6). The coupling of time-space paths sets material preconditions. Individuals who come to share domains of particular places must necessarily confront the meaning of such interactions. In each person's individual biography, "language is acquired, personality is developed, a not always articulated or self-understood ideology evolves and consciousness develops" (Pred 1986, 18). When such time-space bundles are relatively stable and continuous, communicatively negotiated understandings, meanings, and values may become deeply ingrained; individuals may come to see commonalities in their experience. They may come to identify with each other and view themselves in collective terms. As Rustin (1987, 34) observes, "collective identities are formed through the common occupancy of space."[2]

The role of the state parallels that of the economy in shaping lived experience. The local state, for instance, can play a significant role in shaping place-specific social practices as it formulates and enacts policy regarding virtually all aspects of social reproduction: the planning and operation of schools, the development and preservation of residential areas, the provision

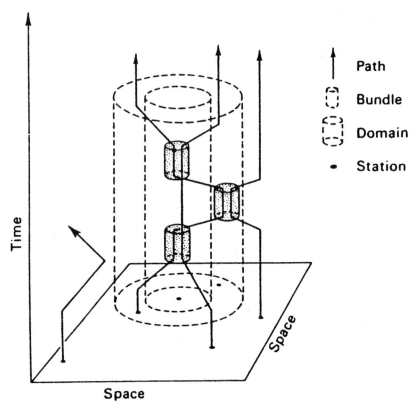

Path
Bundle
Domain
Station

Time

Space

Space

Figure 6. Hagerstrand's web model. Source: Gregory 1985.

of open space and recreation, and the selection of the types and locations of commercial and industrial development for particular communities.

As Routledge points out, "each locale produces its own set of circumstances, constraints and opportunities" (1993, 140). Place-specific circumstances lead to processes of collective identity construction that vary from place to place, even when the identities being formed are not necessarily place-based. Moreover, the daily life-paths of most individuals course through a variety of places and activities, from home to work to school to stores to public offices and spaces, leading to the construction of multiple and sometimes contradictory identities and roles (Laclau and Mouffe 1985; Staeheli 1994; Staeheli and Cope 1994; Cope 1996; Brown 1997a, 1997b). A multiplicity of identities is not necessarily a hindrance to action, however. Although social actors always act in place-specific contexts, they not infrequently draw on multiple experiences, roles, and identities as they mobilize around causes that span particular places and scales (Staeheli and Cope

1994). Such multiple identification can be a source of strength for social movements—providing organizations with diverse perspectives and insights, or of internal conflict—based in inequities in power associated with group differences.

Appeals to explicitly place-based identities can be extremely important in social movement mobilization. Place-based collective identities—constructed at a suitably broad scale—can offer social movements a very effective means (although certainly not the only means) by which to bridge or partially transcend identities constructed along lines of class, race, ethnicity, gender, and sexuality. It is important to emphasize, nonetheless, that "sense of place" can be either positive or negative and that negative associations with place rarely act as effective bases for mobilization.

How people come to identify with a place may be determined in large measure by the collective experiences groups have living in a place, including the power group members have to influence decisions affecting their lives. As Relph explains:

> [T]hrough interest groups . . . communities can develop and an image be projected in which the identities of places of significance to that group are a reflection of group interests and biases. Thus a particular city presents a different identity to those living in its slums, its ghettos, its suburbs; and to developers, planners, and citizens' action groups. Such differences in identity are never more apparent than in confrontations between different groups. (1976, 57–58)

The outcome of such confrontations plays a major role in determining whether group members identify positively or negatively with a place and whether that identification is strong or weak.

Place-based identification is far from a straightforward matter. The geographic scale at which place is constructed is at issue as well. Few processes can be exclusively tied to a specific scale. For instance, the economic processes that shape many of the characteristics of places "are directly or indirectly connected to the dialectics of more macro-level structuration" (Pred 1984, 283). Likewise, decisions made within local states occur within a broader system of local-central and local-local state interactions. Generally, people tend to identify more strongly with a place they know firsthand. This is not always the case, however. Discussing regional identity—a particular type of place identity—Markusen (1987, 42) observes:

> The proximity and concreteness of the region suggest a tractability, a chance to shape the environment, that is not there for most people on a larger scale.

People know firsthand the local power structure, and they see daily changes wrought in their milieu. Not all groups, of course, express this affinity with the region in which they live. Many are forced by economic circumstances to stay in a place where they feel insecure and powerless. Others may feel more grounded in a remote cabin, a neighborhood, or a cosmopolitan circuit.

Places are constructed at different scales and, depending on lived experience, some scales may arouse a stronger sense of place than others. Although a wide range of factors influence place-based identity construction, experiences in political arenas must be considered of relatively greater significance among politically concerned and active citizens.

The relationship between political experience and local identification can be observed among many community activist groups. The political opportunities afforded community groups by the local state, for example, shape these groups' ability to participate in and influence local state policies. Members of groups that can control or influence the actions of the local state more frequently feel empowered and are more likely to develop a positive local identification. Members of groups that are excluded from local state decision making, conversely, more frequently develop a sense of political alienation and are more likely to develop a weaker, or even negative, local identification.

Although place-based identification is not the only relevant form of collective identity, it does represent one means by which the free-rider problem may be overcome. A strong place-based identity may provide a level of collective identification sufficient to transcend free-ridership tendencies, while a weak or negative place-based identity may lead a potential participant in political struggle to ask, "What's in it for me?" and to reject political activism unless the benefits appear to outweigh the costs.

One can posit some general relationships between local state structures, sense of place, and political mobilization (figure 9). Political opportunity structures, which can include or exclude particular groups from decision-making processes, can vary considerably among local states. The empowerment or disempowerment of particular groups is likely to affect the degree to which members of those groups consider the territory of the local state to be "their place." A strong positive sense of place represents a form of collective identity that may lead an individual to put the good of the place-based community before the individual costs and benefits of political action. A sense of place of this nature may foster place-based political mobilization. On the other hand, experiences of disempowerment may lead individuals to act solely on their individual interests. Although a shared sense of place may

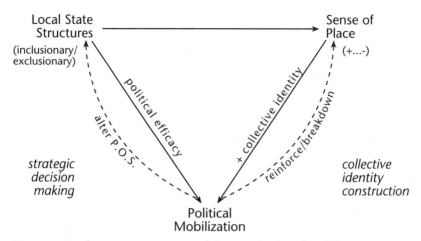

Figure 7. Local state structures, sense of place, and political mobilization.

provide a basis for solidarity necessary in political movements, solidarity alone does not produce mobilization. Mobilization is also affected by the prospects of success. Expectations of political efficacy foster mobilization, while unfavorable prospects may prevent mobilization even when solidarity is relatively strong.

In short, economies, states, and lifeworlds all vary geographically. Geographically uneven development, geographically differentiated state structures, and the time-space paths of identity construction articulate in different ways in different places, giving rise to an uneven geography of social movement mobilization. Not surprisingly, different places exhibit different propensities for protest. Katznelson (1976), Wright (1978), and Agnew (1987) use the term *capacity* to refer to the ability of individuals to come together as a group to pursue their common political aims. Agnew (1987) observes that "different places produce different degrees and orientations of organizational capacity" (59). In other words, different places exhibit different capacities for social protest, not only because of their "internal" characteristics, but also because of their location in the geography of broader-scale social forces.

A Geographic Theory of Communicative Action: Summary and Implications

By examining Habermas's conceptualization of the operation of society from an explicitly geographic perspective we can begin to understand not only the genesis of social movements, but also the geographically uneven nature of social movement mobilization. Social movements cannot be explained on the basis of singular processes, but rather as the result of a variety of systemic and lifeworld processes that articulate in different ways in different places. When Pred (1984, 279) refers to place as a "historically contingent process . . . of becoming," he puts geography and history front and center in any examination of social processes. The geographical and historical constitution of social processes, moreover, fluctuates. As Brown (1997b, 191) explains, "spaces restructure [in ways that] are not necessarily linear or absolute." One can see this in the shifting geography of economic restructuring, the opening and closing of political opportunities, patterns of migration, and the flux of culture. A variety of forces, which vary in terms of both geographic extent and temporal frame, are relevant to the explanation of social movements.

A central force contributing to the differentiated geography of social movements is the fluctuating and uneven nature of capitalist development. Uneven development means that different places will have different class structures, skill mixes, resources, and material interests. People living in a particular place must confront their shared material circumstances and collectively construct a meaningful world. When a significant threat to their well-being arises, they must have the requisite cohesion, skills, and resources if they are to mount a credible political response.

Mutual understandings are reached within geographically differentiated lifeworlds. Sometimes these understandings are shared across multiple lifeworlds, sometimes they are specific to particular lifeworlds. More accurately, the social cleavages dictated by the spatial division of labor, social constructions of class, race, and gender, and geographically specific patterns of interaction give rise to multiple, partially overlapping, partially segregated patterns of understanding. This structuring of lived experience gives rise to the construction of multiple identities, some strongly *associated with places* and all *constructed through places*.

A strong sense of collective identity (including, but not limited to, sense of place) bolsters the capacity of individuals to come together in organizations to act collectively. Not all organizations are held together by means of collective identity; some organizations draw participants operating strictly from strategic or instrumental motives, but these organizations must provide selective incentives or sanctions.

The capacity to come together in organizations does not necessarily lead to political action. Mobilization rarely occurs without clear and significant grievances. Grievances usually stem from actions taken within the system. Corporate disinvestment or relocation decisions, cutbacks in state funding of any variety of social programs, or state actions promoting or allowing discrimination against specific groups can undermine the reproduction of lifeworlds and spur political organizations to action. In the case of grievances stemming from corporate decisions, political movements (e.g., labor) may attempt redress by direct confrontation. However, class struggle in Western industrialized societies has been largely displaced to the state. It is in the arena of the state that struggles of economic production as well as social reproduction are usually fought. Both forms of struggle involve the material interests of particular groups and communities. Although it is usually argued that traditional social movements, such as the labor movement, address issues stemming from conflicts in production spaces and that new social movements, such as the women's movement, address conflicts stemming from lifeworld spaces, it is increasingly clear that such a simple dichotomy is untenable. Most individuals live their lives in a variety of lifeworld and systemic spaces, develop multiple and crosscutting identities, and recognize their multiple locations in their political activities. Certainly, cognizance of the links between systems and lifeworlds is recognizable in the contemporary demands of both the labor and women's movements.

There is no necessity for social movements to express their grievances at a particular level of the state, at least not initially. In a state system differentiated by place and geographic scale, opportunities for successful political action may be relatively favorable at some places and scales and unfavorable at others. Many political movements opt to fight their early battles on favorable turf (often the local state) even though central state action is ultimately required to redress their grievances. The disjuncture between many broadscale systemic processes and often favorable but locally circumscribed local state political opportunity structures means that the local state may function as a mere crisis-avoidance mechanism for the central state. But this need not always be the case; mobilization aimed at numerous local states can be redirected to toward the central state and influence central state policy in a manner not possible without initial local mobilization.

Perhaps the biggest issue facing social movements is the frequent disjuncture between the geographies of lifeworlds and the geographies of systemic processes. Movements challenge the operation of systemic processes from particular social and geographic locations. Collective identities are usually the primary basis for mobilizing movements, yet the demands of social movements can have systemic repercussions considerably beyond the location of the mobilized collectivity. Forming alliances that span several collectivities, as well as considering implications of movement demands for other groups, are central dilemmas for social movements—dilemmas that require building bridges across spaces and places. Such bridge building is by no means an easy task, requiring, as it does, the establishment of meaningful dialogue among multiple, geographically differentiated lifeworlds that do not necessarily share common views, values, or experiences.

A geographically sensitive model of social movement mobilization is needed if we are to begin to understand the geographically uneven landscape of social protest. But such a model tells us little about how social processes operating at a variety of geographic scales articulate in different ways in different places. To gain a better understanding of how these processes articulate "on the ground," comparative case study is required. It is to just such a study that we now turn.

Chapter 3 investigates the geographic patterning of interests, resources, and opportunities in Cambridge, Lexington, and Waltham, Massachusetts. In chapter 4 the sociospatial recruitment strategies employed by local peace organizations in these municipalities and their implications for resource mobilization and alliance building are examined. Chapter 5 returns to Lefebvre's conceptions of space to analyze scale disjunctures between the material geography of defense investment and its representation; emphasis is placed on how these scale disjunctures affected peace politics. Chapter 6 explicitly examines scale differences in political opportunity structures and how these affected peace movement strategies and outcomes. The Conclusion completes the book with an examination of the variety of ways the geographic structuring of the peace movement affected its successes and failures and how attention to geographic structuring enriches our understanding of social movements in general.

3

Place Matters: Interests, Resources, and Opportunities

> This is the paradox of the contemporary movements: they address the
> whole of society in the name of a category or a group, or on the basis of a
> particular place within the social structure. (Melucci 1994, 118)

The disjuncture between the geographies of lifeworlds and the geographies
of systems represents one of the most intransigent and paradoxical problems
facing social movements. On the one hand, most major political grievances
derive from processes that are systemic in nature; they stem from the functioning (or disfunctioning) of the economy or the state. On the other hand,
social movements mobilize around shared lifeworld identities and values
that have their own geographies, usually different from those of systemic
processes. Social movements are necessarily rooted in places—and not just
the metaphorical "places" to which Melucci alludes, but rather in real places,
each with its own "circumstances, constraints, and opportunities for social
action" (Routledge 1993, 140).

The peace movement is no exception in this regard. Although questions
of peace necessarily entail issues of national policy and international relations, peace mobilization occurs in a constellation of place-specific contexts.
Although movement objectives and core messages may exhibit some national
consistency, the reception of those messages is shaped by the constituent characteristics of place. As former Speaker of the U.S. House of Representatives
Tip O'Neill succinctly observed, "all politics is local." Even national politics
must be anchored in particular places.

For individual actors, the ways in which place structures experience can be analyzed by tracing the "paths" and "projects" of everyday life (Pred 1984, 1986). In broader terms, Agnew (1996) reminds us of several processes that shape the political activity of particular places, including the spatial division of labor, the characteristics of local and central states; class, gender, and ethnic divisions; place-based identities oriented to the local, regional, or national level; and the geography of everyday life.

Although I argue that attention to place is a prerequisite for any nuanced understanding of political mobilization, I would be remiss to neglect the historical—as well as geographic—constitution of political processes. Clearly, the mobilization of a social movement—or any political activity, for that matter—is constituted both temporally and spatially. Indeed, as Pred (1984, 279) stresses, place is a historically contingent *process*. Attention to process precludes the analytic reduction of political activity to static phenomena, explainable through the association of purportedly stable variables. In the geographic and temporal flux of any process, however, there are crucial *moments* in which significant forces and transformative opportunities emerge. Such moments vary in duration. As Melucci (1994, 106) puts it: "We must seek to understand . . . [the] multiplicity of synchronic and diachronic elements. Then we can explain how they combine into the concrete unit of a collective actor."

This chapter focuses on conditions created by systemic processes—the uneven geography of material interests, resources, and political opportunities in the Boston metropolitan area—rather than on the systemic processes themselves. Although these conditions laid the foundation for the uneven geography of peace mobilization in the Boston metropolitan area during the 1970s and 1980s, it must be remembered that they were themselves the result of long and complex processes. The next three chapters address the historical and geographical *unfolding* of peace mobilization in the Boston metropolitan area in considerably more detail.

There is a substantial, although largely aspatial, treatment of systemic conditions in the social movements literature that can serve as a useful starting point for analyzing the geography of material interests, resources, and political opportunities. In one of the most wide-ranging contemporary treatments of class, Eder (1993, 162) argues that class matters in the analysis of social movements in two principal ways: (1) class-specific social position defines what is essentially a "social opportunity structure" that "anchor[s] protest practices" and helps to explain their "strength and durability" among particular classes; (2) cultural definitions of class are constructions that serve to group and separate classes of people through the creation of collective identities that form the bases for mobilization. Perhaps the most innovative aspect of Eder's constructivist approach to class is the way in which class agency and context are linked. The "social-structural processes (occupational differentiation, educational differentiation, income differentiation, life-style differentiation etc.) that open up the social space for class differentiation and class relations" are themselves viewed in the context of "countervailing processes on the level of [political] institutions" (1993, 176). Eder essentially lays out a schema that in broad outlines mirrors the Habermasian model of interactions between the economy and state (with implications for lifeworld processes) detailed in chapter 2. However, like most theorists of social movements, Eder says little about the geographic structuring of social movement processes and how that structuring affects key processes and interactions.

In work that dovetails nicely with Eder's, Wallace and Jenkins (1995) examine three explanations of the nature of contemporary social protest: (1) *New class arguments* emphasize the rise of a class of "knowledge workers" who demand high levels of autonomy and who are frequently at odds with the traditional profit-oriented managerial class and the socially conservative working class; (2) the *postindustrialism thesis* stresses that social and demographic changes such as expanded higher education, a larger youth cohort, and greater affluence have "loosened traditional social controls and nurtured a new postmaterialist political culture"; this, in turn, has created "greater cognitive mobilization, broader support for a postmaterialist or "self-fulfillment" ethic, and demands for direct participation in decision-making" (99); (3) *neocorporatist and dealignment arguments* focus on changes in systems of political representation. Relatively clear party identities have been lost and in their place "broad 'catch-all' parties" have evolved, creating a more volatile electorate, more open to political alternatives" (ibid.). Hand in hand with changes in party structures has come strong corporatist bargaining between capital and labor, which is frequently associated with stronger social controls, less political accountability, increased alienation, and social protest.

Wallace and Jenkins conduct a cross-national analysis of eight Western democracies to assess the validity of the new class, postindustrial, and neocorporatist/dealignment arguments. Their findings are of interest for a variety of reasons, not least of which because they show significant cross-national variation in characteristics related to social protest. They find that differences in political representation systems profoundly affect the nature and incidence of political protest; the new class is a significant source of protest in five countries, including the United States; class identification varies in its effects but is particularly strong in the United States (where non-class identification is also strong); education is significantly related to protest in four countries, including the United States; left political identification is associated with protest; religiosity is significantly related to reduced protest participation in four countries, including the United States (except among Catholics, who protest more); and the life-cycle effects of age are negative and significant in all eight countries.

Eder's (1993) and Wallace and Jenkins's (1995) work points to the varying significance that class, political structures, and culture can play in political protest activities and begins to suggest some of the ways in which economic, political, and cultural processes may interact. Inattention to the geographic constitution of crucial processes, or reduction of geographic constitution to national-level differences, however, obscures important variations within countries, how place-specific conditions may alter the significance of particular processes, and how the strategies and actions in particular places can shape a national movement.

Certainly a crucial process leading to antinuclear weapons-focused peace mobilization was the escalation of the nuclear arms race, a process that was international in scale. Yet, as numerous resource mobilization and political process scholars have demonstrated, the emergence of broadscale "objective" grievances does not necessarily translate into political mobilization. The tremendous geographic variation of peace mobilization in the United States confirms this point. Some places within the United States exhibited extremely high levels of peace activism during the arms race, while in other places activism was virtually nonexistent.

During the 1970s and 1980s the Boston metropolitan area was widely recognized as one of the centers of peace movement activism in the United States, yet this perception too was somewhat misleading. Certain municipalities within the metropolitan area, such as Cambridge, were extremely influential in peace politics, while other municipalities exhibited lower levels of enthusiasm and support.

In examining the mobilization of the antinuclear weapons branch of the peace movement in the Boston metropolitan area, care was taken in this study to select places for comparative analysis that differed in significant ways. The mobilization of four Boston-area antinuclear weapons-oriented peace organizations—Cambridge SANE/Freeze, Boston Mobilization for Survival (Cambridge members), Lexington Committee for a Nuclear Weapons Freeze, and Waltham Concerned Citizens—must be understood in the context of differing systemic and lifeworld geographies. The cities in which these organizations have operated differ greatly in terms of their place in the spatial division of labor and the openness of local state structures— differences that have had significant implications for organizational strategies, successes, and failures. Lifeworld considerations are also crucial and will be taken up in chapter 4. An initial, and fundamental, question to be addressed here is how the geographic structuring of material interests and resources can affect political action, and so it is to the spatial division of labor that we turn first.

Spatial Divisions of Labor: Material Interests and Potential Resources

In the past century, military spending has often been a powerful accelerant to economic growth. That is one reason—perhaps the main reason—it is so very difficult to curb.

—David Warsh, *Boston Globe*

Do you really want to kill the goose [defense contracting] that lays the golden egg?

—Ronald Mills, Foundation for Economic Research

The peace movement is not simply a symbolic movement; it strives to effect material change. In the early 1980s the moderate wing of the movement worked toward a bilateral freeze of the nuclear arms race; more radical wings worked toward the elimination of all nuclear weapons. Achieving either objective would have had very significant economic implications: millions of jobs nationally, and hundreds of thousands of jobs in Massachusetts, depended (and still depend) on defense spending. In Massachusetts, the high-tech defense industry played the leading role in the "Massachusetts Miracle," as the state's phenomenal economic turnaround came to be known. Halting or reversing the arms buildup would have likely meant halting or reversing Massachusetts's economic recovery.

Against such a backdrop, one would not expect the most vibrant peace movement in the country to develop, yet that is precisely what happened. The explanation for such a paradoxical situation is not to be found in a simple analysis of material interests prevailing in Massachusetts; still, such interests have played a vital role in the dynamics of peace politics and were the Achilles' heel of the 1983 Nuclear Free Cambridge campaign that sought to ban all nuclear weapons-related research and development in Cambridge.

The economic history of three quite different places—Cambridge, Lexington, and Waltham—is an important starting point in any attempt to understand the complex processes that produced both a tremendous mobilization of resources for the cause of peace and a rejection of binding measures to halt the arms race. All three municipalities have long histories, with some important differences that help to explain place-specific variations in peace mobilization.

Cambridge was founded in 1630 and holds a central position in American revolutionary history. It grew substantially during the nineteenth century, but remained largely distinct from Boston until 1912, when subway connections fostered stronger economic links and stimulated rapid industrial growth. Publishing, scientific instruments, rubber goods, leather goods, and fabricated metals all became important industries, in addition to education. Most of Cambridge's traditional industries declined during the twentieth century as manufacturing firms moved elsewhere, but a very large proportion of Cambridge's population remains working-class, contrary to the city's popular image. Lost industrial jobs have been at least partially offset by high-tech defense-related manufacturing and service jobs, although the working class remains in very precarious economic circumstances. MIT and Harvard are the major economic forces in the city, both in terms of direct employment and the firms and research and development (R&D) labs that spin off from them.

Lexington was founded at about the same time as Cambridge—around 1640. Lexington has continuously maintained its tranquil image as well as its historical notoriety as a significant site of the American revolution. The town remained an agricultural community until 1951 when the expansion of Route 128 into a four-lane highway made the area attractive to growing high-tech firms. Although a significant amount of high-tech industrial development has taken place in and adjacent to Lexington, the town has grown mainly as an exclusive bedroom community for professional, managerial, and upper-level technical employees of Route 128 high-tech industries.

Waltham stands in considerable contrast to both Cambridge and Lexington. It too was settled in the 1630s, but historical similarities end there. The waterpower of the Charles River offered major advantages to developing industries in the eighteenth and nineteenth centuries. The first paper mill was built on the river in 1788 and the first textile mill to combine all stages of cotton cloth production under one roof was founded by the Boston Manufacturing Company in 1813. The Waltham Watch Company, for which the city became well known, opened in 1854. The Metz Company, which manufactured cars and bicycles, opened in 1909. Waltham became the quintessential working-class manufacturing city of the nineteenth century. The twentieth century brought the decline of Waltham's traditional manufacturing base. The Metz Company closed in 1924, textiles ceased to be significant after 1930, and the Waltham Watch Company closed in 1950. A severely depressed city, Waltham's economy began a slow rebound with the construction of Route 128, the growth of high-tech defense-related industry, and increased defense spending. Its largest employer is Raytheon, which opened its first manufacturing plant in Waltham in 1934. The city's economy today is based largely on the manufacture of precision instruments, electrical machinery, cameras, electronic systems, missiles, and fabricated metal products, as well as electronic R&D.

Although these three municipalities have significantly different economic histories, they share one very important characteristic: economic dependence on the "golden goose" of high-tech defense-related industry. This dependence is especially significant in the context of the decline of Massachusetts's manufacturing economy that began after World War I and continued until the late 1970s. As Harrison (1984, 64) argues, "the contextual importance of the long history of high unemployment in New England can hardly be exaggerated." Massachusetts unemployment rates were above the national average in twenty-two of the twenty-eight years between 1951 and 1978. Unemployment rates were especially high in the late 1940s and early 1950s as capital fled Massachusetts for even cheaper and, more importantly, nonunionized and docile labor of the South. As a result of the space race and Vietnam War–related defense spending, the Massachusetts economy recovered to a degree between the late 1950s and the mid-1960s. But with the winding down of the Vietnam War and National Aeronautic and Space Administration (NASA) spending, the Massachusetts economy again went into a tailspin with unemployment running 37 percent above the national average in 1973; by 1975 unemployment was 11.2 percent—worst in the nation and 32 percent above the national average (statistics compiled by Ross and Trachte 1990, based on Bureau of Labor Statistics and Massachusetts Division of Employment Security data).

The postwar economic history of Massachusetts has primarily been the result of two opposing economic forces: rationalization and geographic restructuring serving to discipline the labor force through lower wages and unemployment; and stimulation of the Massachusetts economy through defense- and space-related government spending. One can readily see why high-tech defense-related industry has taken on such significance to Massachusetts workers. High-tech defense-related jobs represent one of the few sources of replacement employment for working-class production workers who have experienced decades of economic disciplining. Most professional and technical workers in Massachusetts directly owe their jobs to such industry.

Firms engaged in defense contracting account for an especially large number of jobs in Cambridge, Lexington, and Waltham. Between 1979 and 1985—the period of significant peace mobilization—defense contracting represented a major and growing source of economic stimulus to all three of these municipalities (table 4). By 1985, total prime contracts represented an almost billion-dollar infusion to their collective economies—a phenomenal amount for three municipalities with a combined population of fewer than two hundred thousand people.

Some of the key weapons systems of the Carter/Reagan arms buildup were developed in Cambridge, Lexington, and Waltham. In Cambridge, Draper Laboratory, formerly the MIT Instrumentation Laboratory, played a central role in the development of the missile guidance system for the Trident II submarine's nuclear missiles; the lab also worked on the MX missile and Ballistic Missile Early Warning System (BMEWS) radars. Also in Cambridge, Bolt, Beranek, and Newman produced computer and communications networks for the Pentagon. Raytheon, Massachusetts's largest defense contractor, contracted for work on the Trident II submarine and BMEWS radars; its Waltham plants produced, among other items, microwave equipment, infrared detectors, and various computer and communications equipment; its Lexington plant produced a variety of items, most likely including radar and sonar systems, missile guidance systems, and air traffic control systems. MIT's laboratories (primarily Lincoln Laboratory) at Hanscom Air Force Base were involved with AWACS radar and planes, strategic missile warning radars, and Distant Early Warning Line anti-bomber radars. Itek, also in Lexington, produced ground and airborne camera systems and various electro-optical equipment (Hall 1981a, 1981b, 1985a, 1985b; Leavitt 1986).

Table 4 lists the number of employees for each defense-related firm in these municipalities, as well as the dollar value of their prime defense contracts. The employee numbers, however, are not equivalent to the number of jobs directly created by defense contracting, that is, a portion of these jobs would exist even without defense contracting. To estimate the number of jobs produced by defense spending per se we can follow techniques outlined by Leavitt (1986) and generally replicated by Harrison and Kluver (1989). Leavitt, based on a Data Resources model applied to Bureau of Labor Statistics data, estimates that 10,700 direct jobs and 10,600 indirect (subcontracting) jobs are created for every $1 billion of Massachusetts defense contracting. At these rates, 10,544 defense jobs were created in Cambridge at its contracting peak (1984–85), 8,243 defense jobs were created in Lexington at its contracting peak (1984–85), and 5,581 defense jobs were created in Waltham at its contracting peak (1982–83). Of course, not all of these jobs would have been held by residents of these municipalities, but these numbers must still be considered conservative. Applying a conservative multiplier of 2 to account for additional jobs created by defense workers' spending, these numbers double to 21,088, 16,486, and 11,162 jobs in Cambridge, Lexington, and Waltham, respectively. This represents 42 percent, 108 percent, and 37 percent of the jobs held by Cambridge, Lexington, and Waltham residents in 1980 (according to U.S. Census figures), respectively. These numbers may appear high, but even if only direct prime contracting jobs were actually created in the municipalities under consideration (and this would clearly be an underestimation), each municipality still had a very big stake in defense contracting.

The spatial division of labor—substantially driven by the locational pattern of defense-oriented firms and the geography of defense contracting—clearly creates a pattern of material interests favoring defense industries in Massachusetts, generally, and in Cambridge, Lexington, and Waltham, in particular. Why the geography of material interests does not, by itself, determine the dynamics of peace politics is taken up in detail in chapter 5.

Material interests are not the only aspect of the division of labor that is relevant to an understanding of Boston-area peace politics. Also a direct function of the spatial division of labor is the resources potentially available for mobilization in any given place. Resources of particular importance include the financial resources required to run a campaign and the education and skills required to negotiate complex political institutions—in other words, resources related to class.

That class characteristics differ greatly among Cambridge, Lexington, and Waltham is immediately apparent from table 5. Of all persons active in the paid labor force, approximately half in Cambridge, a third in Lexington, and a quarter in Waltham work in professional and related service industries. The ratios are almost reversed in manufacturing industries: an eighth of Cambridge workers, a fifth of Lexington workers, and a quarter of Waltham workers are employed in manufacturing. Occupational compositions are no surprise: half of the employed Lexington residents are in managerial and professional occupations, a slightly lower percentage hold the same occupations in Cambridge, and only a quarter of employed Waltham residents are in such occupations. Manufacturing production occupations account for a small proportion of all occupations in Cambridge and Lexington, but are as significant as managerial and professional specialty occupations in Waltham. Technical, sales, and administrative support occupations account for about a third of all positions in all three municipalities; services play a relatively small role.

Mean and median incomes are somewhat surprising. Lexington residents have by far the highest incomes, which is not surprising, but Cambridge residents have the lowest incomes, which perhaps is. The low mean and median

Table 4. Prime defense contracts over $1 million in Cambridge, Lexington, and Waltham (1979–85)
(employees and millions of dollars in contracts)*

Contractor	Employees	Contracts, millions of dollars				
		79–80	80–81	81–82	82–83	84–85
CAMBRIDGE						
Adaptive Optics	NA	—	—	—	—	5
B & M Technological Services	NA	—	—	—	—	1
Block Engineering	140	1	1	1	3	—
Bolt, Beranek, and Newman	1,530	25	21	41	42	61
Brown Daltas & Sipican	250	4	4	4	2	—
Charles Stark Draper Lab	1,000	77	86	125	111	338
Computer Corporation of America	115	2	2	4	3	5
Harvard University	10,975	5	3	3	6	5
Higher Order Software	NA	2	2	—	—	—
Input Output Computer Services	NA	—	2	2	—	—
Intermetrics	350	3	4	6	9	9
Little, Arthur D.	1,000	6	6	10	13	12
MIT	1,000	27	28	31	52	42
National Council on Soviet and Eastern European Research	NA	1	—	—	—	—
Polaroid	NA	—	—	2	2	—
Scientific Systems	NA	—	—	—	2	2
Thinking Machine	NA	—	—	—	—	3
Vi Mil	360	5	3	4	—	—
TOTAL**	16,720	164	168	242	252	495
LEXINGTON						
Emmanuel College	NA	—	—	—	1	—
Honeywell	5,000	28	45	63	18	26
Horizons Technology	NA	—	—	—	—	9
Itek	1,000	8	7	9	8	18
Logicon	NA	1	1	1	—	—
MIT (Hanscom AFB)	NA	129	138	188	198	322
Raytheon	6,000	3	13	108	60	2
Signatron	50	1	3	3	2	1
Support Systems	NA	—	—	—	—	4
Systems Integration Engineering	NA	—	—	—	—	1
TOTAL**	12,050	173	210	376	290	387

Table 4. (continued)

Contractor	Employees	Contracts, millions of dollars				
		79–80	80–81	81–82	82–83	84–85
WALTHAM						
Adams, Russell Company	480	1	—	—	3	1
Corporate Technology Planning	NA	—	1	—	—	—
First Petroleum	NA	—	—	—	—	2
Foster Miller Associates	200	1	—	2	4	8
General Electric	NA	—	—	—	—	2
GenRad	3,000	—	—	—	2	3
GTE Laboratories	327	—	—	1	2	2
Helix Technology	350	4	2	—	2	1
Hewlett Packard	1,100	4	—	—	—	4
Input Output Comp Serv	49	—	—	2	4	—
Nichols, W. H. Company	400	—	—	2	1	1
North Atlantic Petrol	NA	—	—	3	—	—
Raytheon	3,375	41	120	158	221	31
Softech	350	10	10	8	12	12
Stein Associates	NA	1	—	—	—	—
Thermo Electron	249	—	—	—	1	1
Waltham Precision Instruments	130	3	3	4	1	3
TOTAL**	10,010	75	148	190	262	81

* Employee estimates based primarily on George D. Hall's *Directory of Massachusetts Manufacturers 1981–1982* (1981) and George D. Hall's *Massachusetts Service Directory 1981–1982* (1981); when reliable estimates were not available in these directories George D. Hall's *Directory of Massachusetts Manufacturers 1985–1986* (1985), George D. Hall's *Massachusetts Service Directory 1985–1986* (1985), and a 1982 unpublished AFL-CIO memorandum were used. Prime contracts data are taken from the Department of Defense series *Prime Contracts by State, City, and Contractor.* The Department of Defense did not publish prime contract data by city and contractor for fiscal year 1983–84.

** Employee totals are low because of lack of employee estimates for several plants. Especially significant are the lack of estimates for Polaroid, MIT's laboratories at Hanscom Air Force Base, and General Electric. Total value of defense prime contracts is for all contractors in each city, that is, the value of small contracts (less than $1 million), not individually shown in this table, is included in the totals.

Table 5. Socioeconomic characteristics of Cambridge, Lexington, and Waltham (1980)

	Cambridge	Lexington	Waltham
Population	95,322	29,479	58,200
Mean income (1979)	$18,434	$36,502	$21,025
Median income (1979)	$14,211	$31,605	$18,615
Selected industries			
Manufacturing	13%	20%	25%
Wholesale/retail trade	12%	15%	19%
Professional & related services	47%	36%	26%
Class of worker			
Private wage & salary	80%	76%	82%
State & federal government	8%	6%	6%
Local government	7%	10%	8%
Self-employed	5%	7%	4%
Occupation			
Managerial/professional specialty	40%	50%	26%
Technical sales, administrative support	30%	30%	35%
Service	13%	7%	13%
Production, machine operator, etc.	16%	13%	26%
Four or more years of college (25 years and older)	55%	65%	35%
Enrolled in college	25%	6%	13%
Owner-occupied households	24%	85%	46%
Same SMSA 5 years ago	68%	89%	85%
Same house 5 years ago	40%	68%	56%
Median age	29	37	30
Race (non-Spanish origin)			
White	81%	95%	95%
Black	11%	1%	1%
Asian/Pacific islander	4%	3%	1%
Spanish origin	5%	1%	2%

Source: U.S. Bureau of the Census (1983a).

income in Cambridge is undoubtedly explained by the very high percentage of college students (25 percent of the population) and the presence of a significant working class. Somewhat higher incomes, compared to Cambridge, are found in Waltham, due in large part to a substantially smaller college student presence. Cambridge, with significant black, Asian, and Hispanic populations, is much more ethnically diverse than Lexington and Waltham; Waltham, however, retains some ethnic identity based in the Irish and Italian heritage of many of its residents.

In short, Cambridge has a strongly bifurcated class structure with substantial numbers employed in well-paying, highly skilled occupations—many of them in high-tech defense-related fields—and a substantial working class employed in old and new manufacturing and service and support occupations. A substantial college student population adds another axis of social division; the city's social structure might best be called trifurcated—a fact with significant implications for peace mobilization, as will be discussed in subsequent chapters. Lexington has the most homogeneous class characteristics: the town is predominantly a bedroom community for well-paid, highly educated white employees of high-tech defense-related industry. Of the three municipalities, Lexington has the highest percentage in managerial and professional specialty occupations (50 percent) and the lowest percentages in all other categories. College students are only a small proportion of the population and there are no major institutions of higher learning. Waltham, despite the growth of high-tech industry, Brandeis University, and Bentley College, is still predominantly working-class. Managerial and professional specialty occupations associated with high-tech defense-related industry have grown, but manufacturing production occupations are just as prevalent. A plurality of the population is employed in service and support occupations. College students have a greater presence than in Lexington, but still barely half of what is found in Cambridge.

Municipality-wide statistics, however, do not give the whole story behind the potential organizational resources of municipalities (at least as suggested by U.S. Census measures). There is significant spatial variation in socioeconomic characteristics in each municipality. This variation frequently has important implications for the recruitment strategies of organizations and, in turn, the social groups that have been incorporated into the peace movement, either directly as members or indirectly in alliances.

Figure 8 illustrates the geographic distribution, by census tract, of Cambridge residents employed in managerial and professional specialty occupations. Cambridge has a clearly bifurcated—and geographically segregated—class structure. Extremely high concentrations of persons in managerial and

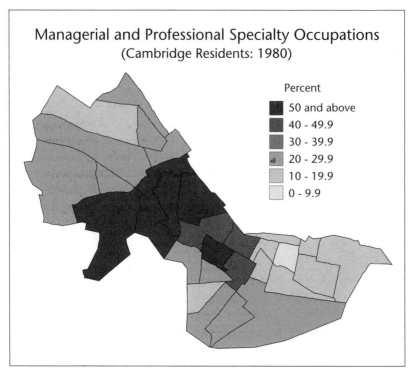

Figure 8. Managerial and professional specialty occupations for Cambridge residents, 1980. Source: U.S. Bureau of the Census (1983a).

professional specialty occupations (more than 50 percent) occur in the census tracts around Harvard Square (in the center of the city) where professors, professionals, and students cluster. As one moves away from Harvard Square, the concentration of such occupations declines. Working-class East Cambridge (in the northeast of the city), which also includes the city's largest Portuguese community, poses a particularly stark contrast to the elite Harvard Square area; in one East Cambridge census tract fewer than 10 percent of all working residents are in managerial and professional specialty occupations; in all other East Cambridge census tracts the percentage is still low. The Central Square area, also in East Cambridge immediately west of MIT, and Cambridgeport, in the southeast of the city, have only slightly higher percentages of residents in managerial and professional specialty occupations. North Cambridge (in the northwest of the city) includes census tracts in the lower ranges. These latter areas are also predominantly working-class and include higher than average concentrations of minority groups. They are areas that are far removed (metaphorically speaking) from the

Harvard/MIT power axis, although Cambridgeport, which in the words of one Cambridge activist is "being yuppified," is not as poor or as distant from the levers of power as it once was.

Lexington presents a significant contrast to Cambridge. Whereas Cambridge has very diverse neighborhoods reflecting its long and varied economic history, Lexington is a model of a homogeneous middle- and upper-class suburb (figure 9). The town is 95 percent white, with only 1 percent of

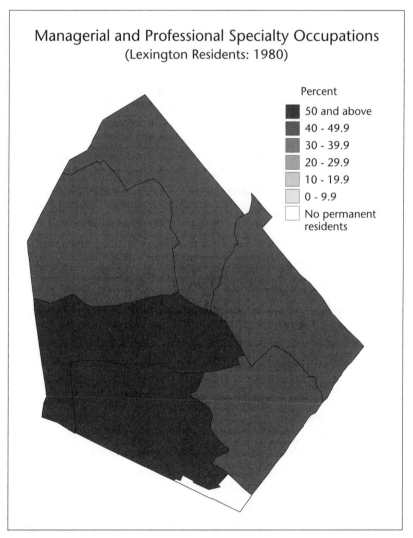

Figure 9. Managerial and professional specialty occupations for Lexington residents, 1980. Source: U.S. Bureau of the Census (1983a).

the population black and 1 percent Hispanic. Half of all employed residents are in managerial and professional specialty occupations; especially high concentrations (more than 50 percent) are found in the southwestern third of the town. This is not, however, to suggest that other parts of the town are significantly different; all other census tracts have concentrations of managerial and professional specialty occupations that are almost as high. The town's extremely high concentration of managers and professionals stems from the town's proximity to high-tech defense industries along Route 128 and its pleasant, well-planned residential environment. Although clearly not all Lexington residents are wealthy, upper-middle-class, or even middle-middle-class, there are no major geographical concentrations of working-class, poor, or minority residents.

Waltham, bordering Lexington to the south, represents almost a mirror image of Lexington (figure 10). Waltham retains the working-class characteristics for which it has been known for a century and a half. Although the growth of high-tech defense-related industries in Waltham has created more managerial and professional specialty jobs, relatively few persons taking those jobs take up residence in Waltham. The highest concentrations (in the low 30 percent range) of residents in managerial and professional specialty occupations are in the eastern part of the city. The entire western half of the city is in the 20–29.9 percent managerial and professional specialty occupation category, while the two census tracts to the southeast—comprising part of the city's old industrial district—are in the 10–19.9 percent category. The city's Hispanic population is also concentrated in the poorer, older industrial areas in the southern part of the city.

In short, peace movement organizers in Lexington have a tremendous, concentrated base of well-educated, highly skilled, financially well-off people to draw from; although the skills potentially available to Lexington organizers are considerable, they must also contend with the drawbacks associated with a lack of diversity and the strong ties of residents to high-tech defense-related industries. Cambridge organizers also have a tremendous base of well-educated, highly skilled, financially well-off people to draw from; these people are concentrated around Harvard Square in the center of the city. Cambridge organizers can also recruit from the substantial student population, which has considerable skills to offer as well as more flexible schedules than most people who are in the workforce full-time. Also a potential resource to peace movement organizers is Cambridge's substantial working-class and minority populations; although these groups' educational and income levels are not as high as those of groups that are usually recruited into the movement, they represent an opportunity to, among other things, broaden the movement's under-

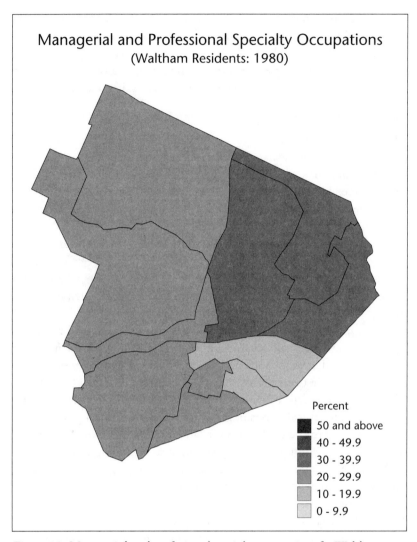

Figure 10. Managerial and professional specialty occupations for Waltham residents, 1980. Source: U.S. Bureau of the Census (1983a).

standings and base of support. In Waltham, peace movement organizers have a smaller financial and skill base to draw from. Certainly Waltham's class structure is not one typically associated with support for the peace movement; although this is in many respects a disadvantage, it is also an opportunity to widen the base of the movement in very meaningful ways.

The economic geography of Cambridge, Lexington, and Waltham sets the stage for social movement mobilization—in terms of both the geography of material interests and the geography of potential resources. But other systemic characteristics are also highly important—and vary significantly among places. Local state structures are especially important to local peace mobilizations, and differ substantially among Cambridge, Lexington, and Waltham.

Local States and Political Opportunity Structures

The local state literature within geography only touches on issues of political participation. The local state literature has focused primarily on the structures and functions of local states, while the related locality literature has paid considerable attention to the potential of local states to serve as vehicles for broader-scale social change (see chapters 1 and 2). More recent developments in local state theory emphasize the geographic and temporal contingency of state structures and functions and the role of local historical relations in shaping place-based modes of social regulation (Peck and Tickell 1992; Goodwin, Duncan, and Halford 1993; Bakshi et. al. 1995; Peck 1993). Little attention, however, has been given to the ways in which local state structures may vary in their openness to political participation.

Openness of local state structures and local modes of social regulation are not separate issues, of course. States are not static or independent entities separate from the rest of society. They are, rather, the outcomes of social struggle, which, in turn, affect social struggle. Peck and Tickell (1992) identify a variety of social regulatory forms and mechanisms operating at the local and regional scales: business relations (including local growth coalitions and interfirm networks), labor relations (including local labor market structures and institutions), money and finance (including venture capital, credit, and housing markets), civil society (including union politics and the gendering of household structures), and state forms (including forms and structures of the local state and local economic policies). These regulatory forms and mechanisms are, in many instances, rooted in the spatial division of labor. As is readily apparent, the spatial division of labor structures place-specific material interests and gives impetus to the creation of institutions serving politically dominant interests in particular places. Certainly, the creation of urban political and economic coalitions—growth coalitions or otherwise—is "necessarily related to changing wider divisions of labor and modes of regulation" (Jonas 1993, 286). Such coalitions are key actors in the structuring of local states, of which there are a wide variety of forms. Such forms affect not only the balance of power, but who participates in politics.

Agnew argues that the variety of barriers "put in place by locally dominant parties or coalitions and designed to restrict electoral competition" largely accounts for the "long-term net decline in [voter] turnouts and the peculiar geography associated with it" (1987, 220). Agnew not only links state structures to political participation, he furthermore argues that "some systems of local government, some political party systems, some electoral systems, and some experiences of political integration, particularly those encouraging territorial commitments in political outlook, encourage a place-based political life" (ibid., 41). Differences in local state structures, then, affect both political participation and the place-based focus of politics.

Agnew's thesis on state structures and political participation can be further developed using Tarrow's (1983, 1989) concept of "political opportunity structure." According to Tarrow (1989, 34), political opportunity structures can be defined in terms of four political characteristics that affect the outcome of political movements: (1) "the openness or closure of formal political access," (2) the "stability or instability of alignments within the political system," (3) the "presence or absence of allies and support groups," and (4) "divisions among the elite and its tolerance for protest."

The "openness or closure of formal political access" in Tarrow's formulation refers to both the formal properties of the state—whether the local state is "reformed" or "unreformed," whether councilpersons are elected by wards or at large, the ease of placing initiatives on the ballot, and so on—and the role of the dominant political coalitions in allowing nongoverning groups access to state power.

The "stability or instability of alignments within the political system" is considered to be a crucial determinant of both protest and the propensity for governmental action. Citing Piven and Cloward (1979), Tarrow argues that "electoral instability—whether related to protest or simply perceived as a danger by elites—would be the source of a more tolerant attitude to protest whatever its sources" (1983, 30).

Allies and support groups are seen as crucial to the success of protest movements. Tarrow asserts that "insurgent groups do best when they succeed in gaining support from influential groups within the system" (ibid., 32). It is not only important that such allies exist; their existence must be widely recognized by those who are to be mobilized. Subjective perceptions of the potential for success are as important as objective support.

Political conflict among elites also creates openings for social movements. When ruling political coalitions weaken, they are less able to repress, combat, and exclude dissident groups from government coalitions and policy decisions. Elite disunity may lead to the formation of new coalitions that include formerly excluded groups.

More open local state political opportunity structures have at least two implications for collective action: (1) they broaden the scope for open debate and discussion, scope that increases the possibility that conflicting parties may come to a common understanding through communicative action; in other words, they present the possibility of a closer approximation of Habermas's "ideal speech situation"; (2) they lower the perceived costs of participation in political movements, thereby affecting actors' strategic calculations; this perception of lower costs may lead to political mobilization that would otherwise appear to be too costly for potential participants. Local state political opportunity structures are likely to affect not only activists' sense of inclusion or exclusion, but also movement success or failure (see chapter 2). Over the long run, such experiences are likely to shape activists' perceptions of the place in which they live and the development of place-based collective identities that may serve to overcome the free-rider problem.

The Boston area exhibits a variety of local state forms. Under the Massachusetts constitution, city governments may adopt one of six different charters; a variety of additional charters are available to smaller-sized municipalities. Differences in municipal charters reflect the history of dominant urban coalitions, while differences in political opportunity structures reflect contemporary constellations of local interest groups as well as the inherited structural characteristics of charters. The cities of Cambridge and Waltham and the town of Lexington represent a range of the charters and political opportunity structures to be found in Massachusetts local states.

For much of the nineteenth and twentieth centuries Cambridge's charter mandated a ward-based system of representation with a strong mayor favoring the city's dominant industrial interests. Under the old charter, the city became known for machine politics and corruption. Largely in response to the problems of corruption Cambridge adopted a new charter in 1940 that produced an extremely open local state based on a council-manager form of government with proportional representation. Under the council-manager system, the city manager serves at the pleasure of the council, and the mayor, who has no veto power, is appointed by the city council. This gives councilpersons a strong voice. More significantly, councilpersons are elected by proportional representation (P.R.), a method that is relatively rare in United States municipalities today, but used to be quite common.

Under P.R., instead of voting for one candidate, voters rank candidates. Candidates who get enough number one votes to reach the quota for election—calculated by dividing the total number of ballots cast by nine (the number of council seats) then adding one—are automatically elected. The extra votes of those candidates with more than the quota of number one votes are allocated to other candidates based on number two preferences.

Table 6. Baseline characteristics of political opportunity structures in Cambridge, Lexington, and Waltham, Massachusetts

I. Cambridge—very favorable to peace movement

Charter: council-manager with proportional representation

Nonbinding referendum: 10 signatures + city council approval or signatures of 10 percent of registered voters to put on next ballot

Initiative petition (binding): signatures of 8 percent of registered voters to put on next ballot or signatures of 15 percent of registered voters to call special election

Referendum petition (challenge city council or school committee action): signatures of 12 percent of registered voters to suspend action and place on next ballot

City council composition: usually a 5 to 4 split between liberals and conservatives/moderates—shifting coalitions/openness to alliances

Influential allies/support groups: faculty and students of Harvard, MIT, and other education institutions

II. Lexington—favorable to peace movement

Charter: town meeting with 189 members elected from 9 precincts

To bring an issue before the town meeting: 10 signatures + Board of Selectmen approval or signatures of 10 percent of registered voters to put on next ballot

Referendum petition (challenge town meeting action): signatures of 3 percent of registered voters in 5 days to call special election within 24 days

Town meeting composition: predominantly neoliberal/liberal—fairly homogeneous reflecting upper-middle-class social composition

Influential allies/support groups: no major institutional allies

III. Waltham—unfavorable to peace movement

Charter: mayor-city council with mayor and 6 councilpersons elected at large and 9 councilpersons elected by ward

Nonbinding referendum: 10 signatures + city council approval or signatures of 10 percent of registered voters to put on next ballot

Initiative petition (binding): signatures of 8 percent of registered voters to put on next ballot or signatures of 15 percent of registered voters to call special election

Referendum petition (challenge city council or school committee action): signatures of 12 percent of registered voters to suspend action and place on next ballot

City council composition: heavily conservative

Influential allies/support groups: no major institutional allies

This process is continued down through the ballot rankings, thereby ensuring that all candidates representing more than one-ninth of the electorate are seated. According to the National Municipal League,

> in a city where 60 per cent of the voters are Republicans, 30 per cent are Democrats, and 10 per cent Independents, under [a nonproportional] system, the Republicans would probably win 100 per cent of the council seats. Under P.R., 60 per cent of the councilmen would be Republican, 30 per cent Democrats, and 10 per cent Independents. The majority rules. But the minority would be represented in exact ratio to its numerical strength. (*Cambridge Magazine* 1972, 15)

Cambridge's P.R. system is widely credited with "mobilizing previously paralyzed minorities whose combined forces now constitute . . . a rousing majority" (Cambridge Editorial Research, Inc. 1965, 34). In Cambridge, P.R. has greatly broadened the scope for political discussion so fundamental to a functioning democracy.

In addition to an extremely open electoral system, Cambridge provides for relatively easy placement of initiatives on the ballot, again allowing greater scope for citizens' voices to be heard. Nonbinding referenda addressing questions of public policy can be placed on the ballot if ten registered Cambridge voters present a petition to the city council and the council approves its inclusion on the ballot. If the council does not approve its inclusion, the question may still be placed on the ballot if a petition is signed by 10 percent of Cambridge's registered voters. Initiative petitions, which are binding, must either be approved or placed on the ballot in the next regularly scheduled election by the city council or school committee if 8 percent of Cambridge voters sign a petition. If 15 percent of the voters sign a petition, a special election must be held within forty-five days, unless a regular election follows within ninety days of signature certification. The initiative becomes law if at least one-third of the registered voters approve the measure and the majority of votes cast favor the measure. Referendum petitions, which challenge an action taken by the city council or school committee, require the signatures of 12 percent of Cambridge voters; acquiring the necessary signatures automatically suspends the measure being challenged and brings it to vote at the next regularly scheduled election if it is not first rescinded by the city council or school committee.

In addition to the extremely open structural features of the Cambridge local state, Cambridge has a very diverse social structure which tends to produce a substantial degree of contention in local politics and a five to four split of the city council among liberals and conservatives. This split often

128, it remains a predominantly working-class city. Working-class interests and peace politics sometimes can be fused, and although dedicated peace activists have made great strides in this respect, city politics has long been dominated by conservative representatives of real-estate interests who have little interest in, and are often hostile to, the issues of concern to new social movements: peace, the environment, and gender. Moreover, although two major educational institutions—Brandeis University and Bentley College—are located in Waltham, they are, for most practical purposes, separate from the city and provide very little in the way of institutional support to the local peace movement. In sum, peace activists in Waltham have little opportunity to press their agenda in the Waltham local state arena; they are frequently shut out of local state politics from the outset.

The local states of these three municipalities, then, present a range of political opportunities to local peace organizations ranging from very favorable in Cambridge, to favorable in Lexington, to unfavorable in Waltham. The existence of political opportunities—which vary from place to place—can have a significant effect on the ability of an incipient movement to recruit and energize members and supporters. Potential movement participants weigh the personal costs and likelihood of political (and public) benefits involved in supporting a movement before deciding to join. The structure of political opportunities is likely to affect those calculations, as is potential participants' place-based identification. These issues will be taken up in greater detail in the following chapter.

Summary and Implications

For several decades, Massachusetts workers have been subjected to a variety of forms of economic disciplining. Unemployment has usually been high, job security precarious, and wages generally below the national average. Massachusetts's defense-led high-tech boom offered significant job growth and hope for long-term economic prosperity to a workforce that had long experienced just the opposite. Within Massachusetts, the places that benefited the most from the defense-related high-tech boom were municipalities along or inside the Route 128 semicircle, including Cambridge, Lexington, and Waltham. The successes and failures of this cycle of peace activism cannot be reasonably analyzed without accounting for the seeming conflict between jobs and peace. Nonetheless, the political dynamics of peace activism cannot be read off material interests in any simple or direct manner.

The availability of resources—which are by and large a function of the spatial division of labor—is crucial to the success of any movement. The most important resources to the peace movement—money, education, and discretionary time—exhibited substantial geographic variation not only among Cambridge, Lexington, and Waltham, but also within these municipalities, raising further issues about spatial recruitment strategies employed by peace organizations.

During the most recent cycle of peace protest, much of the activity of the movement was locally focused. Local political opportunity structures would prove to be important features of the political landscape that also exhibited substantial variation. The three local states examined here presented a range of political opportunities to local peace organizations ranging from very favorable in Cambridge, to favorable in Lexington, to unfavorable in Waltham. Opportunities varied in part because of the formal structures of the local states (Cambridge and Lexington favored broad-based participation while Waltham did not) and in part because of the long-standing political alliances governing the municipalities (favoring insurgents in Cambridge, favoring mainstream liberals in Lexington, and hostile to activists in Waltham). As the following chapter will demonstrate, local political opportunity structures would influence organizational recruitment, strategy, and actions.

The geographic structuring of these systemic characteristics is an important part of the explanation of the uneven geography of political activism, but the mere existence of favorable or unfavorable systemic characteristics by no means guarantees a particular political outcome. Potential resources must be recruited and organized, alliances must be built, and effective strategies devised. Doing this effectively means that messages must be crafted, framed, and directed in a way that resonates with place-specific lifeworld values. It is to these processes that we next turn.

4

Space, Place, and Mobilization

Social movements evidently have their own historical geographies, and many of them have a coherent territorial identity which is not incidental to their discursive and strategic evolution. This is true not only of obvious "struggles for place," like the urban social movements which Castells and others have described in such detail, but also of (say) traditional labour movements which are often closely identified with particular regions. (Gregory 1989b, 200)

The historically specific manner in which the establishment, reproduction, and transformation of power relations contributes to the becoming of place is contingent upon the interconnections existing between micro-level, or person-to-person, and macro-level, or inter-institutional, expressions of those relations. (Pred 1984, 291)

Memberships of peace organizations do not represent systematic samples of local populations.[1] Members are recruited through specific channels that skew organizational memberships both geographically and socioeconomically. Recruitment is the primary channel by which most organizations mobilize the resources they need to mount effective campaigns.

Resources can take a variety of forms. Freeman (1979) distinguishes between tangible and intangible assets; the former can include such things as money, facilities, labor, and means of communication; the latter can include such things as organizing skills, legal skills, common identity, and solidarity (Jenkins 1983). Organizations may employ a variety of recruitment "technologies," that is, "sets of knowledge about how to do a particular action and what its consequences are likely to be" (Oliver and Marwell 1992, 255), which produce very different results in terms of the types of resources obtained. Oliver and Marwell (1992) distinguish between technologies employed for "mobilizing money" and technologies employed for "mobilizing time." All of these technologies are employed with the aim of getting people involved in a movement, but they vary in terms of who is targeted (e.g., a cross-section of a population versus wealthy donors), what is asked of the recruits (e.g., money versus time), and the associated resources they provide a movement (e.g., status, legitimacy, and legal skills versus strong collective identity, solidarity, and broad-based alliances).

It is well known that most social movement organizations make conscious decisions about the types of resources they are primarily concerned with mobilizing. What is not generally recognized is that these decisions, and the recruitment strategies they entail, often imply particular spatial strategies. These strategies—sometimes explicit, sometimes implicit—have important implications not only for how an organization's message resonates (see chapter 1), but for alliances that are and are not built.

Mobilizing Resources for Peace: Spatial Recruitment Strategies in Cambridge, Lexington, and Waltham

All four organizations considered here—Boston Mobilization for Survival, Cambridge SANE/Freeze, the Lexington Committee for a Nuclear Weapons Freeze, and Waltham Concerned Citizens—employ a variety of recruitment strategies, some with no clear spatial dimension. For instance, all four organizations have placed advertisements in local newspapers (which are circulated throughout their respective cities, although one could argue that there are spatial variations in subscription and readership levels); all four have received media coverage (including newspaper, radio, and occasionally television coverage), which is, again, available throughout the organizations' respective municipalities. On the other hand, a variety of spatially targeted recruitment strategies have also been employed: selection of specific places and routes for demonstrations, marches, walks, festivals, information tables, and the like, and—very importantly—canvassing. Moreover, many people have been recruited not through the active efforts of organizations, but through word of mouth; these recruitment channels also have their own geographies. The net result is patterns of recruitment that exhibit varying degrees of spatial and socioeconomic differentiation.

Of the four organizations considered here, only Boston Mobilization for Survival existed prior to the Freeze campaign. Mobilization for Survival ("Mobe") was founded in 1977 when more than one hundred peace, religious, environmental, feminist, and public interest organizations joined forces (Leavitt 1983a). The Boston chapter, one of the nation's largest (with a budget of more than $100,000 and a mailing list of 1,300 in 1987 [Grasek and Emigh 1987]), was founded the same year. As a wide-ranging multi-issue peace and justice organization, Mobe has been involved in a variety of campaigns. For this reason, it is difficult to point to primary recruitment activities.[2] Protest and educational activities are simultaneously recruitment activities; as issues and campaigns change, venues and audiences—to varying degrees—change. Nonetheless, Mobe tends toward particular types of activism. As a "radical" organization, it tends to downplay legislative campaigns and instead emphasizes highly visible public demonstrations, forums, conferences, and training sessions that facilitate its educational objectives. Many activities, accordingly, are held at major public places—including weapons facilities and governmental offices. As a metropolitan-wide organization, it is not focused on any one municipality, although most of its work takes place in Boston and Cambridge. Its office is located in Cambridge (just off Harvard Square). Although much of Mobe's action is local and direct, its issues are usually national and international; because few of its issues are of a strictly local nature, it has relatively little impetus to canvass throughout municipalities and even less need to build broad-based (majority) municipal coalitions. A variety of forms of identity politics play a role in the dynamics of Mobe. In short, Mobe is oriented toward long-term, radical change through public education rather than short-term majoritarian reform. Accordingly, it has fairly specific, rather than broad community-wide, recruitment channels.

The other three organizations considered here were all founded during the early days of the Freeze campaign. The Cambridge Lobby for a Nuclear Weapons Freeze (later to become Cambridge SANE/Freeze and, later still, Cambridge Peace Action) was founded in early 1981 by Anne Crumm and Louise Coleman, whose concern over the escalation of the arms race under Ronald Reagan intensified after viewing a Helen Caldicott film on the dangers of nuclear war. They approached George Sommaripa, who, in addition to his national Freeze organizing work, was helping to organize the Massachusetts Council for a Nuclear Weapons Freeze. Sommaripa encouraged Crumm and Coleman to start a Cambridge Freeze chapter, which they did by contacting a variety of local peace-oriented political groups, especially WAND (Women's Action for Nuclear Disarmament). WAND clearly represented a fusion of the women's and peace movements, as demonstrated by the gendered identity base of the organization. Through Crumm and Coleman's contacts, the initial core of the Cambridge Freeze chapter was formed, including Olivia Abelson, Shelagh Foreman, and Christie Dennis, wide, and its participation in city politics (including the participation of a key member in the city Democratic Party Committee), which helped promote the image of the organization as a significant citywide actor.

The Lexington Committee for a Nuclear Weapons Freeze was founded in 1980 by Lester Arond, who was inspired not only to found the Lexington Freeze chapter, but also co-found the Massachusetts Council for a Nuclear Weapons Freeze (with George Sommaripa), after participating in a fundraising event for Helen Caldicott at the urging of his daughter. Arond initially tried to organize a chapter in Melrose, without success. After the Melrose meetings fizzled, Arond decided to try to start an organization in Lexington, where he lived. He and a group of people he contacted through a Quaker friend met in December to discuss material he had obtained from Randall Forsberg, who wrote the Nuclear Freeze proposal, *Call to Halt the Nuclear Arms Race* (and had studied arms control policy at MIT). The Lexington Committee for a Nuclear Weapons Freeze was founded at that meeting. Jim Driscoll, an MIT Business School professor and Vietnam veteran, emerged as chair of the organization and urged the committee to try to attract interest from all of Lexington's precincts to facilitate a petition campaign. In the spring of 1981 the committee placed an advertisement in the Lexington newspaper announcing a public potluck supper and planning meeting. Several more people attended, including Rachel Rosenblum, Kay Tiffany, and Ed Lieberman—all of whom were well connected across town and would come to play central roles in the organization.

The Lexington Committee for a Nuclear Weapons Freeze (CNWF) focused on legislative action and, not surprisingly, framed its message in a manner very similar to that of the Cambridge Freeze chapter. One of the Lexington Committee's first acts was to start a petition drive to convince the Massachusetts congressional delegation to support a nuclear freeze. Between 150 and 175 activists canvassing the town door-to-door and at supermarkets were able to collect more than five thousand signatures on a Nuclear Freeze petition that was presented to Representative Jim Shannon and Senators Ted Kennedy and Paul Tsongas (Arond 1990). Convinced of the grassroots appeal of the Freeze, Kennedy, Tsongas, and Shannon's successor, Representative Ed Markey, would go on to play a major role in national Freeze legislative efforts. The organization also worked through the Lexington town meeting, tapping into the network of town meeting members who are distributed equally among the town's nine precincts (Arond 1990; Tiffany 1990). Many members became active in the Democratic Town Committee and the committee also cooperated with a variety of local churches, synagogues, and organizations—including the local Chamber of Commerce,

Rotary, and the Sierra Club chapter. The committee sponsored or participated in a variety of educational programs at local schools, parades through
the town's historic center, runs, walks, vigils, and metropolitan area-wide
events. It also received good local news coverage (Arond 1990; Rosenblum
1990; Tiffany 1990). In short, the Lexington Committee for a Nuclear
Weapons Freeze engaged in a number of activities that served to attract
members from all parts of relatively homogeneous Lexington.

The origins of Waltham Concerned Citizens (WCC), which became
Waltham's Freeze organization, differed considerably from those of the
Cambridge and Lexington Freeze chapters. WCC was founded in 1981 by
Jennifer Rose, who had been involved in a number of Cambridge peace and
women's organizations but became "tired of waiting for Cambridge groups
to do outreach" to Waltham (Rose 1990a). Rose contacted several progressive organizations and magazines—for example, Boston Mobilization for
Survival, Boston Alliance Against Registration and the Draft, American
Friends Service Committee, *Dollars and Sense,* and *Radical America*—to get
names and addresses of people of a progressive bent in Waltham. Letters
inviting people to a meeting to start a multi-issue progressive organization
yielded only three new people—Marc Rudnick, who had run for Boston
City Council; Joel San Juan, a social psychologist; and Mary Loan of the
Gray Panthers. Those present, however, decided to try again. The group got
permission to use a downtown church, obtained the Helen Caldicott film on
the arms race, and publicized the event. Approximately fifteen more people
attended the second meeting, including Dee and David Kricker, Sue and
Gene Burkhart, Dick Crowley, Marianne Lynnworth, and others who would
play central roles in the organization.

Although WCC was constituted as a multi-issue organization, the main
emphasis in its early days was peace. Many of the initial organizers were of a
"radical" bent, had substantial experience in left politics, and were not longtime Waltham residents. Many, in fact, felt shut out of local politics and culture, being labeled "breezers" (i.e., people not born and raised in Waltham,
"breezing" in and out of town) by longtime residents. As the organization
grew and broadened its base, however, WCC began to frame its message to
resonate with Waltham's working-class culture and politics. WCC's expanding liberal, not radical, membership forced the organization to "get real
about who was out there" (Rose 1990b) and temper its political stance.

Working with local churches became an important aspect of connecting
with longtime Waltham residents. The Waltham Conference for Church
Unity, representing most churches in Waltham, frequently cosponsored the
Freeze-related events organized by WCC. The Waltham Conference for

registered Lexington voters. A petition signed by one hundred registered Lexington voters will place any issue on the agenda of a special town meeting.

Citizens can bring issues before the town meeting with relative ease: ten signatures of registered Lexington voters on a petition plus approval by the Board of Selectmen will bring an issue before the annual town meeting; if the Board of Selectmen does not approve the petition, the issue can still be brought before the annual town meeting or placed on the ballot in the annual town meeting election if the petition is signed by 10 percent of registered Lexington voters.

With a referendum petition signed by 3 percent of registered Lexington voters within five business days of adjournment of a town meeting, citizens can call a special election to override specific types of action taken by the town meeting. The election must be held no more than twenty-four days after the petition is filed; the action of the town meeting is overturned by a majority vote if the majority also represents at least 20 percent of the registered voters.

Although the formal structure of the Lexington local state is very open, the social structure of Lexington is somewhat less conducive than Cambridge's to giving voice to insurgent groups. Lexington is a very homogeneous upper-middle-class town that produces a much smaller percentage of radical activists than Cambridge. The lack of clear social groupings vying for power provides little incentive to mainstream groups to ally with insurgent groups to improve political position. Moreover, there are no universities or other entities that might provide institutional allies and support for the peace movement, and the occasional failure of the Board of Selectmen to place particular peace issues before the town meeting has at time frustrated the Lexington peace movement.

The third local state, Waltham, is considerably less open. Waltham's charter has been only moderately modified since the heyday of the industrial revolution when a ward-based system of representation with a strong mayor was established. Waltham, like Cambridge before its charter reform, was known for industrial paternalism and machine politics. In 1978 the charter was amended to establish a mayor–city council form of government. Today, the mayor and six city councilpersons are elected at large and nine additional councilpersons are elected by ward. The at-large positions, which are rarely captured by minority candidates, ensure the dominance of the political plurality. Referenda provisions are the same as Cambridge's. The social structure of Waltham, when combined with Waltham's electoral structure, does not favor peace activism. Although the social structure of Waltham has become somewhat more diverse since the growth of high-tech industry along Route fosters an openness toward strategic alliances with insurgent groups as each block tries to maintain or improve its position; this has proven advantageous to local peace organizations, which have developed good relations with several council members who introduce, support, and routinely pass peace-related proposals (Abelson 1990a). Moreover, influential allies of the peace movement can be found among the faculty and students of Harvard, MIT, and other universities and colleges. In sum, Cambridge meets all of Tarrow's criteria for a political opportunity structure that is extremely favorable to the peace movement.

The charter of the town of Lexington dates back to its Revolutionary War form and exhibits a high levels of openness in many respects. Lexington is governed by a town meeting system of government. Under this system 189 people are elected to govern the town—twenty-one from each of nine different precincts. Each precinct is essentially a neighborhood and those elected to the town meeting are often personally known to the electorate. Community organizations can readily tap into the network of town meeting members to initiate discussion around their concerns. The town meeting system ensures a high level of familiarity with and accessibility to those who govern. The large number of town meeting members from each precinct usually ensures that a wide range of views are represented at town meetings and that backroom politicking and strategic deal making is limited. The relatively homogeneous socioeconomic makeup of Lexington also inhibits extreme political polarization. In short, Lexington's local state structure and the characteristics of its population foster a relatively high degree of genuine communication among its citizens and town meeting members alike. As one member of the Lexington Committee for a Nuclear Weapons Freeze explained, the "unique political structure of Lexington [means that] Lexingtonians don't leave their government to the officials" (Tiffany 1990). The strong sense of free political space to talk out solutions to problems promotes a sense of empowerment and broadly positive feelings about the town. Nonetheless, it should be noted that it is possible, under the town meeting system, for the plurality within each precinct to capture most seats to the town meeting, and to grant less than proportional representation to those holding minority positions.

Other structures of the Lexington local state also promote substantial citizen input and control. The day-to-day affairs of the town are decided by a five-member Board of Selectmen who are elected by the members of the town meeting. Any decision of the Board of Selectmen can be overridden by the town meeting and special town meetings can be called at any time at the request of the Board of Selectmen or with a petition signed by two hundred

Church Unity sponsored several church events of its own, such as a very well attended Interfaith Service for Nuclear Sanity. WCC's link with local churches conferred a degree of legitimacy on the organization that made it difficult to dismiss, as well as opened up important recruitment channels. WCC also broadened its issue base to include housing, environmental, and women's issues—issues that were of more immediate concern than peace issues to some people—which further broadened the organization's base of support. WCC also turned more toward electoral issues, working not only to enact local measures but also meeting with Speaker of the House Tip O'Neill, Waltham's as well as Cambridge's U.S. representative.

WCC has been active in a wide range of community activities. In the early 1980s it organized and sponsored public forums, library exhibits, films, voter registration drives (with tables on the Waltham Common and at shopping centers), rummage sales, fairs, parades, vigils, and petition drives—including one in support of a Freeze resolution that targeted the city's first ward (in the West Central part of the city, which is not especially liberal). WCC also participated in metropolitan area–wide peace events, developed connections with local civic and fraternal organizations, challenged the city council on a number of peace issues, and received extensive and generally good local press coverage. Although WCC never canvassed the entire city, it has organized a number of activities to attract citywide attention and interest.

The activities that Boston Mobilization for Survival, Cambridge SANE/Freeze, the Lexington Committee for a Nuclear Weapons Freeze, and Waltham Concerned Citizens engaged in set the parameters through which recruitment occurred. Table 7 illustrates the actual recruitment channels for the organizations' 1990 memberships, as indicated in the membership survey.

Of all the recruitment channels only two—ads and notices in newspapers and newspaper, television, and radio news—do not imply high degrees of spatial differentiation. These two media channels account for a relatively small percentage of recruitment into all of the organizations, with the exception of the Lexington Committee for a Nuclear Weapons Freeze (perhaps because of greater readership of the local newspaper in Lexington).

Information from other peace and justice organizations was an extremely important means of attracting members for some organizations. Virtually half of all Cambridge Mobe members and a third of all Cambridge SANE/Freeze members became interested in those organizations through other progressive organizations. This channel is spatially differentiated to the extent that the originating organizations exhibit spatial differentiation. It also indicates a reliance on attracting people who are already very much of a progressive

Table 7. Organizational recruitment channels* (percentage of members)

	Mobe	Cambridge SANE/Freeze	Lexington CNWF	WCC
Canvassers	12	21	8	2
Info at parades, demos, etc.	33	10	19	13
Friends/acquaintances from neighborhood	24	32	35	22
Family/persons living with you	11	8	6	17
Church	2	0	13	15
Coworkers	9	8	5	3
Friends/acquaintances outside neighborhood	23	15	35	22
Info from other progressive organizations	49	34	23	12
Ads or notices in newspapers, etc.	9	5	15	11
Newspaper/TV/radio news	4	5	23	10

*How members became interested in their organization. Recruitment channels are not mutually exclusive.

bent; this is especially understandable in the case of Mobe, which is more of a "radical" than a mainstream liberal organization. The disadvantage for organizations relying on this channel is that it does little to incorporate nontraditional support groups.

The recruitment channel with the clearest spatial differentiation is canvassing. Somewhat surprisingly, canvassing is a relatively unimportant means of recruiting members for all four organizations; it was most significant for Cambridge SANE/Freeze. As discussed earlier, Cambridge SANE/Freeze's canvassing strategy was likely to bias recruitment toward upper-income, professional people. Information distributed at parades, demonstrations, marches, and so on is also spatially differentiated—toward the locations at which events are held—but this turns out to be a significant recruitment channel for only two organizations: Mobe and, to a lesser degree, the Lexington Committee for a Nuclear Weapon Freeze.

The remaining recruitment channels all involve personal friendship and acquaintance networks. On a superficial level, the characterization of new social movements as lifeworld rather than systemic-oriented movements is confirmed by the fact that few members of any of the four organizations became interested in their organizations through information they received from coworkers. (Of course, systemic processes come into play in other important respects.) Churches were insignificant recruitment channels for Mobe and Cambridge SANE/Freeze, but were of moderate importance for the Lexington Committee for a Nuclear Weapons Freeze and Waltham Concerned Citizens. Both of the latter organizations have worked closely with their municipalities' churches and synagogues.

Recruitment through a variety of noninstitutional personal friendship and acquaintance networks is very important in all four organizations. Information from neighborhood friends and acquaintances was a significant recruitment channel in all four organizations, as was information from friends and acquaintances outside members' neighborhoods. Family and cohabitating friends and acquaintances were a moderately important recruitment channel for Mobe (perhaps due to members living together in housing cooperatives) and WCC (likely reflecting the involvement of a number of couples in the organization). The significance of these recruitment channels indicates the importance of preexisting channels of communication and points to the importance of personal bonds, collective identity, and solidarity among members.

Clearly, there are important differences in the recruitment channels of Mobilization for Survival, Cambridge SANE/Freeze, the Lexington Committee for a Nuclear Weapons Freeze, and Waltham Concerned Citizens that reflect differences in recruitment strategies, place-specific characteristics of the municipalities in which the organizations operate, and the part of the political spectrum the organizations occupy. Looking at Mobilization for Survival, we see that its two most important recruitment channels are information from other peace and justice organizations, and information distributed at demonstrations, marches, and so on. Both of these recruitment channels are skewed toward people who are already active and of a progressive bent; they are also very location-specific channels (assuming the memberships of other peace and justice organizations are spatially differentiated). The most important recruitment channel for Cambridge SANE/Freeze is also other peace and justice organizations, although less so than for Mobe. Neighborhood friends and acquaintances is Cambridge SANE/Freeze's second-most important recruitment channel and canvassing is third in importance; both of these channels suggest strong socioeconomic and spatial differentiation.

The primary recruitment channels of the Lexington Committee for a Nuclear Weapons Freeze and Waltham Concerned Citizens differ considerably from those of the two Cambridge organizations. Neighborhood friends and acquaintances and friends and acquaintances from outside the neighborhood are tied as the most important recruitment channels for the Lexington Committee for a Nuclear Weapons Freeze. While the former channel suggests spatial clustering of members, the latter does not. What seems most important is that the organization tends to recruit people through friendship networks and these extend across the town as well as focus on neighborhoods. This is most likely linked to the way in which the town meeting system of government promotes townwide interaction of politically active people. Tied for the second-most important recruitment channel of the Lexington Committee for a Nuclear Weapons Freeze are information from other peace and justice organizations and newspaper, radio, and television news. Although there are spatial biases associated with the former channel, the latter is for the most part available to all Lexington residents regardless of location within the town or socioeconomic position.

Although the primary recruitment channels of Waltham Concerned Citizens are the same as those of the Lexington Committee for a Nuclear Weapons Freeze, they are important for smaller percentages of WCC's membership. What is most striking about WCC's recruitment is that all channels, with the exception of canvassing and information from coworkers, are important. Personal friendship networks are extremely important. Other channels such as ads or notices in newspapers and newspaper, television, and radio news are also of moderate significance. WCC thus recruits through a wide array of channels, some of them spatially, socioeconomically, and politics-specific, others operating citywide. It seems that once people become interested in WCC, they tell their friends and bring in more members.

The spatial patterns of organizational membership resulting from reliance on particular recruitment channels are readily apparent in figures 11 through 14. The map of Cambridge Mobilization for Survival members (figure 11) shows a heavy concentration in the central part of the city around Harvard Square. A fair number of members also concentrate in Cambridgeport in the southeast part of the city, which is shifting toward higher socioeconomic groups, but is still primarily working-class. Mobe has been fairly successful in recruiting members from working-class North Cambridge (in the northwest of the city), but has virtually no members from working-class East Cambridge (in the northeast of the city). In sum, Mobe draws primarily from the parts of Cambridge that are associated with professional occupations and higher education levels, but has also had modest success in recruiting from working-class North Cambridge.

The membership of Cambridge SANE/Freeze (figure 12) is even more spatially concentrated than that of Mobe. Members are almost exclusively from the Harvard Square area in the center of the city, although there are also a fair number of members in Cambridgeport in the southeast of the city. Considering the organization's sociospatial recruitment strategy, it is not surprising that it has virtually no members in working-class North Cambridge and absolutely no members in working-class East Cambridge.

The Lexington Committee for a Nuclear Weapons Freeze has a fairly uniform distribution of members with several members located in each part of town (figure 13). This is what one would expect with the organization's reliance on recruitment through the media and non-neighborhood-based friendship networks. When examining the geographic distribution of Lexington Committee for a Nuclear Weapons Freeze members, however, it is important to keep in mind the relative homogeneity of the population from which the organization recruits, as well as the influence of the town meeting structure of the local state. It is unlikely that the spatial distribution of the

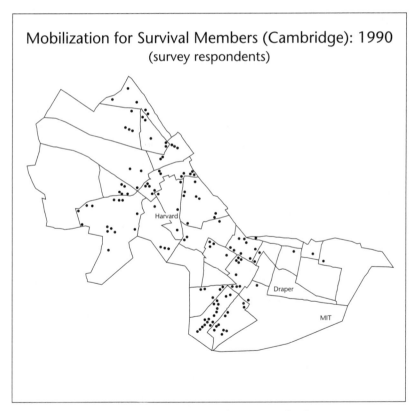

Figure 11. Mobilization for Survival members in Cambridge, 1990.

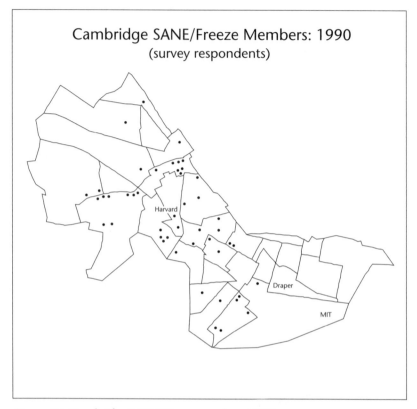

Figure 12. Cambridge SANE/Freeze members, 1990.

organization's membership would be as uniform as it is if the same recruitment strategies had been employed in a town with an array of classes concentrated in different parts of town, or if the structure of the local state did not foster the interaction of substantial numbers of politically active people from across the entire town.

As in Lexington, the spatial distribution of peace organization members in Waltham is fairly uniform (figure 14). Waltham Concerned Citizens members are located in almost all parts of the city, with the sole exception of the city's easternmost neighborhood (a neighborhood of higher rather than lower relative socioeconomic position). WCC's reliance on a wide array of recruitment channels has helped it to draw from across the city, and this in a city that is strongly working-class—not the traditional base of support for peace organizations. If Waltham had a wider mix of classes, including more people in managerial and professional occupations, there might well be a greater concentration of WCC members in neighborhoods of the peace movement's traditional support groups. Even so, it is clear that WCC has been very successful in recruiting members in a working-class city, contrary to conventional expectations.

Of course, although the location of members in particular parts of a city provides an indication of the spatial coverage of an organization's recruitment efforts, it does not necessarily mean that those who join the organization

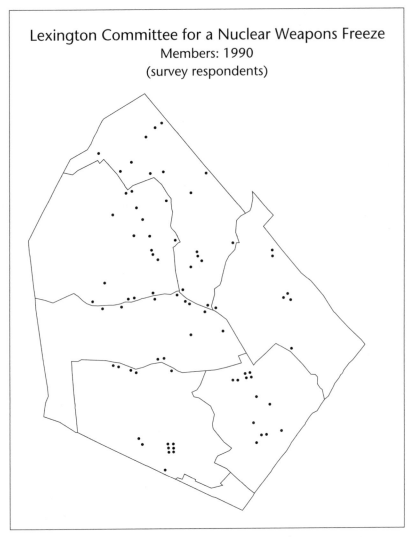

Figure 13. Members of Lexington Committee for a Nuclear Weapons Freeze, 1990.

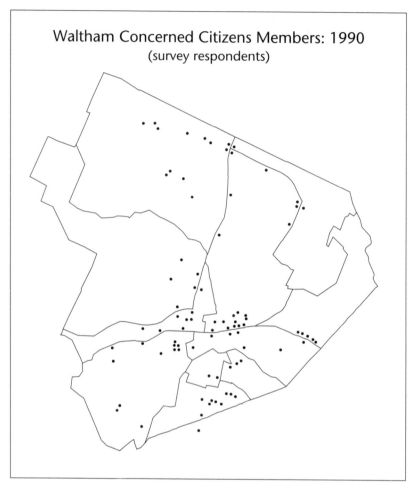

Figure 14. *Waltham Concerned Citizens members, 1990.*

are representative of their part of the city. To find out who joins these organizations, and the organizational resources they bring, we need to examine the socioeconomic characteristics and activism histories of members.

The Fruit of Recruitment: Organizational Resources

> *The peace movement is strong in New England because of bright, intelligent, active people.*
>
> —Elizabeth Campbell Elliot, Massachusetts SANE/Freeze

As table 8 indicates (compare with table 5), the socioeconomic characteristics of members of Mobilization for Survival (in Cambridge), Cambridge SANE/Freeze, the Lexington Committee for a Nuclear Weapons Freeze, and

Waltham Concerned Citizens in part reflect the socioeconomic characteristics of the places (municipalities) in which they are located. Equally important, however, have been sociospatial recruitment strategies that disproportionately attract persons of above-average means and education from each municipality. The characteristics of the organizations' memberships provide important indications of the types of resources available to the organizations and, in turn, possible explanations of varying levels of peace movement activity among the municipalities.

In Cambridge, approximately two-thirds of the members of both Mobilization for Survival and Cambridge SANE/Freeze are in managerial and professional specialty occupations—a considerably higher percentage than that of Cambridge workers on the whole (40 percent), but not an unexpected percentage given the spatial distribution of the organizations' members. Likewise, average household incomes for both organizations are considerably above the norm for Cambridge ($24,272), although lower for Mobe than for Cambridge SANE/Freeze, perhaps reflecting Mobe's inroads in North Cambridge. Educational attainment in both organizations is especially high. Although 43 percent of Cambridge residents age twenty-five and over have completed four or more years of college, 97 percent of Mobe members and 93 percent of Cambridge SANE/Freeze members have done so. Moreover, approximately two-thirds of the members of both organizations hold graduate degrees. Both organizations are also extremely white: neither organization has a single African-American or Portuguese member and only Cambridge SANE/Freeze has a single Hispanic member. The vast majority of members of both organizations do not consider themselves to be part of any ethnic community; 29 percent of the members of both organizations consider themselves Jewish—the only significant ethnic concentration in either organization. In short, the members of both organizations are overwhelmingly white, financially well-off, extremely well educated, and employed in managerial and professional occupations—all well-known characteristics of new social movements organizations. Clearly, Mobe and Cambridge SANE/Freeze draw disproportionately from the city's financial, educational, racial, and occupational elite; they do so even relative to the well-off neighborhoods that have been targeted in recruitment activities.

There are some surprising membership characteristics. Well over 40 percent of the members of both Mobe and Cambridge SANE/Freeze work in education. Although one would expect a relatively high percentage from the education sector, this seems disproportionately high, even for Cambridge. Unfortunately, the U.S. Census does not collect data on education as a separate economic sector, which would allow comparison of employment in education between the city and its peace organizations.

Table 8. Peace organization characteristics—1990 (percent unless otherwise indicated)

	Cambridge Mobe	Cambridge SANE/Freeze	Lexington CNWF	WCC
Household income (mean)	$40,938	$49,099	$52,039	$37,979
Household income (median)	$35,000 to $49,999	$50,000 to $99,999	$50,000 to $99,999	$35,000 to $49,999
Sector				
manufacturing	4	2	4	17
wholesale/retail trade	1	0	6	6
professional and related services	39	38	33	51
government	7	5	8	4
education	47	43	44	22
Class of worker				
private for-profit company	18	14	17	38
private not-for-profit company	42	22	29	27
local government	9	9	16	9
state government	13	10	12	4
federal government	1	0	3	1
self-employed	18	36	24	19
Occupation				
managerial/professional specialty	65	69	64	38
technical, sales, administrative support	11	8	13	22
service	25	23	23	32
production/machine operation, etc.	1	0	1	7
Employment status				
employed	83	71	73	78
unemployed	2	0	0	4
work at home without pay	2	7	8	10
retired	8	22	17	7
full-time student	4	0	2	2
Four or more years of college	97	93	95	85
master's degree	34	41	42	35
doctoral/professional degree	32	27	30	10
Owner-occupied households	59	78	96	66

Table 8. (continued)

	Cambridge Mobe	Cambridge SANE/Freeze	Lexington CNWF	WCC
Same SMSA 5 years ago	98	100	99	92
same house 5 years ago	70	72	92	60
Median age	44	55	56	43
Sex (M/F)	43/57	30/70	40/60	43/57
Ethnicity				
none indicated	63	55	57	60
Irish	4	7	2	12
Italian	2	0	2	5
Jewish	29	29	36	17
African-American	0	0	0	1
Portuguese	0	0	0	0
Hispanic	0	1	1	1
other	2	7	1	5

Also omitted in Census data is employment in private not-for-profit companies. Such employment is very important among members of both peace organizations. In fact, when adding employment in private not-for-profit companies with all forms of government employment, we find that 65 percent of all Mobe members and 41 percent of all Cambridge SANE/Freeze members work in jobs that are not directly driven by market imperatives. Self-employment is also very high among Mobe and Cambridge SANE/Freeze members. Strikingly, only 18 percent of Mobe members and 14 percent of Cambridge SANE/Freeze members are wage and salary workers in private for-profit companies. This suggests a substantial degree of insulation from the direct economic fortunes of large companies (especially defense contractors) and from market forces, generally. As subsequent chapters show, such insulation plays into the formulation of peace movement goals and policies, sometimes with severely detrimental implications.

Another unexpected characteristic of these organizations is the age of members. Although activism is commonly associated with college-age youth, the median age of Mobe members is forty-four and the median age of Cambridge SANE/Freeze members is fifty-five. Moreover, only 4 percent of Mobe members are full-time students and Cambridge SANE/Freeze has no student members.

Perhaps to be expected more, the mix of sexes is substantially skewed toward women in Mobe (57 percent) and heavily skewed toward women in Cambridge SANE/Freeze (70 percent). The disproportionate role of women in these two organizations is not particularly surprising given Mobe's multi-issue politics, including a strong feminist component, and Cambridge SANE/Freeze's roots in WAND.

It would be a mistake to read the age and sex characteristics of these organizations as supporting the conventional wisdom that those outside the commodified workforce (having substantial discretionary time) form the backbone of the peace movement. Those who work at home without pay (e.g., homemakers) and college students form a very small percentage of these organizations' memberships. The vast majority of the members of both organizations are employed; retirees are the only significant subgroup of members outside the remunerated workforce, and then only in Cambridge SANE/Freeze. Members of both organizations are also much less likely to move than typical Cambridge residents, suggesting a stronger rooting in local place-based communities.

In short, the memberships of the two Cambridge peace organizations are older than the stereotype of such organizations, highly educated, skewed toward women, include few students and homemakers but many longer-term residents, and overwhelmingly work for non-market-driven employers.

The membership characteristics of the Lexington Committee for a Nuclear Weapons Freeze are similar in many regards to those of the two Cambridge peace organizations. Average household income for the Lexington Committee for a Nuclear Weapons Freeze members is quite high—higher than that of the two Cambridge peace organizations—but actually somewhat below average for Lexington (which is $62,345). Educational attainment is very high with 95 percent of all members having completed four or more years of college and 72 percent holding graduate degrees. The Lexington peace organization, like the Cambridge organizations, is extremely white: Jewish members (36 percent) are the only significant non-Anglo ethnic group represented. Employment characteristics of the Lexington Committee for a Nuclear Weapons Freeze members are also quite similar to those of the Cambridge organizations. Most members participate in the remunerated workforce. Approximately two-thirds of the members of the Lexington Committee for a Nuclear Weapons Freeze are employed in managerial and professional specialty occupations—not especially surprising given that half of all employed Lexington residents work in such occupations. Members are most frequently employed in education (44 percent), a high percentage work for not-for-profit companies or government (60 percent altogether), and only 17 percent are wage and salary workers for private companies.

Very few of the Lexington Committee for a Nuclear Weapon Freeze's members are college students or work at home without pay; a modest 17 percent are retired. Women outnumber men by a three to two margin in the organization and the median age of Lexington Committee for a Nuclear Weapons Freeze members is fifty-six. Members tend to have relatively long-standing roots in the town and almost all (96 percent) are homeowners—considerably higher percentages than in Cambridge and above the norm for the municipality, as with the Cambridge organizations. In short, the characteristics of the Lexington Committee for a Nuclear Weapons Freeze are for the most part quite similar to those of (Cambridge) Mobe and Cambridge SANE/Freeze.

Of the four organizations, Waltham Concerned Citizens comes closest to representing the characteristics of its host city, and this despite the fact that Waltham's socioeconomic characteristics are not those typically associated with support for the peace movement. Average household income for WCC members is only $2,068 above that of the average Waltham household, and considerably below average household incomes for the Cambridge and Lexington peace organizations. WCC's employment characteristics are skewed away from working-class and middle-class occupations, but only mildly in comparison with the Cambridge and Lexington organizations. Only 38 percent of WCC members are in managerial and professional specialty occupations, and this is only 12 percent more than for Waltham as a whole. (The Lexington Committee for a Nuclear Weapons Freeze is 14 percent above the whole Lexington figure and Cambridge Mobe and Cambridge SANE/Freeze are 25 and 29 percent above the whole Cambridge figure, respectively.) Technical, sales, and administrative support occupations account for another 22 percent of WCC members, 13 percent below the citywide average but considerably more than in the other three peace organizations. Service occupations are also significant for WCC members (32 percent)—again, higher than in the other organizations.

Examining the sector of the economy in which members work, we find only 22 percent of WCC members in education (less than half of the percentages for the other organizations) and 17 percent in manufacturing (making WCC the only organization with a significant portion of its membership in the manufacturing sector); 51 percent of WCC members work in the professional and related services sector (double the city-wide average). While 41 percent of WCC members work for not-for-profit companies or government—the same percentage as for Cambridge SANE/Freeze—this is considerably below the 65 percent for Cambridge Mobe and 60 percent for the Lexington Committee for a Nuclear Weapons Freeze. Also significant is the fact that 38 percent of WCC members are wage and salary workers in private for-profit companies—a considerably higher percentage than for Cambridge SANE/Freeze, (Cambridge) Mobe, and the Lexington Committee for a Nuclear Weapons Freeze.

Like the other peace organizations and the city of Waltham itself, WCC is very white, although WCC differs from the other organizations in that its membership is actually somewhat more ethnically diverse than its host city; 17 percent of its members are Jewish, the largest ethnic group in the organization. WCC membership is disproportionately comprised of women (57 percent)—no surprise given the multi-issue (including feminist issues) nature of the organization and the strong involvement in feminist politics of some of the organization's original founders. The median age of WCC members is forty-three—younger than the other three organizations and closest of the four organizations to the average for the host city. Few WCC members have an employment status that would suggest substantial discretionary time. Members are only slightly less likely to have moved in the past five years than residents citywide, although WCC homeownership is 20 percent above the city average.

Although WCC membership does differ from citywide Waltham characteristics, there appears to be only one socioeconomic characteristic for which the difference is dramatic: education. Whereas 19 percent of Waltham residents age twenty-five and over have completed four or more years of college, 85 percent of WCC members have. Moreover, 45 percent of WCC members hold graduate degrees—obviously a much higher percentage than among city residents generally, but considerably below the percentages for the Cambridge and Lexington peace organizations.

In short, the variety of sociospatial recruitment channels WCC has emphasized is reflected in a membership that is appreciably more diverse than the other peace organizations considered here. WCC is also more representative of its host city than the Cambridge organizations are of theirs, although WCC's membership is still somewhat skewed toward those in managerial and professional occupations, those in types of work that are not driven by market imperatives, and women. What primarily distinguishes WCC from Waltham in general, however, is the educational level of its members.

In sum, the sociospatial recruiting strategies the Cambridge, Lexington, and Waltham peace organizations have pursued attract highly educated persons likely to have the skills necessary to run effective political campaigns.

The Cambridge and Lexington organizations have also effectively mobilized persons capable of making significant financial contributions. Personal friendships are significant recruitment networks in each of the organizations, suggesting a high degree of solidarity and shared identity.

Gender solidarity undoubtedly played a significant role in the early stages of movement mobilization, especially among the women who organized the Cambridge Lobby for a Nuclear Weapons Freeze, and in terms of setting a multi-issue agenda among the organizers of Mobe and WCC. As organizations strove to recruit from across their municipalities, memberships broadened and broader bases for solidarity developed. As Rachel Rosenblum (1992) of the Lexington Committee for a Nuclear Weapons Freeze puts it, "People need to feel they belong to a cause, an effort, or a group. They seek out 'community' in activism and are reinforced when their cause is reflected in the news and the public domain." Indeed, members in all four organizations talk of the importance of a sense of community among local activists. One anonymous survey respondent from WCC points out how "extremely complex and important" the development of her "sense of community" has been to her activism. Specifically, connections to the women's movement, place-based connections developed in Waltham over the two years she has lived there, and broader place-based bonds developed during the thirteen years she lived in a variety of locations in the Boston metropolitan area have all influenced her activism. That activists' sense of community is often intertwined with place-based attachments (addressed later in this chapter) is further suggested by the fact that many tend to have fairly long roots in their local communities.

Surprisingly, none of the organizations have a significant percentage of members with substantial discretionary time. Most members are in the remunerated workforce; students, homemakers, and retirees are a distinct minority in all four organizations. Highly significant is the fact that the majority of members in two organizations (Cambridge Mobe and the Lexington Committee for a Nuclear Weapons Freeze) and a large minority of members in the other two organizations (Cambridge SANE/Freeze and WCC) work in jobs that are not directly affected by market imperatives. Insulation from the market disciplining that has played a central role in shaping the outlook of Boston-area workers has proven to be a substantial hindrance to the effective formulation of goals and strategies (as chapter 5 shows), but another characteristic unrelated to socioeconomic considerations fosters effectiveness: past experience in political activism.

Socialization into Activism: Past Political Campaigns of Boston-Area Peace Activists

After the antinuclear weapons branch of the peace movement "took off" in the early 1980s, there was a tendency among some to view it as a new and distinct social movement. Although this most recent wave of peace mobilization was, by definition, a new wave, in many respects it represented the continuation of past (and ongoing) social movements. Very few of the members of the four organizations examined here became politically active for the first time during the most recent wave of peace mobilization. On the contrary, the overwhelming majority were socialized into political activism long before the most recent cycle of peace protest. These previous political experiences helped members to develop political skills useful to the peace movement and, in many cases, experience the political efficacy that can lead one to view further political activism as worthwhile.

As table 9 illustrates, the civil rights movement and the anti–Vietnam War protests were the key movements that politically socialized Boston-area peace activists. The most recent cycle of peace protest was the first political movement for only 7 to 10 percent of the members of the four organizations considered here. Similarly small percentages were first active in other peace-focused movements such as the national ban the bomb movement and the related H. Stuart Hughes Senate campaign in Massachusetts (which represented an earlier cycle of protest against the arms race).

As table 10 indicates, many peace organization members have been active in a wide variety of political movements. Many members were active in the anti–Vietnam War protests (a majority of members in all but WCC) and substantial numbers also participated in the civil rights movement (a lower percentage in WCC, undoubtedly related to the younger average age of WCC members). Substantial overlapping participation is also found with the women's, environmental, antinuclear power, and housing rights/affordable housing movements, all of which address issues of the integrity of the life-world. These patterns of overlap vary by place and organization, however. The highest levels of overlap are found in Cambridge, somewhat higher in Mobe than in Cambridge SANE/Freeze. Lowest levels of overlap are generally found in Lexington. This geographic variability in overlapping social movement participation can be attributed to a combination of the place-based characteristics of Cambridge, Lexington, and Waltham and the socio-spatial recruitment strategies employed by the four peace organizations.

Participation levels in the labor movement—addressing systemic work-

Table 9. First political movement or campaign in which members contributed time (percent)

	Mobe	Cambridge SANE/Freeze	Lexington CNWF	WCC
Civil rights movement	23	23	18	12
Anti–Vietnam War protests	26	19	17	23
JFK campaign	1	0	7	1
Ban the bomb movement	2	6	7	0
McCarthy campaign	3	6	3	3
Women's movement	3	2	3	1
Environmental movement	0	4	0	8
Peace movement (this cycle)	9	10	7	10
Anti–nuclear power movement	5	4	0	7
Hughes Senate campaign	0	0	2	1
Drinan House campaign	0	0	0	8
McGovern campaign	4	2	2	4
Other local or state electoral politics	4	6	5	5
Other national electoral politics	8	8	22	7
Other local or state nonelectoral politics	4	4	5	5
Other national nonelectoral politics	10	4	2	3

place issues—is considerably more variable than in lifeworld-related movements. Substantial geographic differences in class composition—both among and within the municipalities—in combination with sociospatial recruitment strategies, play a major role in this variability. High levels of labor movement participation are found among Mobe members, moderate levels of participation among WCC members, and low levels of participation among members of Cambridge SANE/Freeze and the Lexington Committee for a Nuclear Weapons Freeze. Not surprisingly, this relates in part to union membership rates: Mobe (24 percent), Cambridge SANE/Freeze (10 percent), the Lexington Committee for a Nuclear Weapons Freeze (18 percent), WCC (16 percent). Yet Mobe and WCC have labor movement participation rates considerably higher than their unionization rates, most likely

Table 10. Political movements or campaigns in which members contributed time (percent)

	Mobe	Cambridge SANE/Freeze	Lexington CNWF	WCC
Ban the bomb movement	16	16	10	3
Hughes Senate campaign	3	1	5	3
Civil rights movement	44	32	29	18
Anti–Vietnam War protests	72	51	53	40
Anti-ABM campaign	9	13	3	3
Environmental movement	37	36	28	47
Women's/Pro-choice movement	57	37	21	33
Anti–nuclear power movement	50	29	14	28
Labor (union) movement	42	8	13	21
Housing rights/affordable housing movement	34	19	20	25
Anti–B1 bomber campaign	6	7	1	5

because of broad-based sympathies with the labor movement among members who work in areas that are not commonly unionized—for example, not-for-profits and self-employment. In Cambridge SANE/Freeze and the Lexington Committee for a Nuclear Weapons Freeze, on the other hand, labor movement participation rates are even lower than the rates of unionization among members; such weak support is likely a reflection of the "professional" positions held by some unionized members who do not think of themselves as working-class labor.

The broad participation of many peace organization members in a variety of movements over a considerable period of time speaks to the continuity of the most recent cycle of peace activism with past cycles of protest and other ongoing movements. As peace organization members have worked to effect political change, they have done so with a strong base of experience and skills: knowledge of political processes, experience in running effective campaigns, a sense that political activism can bring about meaningful change, and links to other potentially allied movements. The importance of these and other resources previously discussed is difficult to overestimate, yet resources alone cannot guarantee the success of a social movement. The political opportunity structures within which a movement operates are also crucial, not only in terms of the opportunities that may be available in any given time and place, but also in terms of the ways in which place-specific political opportunity structures shape place-specific political identities and outlooks.

Political Opportunity Structures, Place-Based Identities, and Activism

> *The movement [to adopt proportional representation] acted as a catalyst, mobilizing previously paralyzed minorities whose combined forces now constituted a rousing majority.*
> —Cambridge Editorial Research, Inc.

> *The unique political structure of Lexington [means that] Lexingtonians don't leave their government to the officials.*
> —Kay Tiffany, Lexington Committee for a Nuclear Weapons Freeze

> *Waltham had a Tammany Hall type of government for many years. Mayor Arthur Clark and his cronies ran the city.*
> —Marc Rudnick, Waltham Concerned Citizens

As elaborated in chapter 2, there are substantial theoretical grounds to expect the place-specific experiences of political actors to influence the attachments actors develop to the places in which they are active, as well as actors' expectations for future political success in those places. Place-based attachments, moreover, constitute a form of collective identity that can promote or, if negative, hinder further activism.

For local peace movement organizations, political opportunity structures have generally been very favorable in Cambridge, favorable in Lexington (especially for moderate organizations), and unfavorable in Waltham (chapter 3). Accordingly, one might expect Cambridge peace activists to be highly satisfied with the political situation in Cambridge, although high satisfaction levels would be more likely among the more moderate members of Cambridge SANE/Freeze than among the more radical members of Boston Mobilization for Survival. Very high political satisfaction levels might also be expected among members of the Lexington Committee for a Nuclear Weapons Freeze. One would expect the greatest political dissatisfaction among members of Waltham Concerned Citizens, who have had to struggle for virtually every achievement in the Waltham local state.

Survey results confirm these expectations (table 11). In 1990, a phenomenal 80 percent of Cambridge SANE/Freeze members were satisfied with Cambridge politics, 63 percent of the Cambridge members of Boston Mobilization for Survival were satisfied with Cambridge politics, 84 percent

Table 11. Political satisfaction by organization and place

"Please indicate whether you are very satisfied (VS), satisfied (S), dissatisfied (D), or very dissatisfied (VD) with the general political situation in each of the following places." (percent)*

	VS	S	D	VD	D+VD	S+VS
Cambridge SANE/Freeze						
Your city	20	59	17	3	20	80
Boston area	3	25	56	14	70	28
Massachusetts	0	19	52	25	77	19
New England	0	26	34	15	49	26
United States	0	8	34	57	90	8
Boston Mobilization for Survival (Cambridge)						
Your city	8	55	28	4	32	63
Boston area	1	14	59	20	79	15
Massachusetts	1	9	43	43	87	9
New England	1	14	44	21	65	15
United States	0	3	21	75	95	3
Lexington Committee for a Nuclear Weapons Freeze						
Your city	19	65	13	1	14	84
Boston area	0	20	66	8	74	20
Massachusetts	1	19	46	29	75	20
New England	0	30	39	3	42	30
United States	0	6	55	38	93	6
Waltham Concerned Citizens						
Your city	3	24	35	30	64	27
Boston area	0	25	42	19	60	25
Massachusetts	2	19	49	26	75	21
New England	3	26	34	6	40	29
United States	1	13	31	50	81	14

*Percentages may not total 100 percent due to "not sure" responses (not shown in table) and rounding.

of Lexington Committee for a Nuclear Weapons Freeze members were satisfied with Lexington politics, but only 27 percent of Waltham Concerned Citizens members were satisfied with Waltham politics. These data not only suggest a strong relationship between favorable political opportunity structures and levels of political satisfaction; the low political satisfaction rate in Waltham demonstrates that satisfaction is not necessarily an outgrowth of the localness of peace politics and local state institutions.

Theoretical expectations suggest that activists' attachment to place should follow a similar pattern. Indeed, this is generally the case (table 12). Peace organization members have strong attachments to the cities in which they live, with the sole exception of Waltham Concerned Citizens members. A full 75 percent of the members of Cambridge SANE/Freeze have strong or very strong attachments to Cambridge, a percentage most likely influenced by the significant local efficacy of their organization. Not surprisingly, the percentage of members with strong or very strong attachments to Cambridge is lower among the members of the more radical Boston Mobilization for Survival—64 percent. A high proportion of the members of the Lexington Committee for a Nuclear Weapons Freeze—71 percent—have strong or very strong local attachments; members could take satisfaction in the widespread consensus reached on a number of local resolutions and campaigns. Waltham Concerned Citizens members, who have often been shut out of the local political process, expressed, as expected, a lower degree of attachment to their city than to any other place.

Chi-square analysis of the relationship between satisfaction with city politics and attachment to one's city shows a strong and significant relationship for three of the four organizations (table 13). Only among members of Cambridge SANE/Freeze is the relationship questionable (significance = .1011), but this stems largely from a smaller sample size. The pattern of responses for Cambridge SANE/Freeze members is similar to those of the other three organizations. Moreover, chi-square analysis of the relationship between attachment to one's city and numerous socioeconomic variables does not indicate any other consistently significant relationships across the organizations. These results support the notion that place-based political experience influences place-based attachments and that the structure of local political opportunities plays a role in this.

Summary and Implications

An uneven geography of potential resources, combined with sociospatial recruitment strategies specific to each organization, created an uneven geography of mobilized resources. Although financial and skill-related resources

Table 12. Place-based attachments by organization and place

"How strong do you consider your emotional ties to each of these places?"
(VS = very strong; S = strong; M = moderate; W = weak) (percent)*

	VS	S	M	W	M+W	S+VS
Cambridge SANE/Freeze						
Your city	27	48	19	6	25	75
Boston area	21	43	33	3	36	64
Massachusetts	18	39	39	5	43	57
New England	28	40	29	3	32	68
United States	31	39	9	3	12	69
Boston Mobilization for Survival (Cambridge)						
Your city	23	42	26	9	35	64
Boston area	17	44	32	6	38	61
Massachusetts	13	28	44	15	59	41
New England	16	37	30	16	46	53
United States	16	39	28	15	43	55
Lexington Committee for a Nuclear Weapons Freeze						
Your city	31	40	24	5	29	71
Boston area	21	53	22	3	25	74
Massachusetts	16	45	33	5	37	62
New England	23	50	21	5	25	73
United States	33	43	21	3	23	76
Waltham Concerned Citizens						
Your city	12	31	37	20	57	43
Boston area	17	40	30	12	42	57
Massachusetts	19	33	33	14	47	52
New England	24	31	28	16	44	55
United States	34	27	29	8	37	61

*Percentages may not total 100 percent due to "not sure" responses (not shown in table) and rounding.

Table 13. Satisfaction with city politics by attachment to city (chi-square)

	Significance
Cambridge SANE/Freeze	.1011
Boston Mobilization for Survival (Cambridge)	.0000
Lexington Committee for a Nuclear Weapons Freeze	.0001
Waltham Concerned Citizens	.0217

are usually considered key, forms of collective identity, social solidarity, and political experience are also extremely important. All show considerable geographical variation: household income and educational levels vary substantially among the organizations, as does the percentage of members involved in the women's movement and the labor movement; the percentage of members asserting an ethnic identity varies as well. Of course, social solidarity is also developed over time in the context of organizational activities; it is clear that such bonds have grown among activists in all four organizations and that attachment to place is a significant dimension of collective identity developed in three of the organizations.

All four organizations adopted sociospatial recruitment strategies that very effectively tapped their municipalities' considerable financial and skill resources, perhaps too well in some regards. For example, in three of the four organizations, approximately two-thirds of the members work in managerial or professional occupations and fewer than one-fifth of the members work for private for-profit companies. Such strong membership biases cannot help but influence organizational outlook and strategy. Ultimately, a narrow membership base hinders the ability of an organization to devise campaigns and frame messages that resonate broadly across a municipality. The one exception to this bias in recruitment is WCC, which successfully recruited a membership base that reasonably approximates the characteristics of Waltham as a whole (with the exception of educational attainment)—and this in a predominantly working-class city. WCC's membership profile can be attributed to, again, WCC's sociospatial recruitment strategy and the way it tapped into Waltham's social geography.

The geographies of resources and recruitment, however, do not by themselves determine the success of organizations. Organizations and political opportunity structures relate to each other in a recursive manner, and there is the geography of political opportunity to consider. Given the uneven geography of both resources and political opportunities in the Boston metropolitan area, one would expect to find an uneven geography of activism.

Table 14. Peace activism levels by organization (percent of members)

	Low	Medium	High
Cambridge SANE/Freeze	27	38	35
Boston Mobilization for Survival (Cambridge)	16	53	31
Lexington Committee for a Nuclear Weapons Freeze	46	31	24
Waltham Concerned Citizens	42	45	13

Extensive organizational resources, very favorable political opportunity structures, and very high levels of attachment to place (representing a form of collective identity) suggest high levels of activism in both Cambridge and Lexington. Indeed, Cambridge has a national reputation for activism, and within the Boston metropolitan area Lexington peace activism is well known. Survey data of the organizations examined here lend credence to these reputations. Based on the composite peace activism index constructed from information supplied by respondents (table 14), the highest percentages of high activism scores are found among members of the two Cambridge peace organizations.[3] Almost a quarter of the members of the Lexington organization are in the high activism category, while a considerably lower percentage of Waltham activists have high activism scores.

In examining the geographic structuring of peace activism, one must not neglect its historical dimension. Just as there is an uneven geography of activism even during peaks of protest cycles, there are cycles of protest even in the geographic centers of activism. Standardized political activism scores show two clear cycles of political activism (table 15).[4] Members of all four organizations show an upswing in activism in the late 1960s and early 1970s (during the wave of civil rights, Vietnam War, women's, and environmental protest). Activism levels decline drastically in the mid-1970s, but then increase again in the late 1970s and early 1980s (during the wave of protest against the arms race), followed by rapid decline. It is highly unlikely that these patterns can be traced simply to fluctuations in resources. Other processes that cannot be reduced to available resources must be at play—processes that are external to individuals and organizations, yet that affect the capacity of organizations to mobilize resources. These processes undoubtedly include changes in "objective" material grievances, ways in which grievances are represented and understood, and shifting structures of political opportunity. These processes are also geographically structured. It is to such processes that we turn next.

Table 15. Standardized political activism scores by organization (years in which members were moderately or most active)

Year(s)	Mobe	Cambridge SANE/Freeze	Lexington CNWF	WCC
55–59	18	43	17	53
60–64	44	42	36	51
65–69	68	62	65	37
70–74	74	63	60	50
75	61	45	32	37
76	61	40	31	34
77	58	41	34	31
78	61	45	34	35
79	61	44	34	36
80	65	55	46	49
81	73	61	50	49
82	78	69	56	56
83	79	70	57	55
84	74	71	68	57
85	70	71	65	58
86	63	69	65	48
87	58	70	66	44
88	54	67	57	47
89	52	67	51	47
90	49	57	46	42

5

Geographic Scale, Mobilization, and the Representation of Defense Investment

> . . . representations of space are shot through with a knowledge *(savoir)*—
> i.e. a mixture of understanding *(connaissance)* and ideology—which is al-
> ways relative and in the process of change. (Lefebvre 1991, 41)

> . . . ideology aims to disclose something of the relation between an utter-
> ance and its material conditions of possibility, when those conditions of
> possibility are viewed in the light of certain power-struggles central to the
> reproduction . . . of a whole form of social life. (Eagleton 1991, 223)

Defense investment, perhaps even more so than with other forms of investment, cannot be understood in isolation from processes operating outside the
site of investment. A variety of processes—economic, political, ideological—
operating on a variety of scales articulate in complex ways to effect specific
investments in particular places. For instance, the economic turnaround of
Massachusetts during the early 1980s (known as the "Massachusetts Miracle")
was driven in large measure by increased defense spending that stimulated
defense-related industries and provided substantial secondary multipliers
through the service sector (Barff and Knight 1988). Understanding how
particular sites in Massachusetts came to benefit from these increases requires an understanding of the international- and national-scale ideological
processes driving the cold war, national-scale political processes affecting defense budgeting decisions, the preexisting spatial division of labor affecting
the ability of particular places to capture defense-spending increases, characteristics of political opportunity structures at the national, state, and local
levels affecting the ability of forces opposing the arms race to mobilize,

and—as is argued in this chapter—how the impacts of defense spending are represented in different places, in turn affecting defense investment politics in those places.

Far too often political and economic processes are analyzed on the basis of what can be gleaned from apparently "objective" data. Although such analyses have their place, it is critical to recognize that there is no necessary relation between the material manifestations of political-economic processes and how that material reality is perceived, understood, and, in turn, acted upon. A variety of individual and institutional actors, operating from differing positions of relative power, frame—that is, represent—political-economic processes in public discourse. It is representations—often multiple and conflicting—that shape political action and economic policy. Representations may vary from place to place and by geographic scale such that similar material circumstances may be understood in very different ways in diverse geographical settings. The politics of defense investment of a particular place, then, cannot be read directly from the apparent material interest (or lack thereof) of that place in defense spending.

The politics of defense investment during the "Massachusetts Miracle" provides an especially clear example of a divergence between material conditions and their representations. This divergence varied by geographic scale with Massachusetts's congressional delegation, governor, and local politicians representing the significance of federally driven defense spending in their jurisdictions in different ways for different reasons. Politically motivated representations of defense spending at the state and congressional district scales had important ramifications for the efficacy of Massachusetts peace organizations and the scale-specific strategies they adopted in opposing the escalation of the arms race during the 1980s.

Before turning directly to the politics of defense investment in Massachusetts and, in particular, three Massachusetts municipalities—Cambridge, Lexington, and Waltham—the theoretical concepts that inform this analysis must be explicated. Of central concern is what Jonas (1994, 257) has called the "scale politics of spatiality," in particular how representations of material practices are politically constructed at a variety of scales. To better understand these scale politics, it is useful to return to some of the spatial concepts of Henri Lefebvre.

Material Practice, Representation, and Scale

Henri Lefebvre (1991) has argued that to understand the production of space one must examine both its materiality and its representation. Many geographers have consistently stressed the materiality of sociospatial processes such as the production of the built environment and social spaces; flows of goods, money, and labor; and the role of the state and capital in regulating and controlling the physical production of space. Several geographers have emphasized the significance, both analytically and politically, of the variety of scales at which sociospatial processes operate. Jonas (1994, 257), for instance, points out that many social objects, "such as neighborhood groups, urban growth coalitions, regional business associations, nation-states, and multinational corporations, have well-defined scales of [material] operation" that affect their capacity to exercise power. Representations of material processes, however, do not always coincide with actual material practice, which also has implications for the exercise of power.

Representations of sociospatial processes are the conceptions through which people perceive, evaluate, and negotiate material spatial practice (see chapter 1). Lefebvre stresses the instrumental production of these representations by those in positions of authority, calling representational spaces "the spaces of scientists, planners, urbanists, technocratic subdividers and social engineers" (38). Harvey (1989) construes representations of space more broadly, acknowledging the representations of space constructed by individuals and communities for themselves. He defines representations of space as "all of the signs and significations, codes and knowledge, that allow such material practices to be talked about and understood" (218). These representations may be strongly contested and bear no relationship to the scale of material practice. Actors dependent on local material and social relationships (see Cox and Mair 1988), for instance, may have a strong interest in representing broad-scale processes in locally idiosyncratic ways to further their local interests. As Jonas (1994, 262) summarizes, "the presentation of scale in political discourse merely provides clues as to the scale of material geographies that are in the process of becoming, but it does not independently 'construct' these scales."

Both material processes and their representations are objects of social and political struggle. Social movement organizations as well as individual actors are always situated relative to the flows and interconnections of sociospatial processes, creating what Massey (1992, 61) calls a "power-geometry." Changing one's position of power frequently involves changing one's position within this power-geometry. "Jumping scales," as Smith (1993) terms it, is an important strategy in the quest for advantageous position. Contrary to conventional treatments, scale should not be taken as an external "given" in social conflict. Scale is simultaneously part of social struggle, "the object as well as the resolution of the contest" (Smith 1993, 101). In some cases, struggles will be over the scale at which material processes—such as labor bargaining or investment in production facilities—take place. In other cases, struggles will be over the scale of representation—such as attempts to portray foreign policy initiatives as inappropriate or infeasible at anything other than the national scale. In still other cases, struggles may be over both scales of material practice and scales of representation. The relative autonomy of these two realms, however, must be stressed; there is no necessary relation between them, scale or otherwise.

In struggles for empowerment, one frequently observes "groups and organizations 'map[ping] out' [i.e., spatially representing] material scales that eventually might liberate them from their existing scale constraints" (Jonas 1994, 262). Counterrepresentations (what Harvey [1989] calls "spaces of representation"), in other words, can communicate the possibility of new spatial practices, including more favorable scales of material spatial practice. The complex interplay of material spatial practice, representation, and counterrepresentation operating at diverse scales is apparent in the politics of defense investment during the Massachusetts Miracle.

Material Spatial Practices: Patterns of Defense Investment

A very curious characteristic of the Massachusetts political scene in the 1980s was the relative paucity of public discussion on the economic significance of the state's defense industries. Although high-tech industries were broadly discussed and directly and indirectly promoted through various state governmental programs and policies, defense industries were generally treated as a separate and comparatively minor concern. Indeed, as will be discussed in the following section, one could have easily developed the impression that defense industries were an insignificant part of the Massachusetts economy. The emphasis on high-tech industries, as opposed to (often high-tech) defense-related industries, moreover, contained an implicit but strong message about the scale at which the processes driving the Massachusetts Miracle operated. Massachusetts's high-tech industries were widely considered to be locally grown and thus their success attributable to the actions of Massachusetts actors, including Massachusetts politicians. Defense industries, on the other hand, are clearly dependent on defense-spending decisions made at the national scale; a defense-driven conception of the Massachusetts Miracle, then, would have made it far more difficult for Massachusetts political figures to take credit for the state's economic turnaround—unless they were to claim credit for increased defense spending. Not surprisingly, the Massachusetts Miracle was widely represented as a phenomenon traceable to Massachusetts conditions and policies. A variety of economic analyses, however, suggest otherwise.

Shift-share analyses performed by O'hUllachain (1987) indicate that increased defense spending played the leading role in the economic turn-around known as the Massachusetts Miracle. Using U.S. Bureau of the Census (1983b) *Current Industrial Reports* data, O'hUllachain classified high-technology industries as high defense-related (the eight most military-dependent high-tech industries accounting for 71 percent of the Department of Defense's goods purchases), low defense-related (high-tech industries with 4 to 10 percent of their sales to the Department of Defense), and non-defense-related (less than 4 percent of sales to the Department of Defense). Examining the period 1977 to 1984, O'hUllachain found that Massachusetts high defense-related high-tech employment grew by 16,300, low defense-related high-tech employment grew by 34,600, and non-defense-related high-tech employment actually decreased by 3,200.

O'hUllachain's shift-share analyses reveal industrial mix effects (how many jobs a state's industrial sector gained or lost in comparison to the expected change based on the national rate of employment growth in that sector, minus its national share) to be particularly strong for Massachusetts's high defense-related high-tech industries (19,100 jobs gained) and low defense-related high-tech industries (24,300 jobs gained), whereas there was very little industrial mix effect for non-defense-related high-tech industries (only 1,200 jobs gained). Regional shift effects (the total shift in employment minus the industrial mix effect, that is, the portion of employment change due to state-specific, rather than industry-specific, conditions), were actually negative for high defense-related high-tech industries (2,000 jobs lost) and non-defense-related high-tech industries (3,600 jobs lost), but positive for low defense-related high-tech industries (11,200 jobs gained). O'hUllachain's analysis gives a clear picture of the overriding importance of the preexisting mix of defense-related industries in Massachusetts's economic revival.

Defense location quotients indicate how concentrated defense contracting is in particular places. O'hUllachain shows Massachusetts with a 1983 defense-shipments location quotient of 1.705, that is, Defense Department purchases from Massachusetts firms were 170.5 percent of Massachusetts's national "share." Barff and Knight (1988) show that the 1977 location quotient for strongly defense-related jobs in New England was 2.01, even higher than that of high-tech industry generally. Although the strongly defense-related quotient declined somewhat by 1984, the location quotient for weakly defense-related manufacturing ballooned from 1.68 to 2.12, most likely explained by Defense Department computer orders. It should also be noted that the location quotients of non-defense-related high-tech industry actually declined, reinforcing the defense-related character of New England's high-tech economy.

The high concentration of defense-related high-tech industry in Massachusetts poised the state for a defense-based economic recovery. The sectoral and spatial distribution of defense contracts clearly creates regional winners and losers (Malecki 1984, 1986; Markusen 1985, 1986; O'hUallachain, 1987), and Massachusetts was a winner. The timing of the turnaround coincided with the U.S. military buildup. Increased defense appropriations began under the Carter administration and accelerated during the first Reagan administration. In real dollars, defense expenditures held steady in 1977 and 1978 and then increased by more than 2 percent in 1979. Defense appropriations more than doubled between 1977 and 1984, increasing from $97.5 billion to $227.4 billion for an annual rate of real growth of almost 5 percent (U.S. Bureau of the Census 1986). Massachusetts's high-tech industries were able to reap the benefits of greatly increased defense spending because they were already defense-oriented when the Carter/Reagan defense buildup began.

Numerous analysts (e.g., Hekman 1980a, 1980b; Malecki 1981, 1982, 1984, 1986; Browne 1984; Saxenian 1985; Markusen and Block 1985; Leavitt 1986; Markusen 1986; O'hUallachain 1987; Barff and Knight 1988; Dorfman 1988; Warsh 1988; Markusen et al. 1991) concur that defense contracting played a significant role in the growth of the Massachusetts and New England economies during the Carter/Reagan arms buildup. Virtually alone in their dissent are Harrison and Kluver (1989), and yet they acknowledge that "Massachusetts military prime contracts rose from $3.7 billion to $7.7 billion" (23) between 1980 and 1985, and that these contracts "accounted for 7 percent of Gross State Product in 1984—*more* than their 6.3 percent share back in 1968, at the height of Vietnam War spending" (23–24). Their principal reservation stems from the fact that figures on industry shipments to the Pentagon suggest that "military production . . . account[s] for only about 4 percent of *all* employment in the state—a bit higher than the national average" (25). Yet, applying a fairly conservative secondary multiplier of 2, to account for expenditures by workers, increases this figure to 8 percent. Considering the advantages gained in nondefense markets as a result of defense-contracting increases this percentage even further.

In sum, the evidence overwhelmingly supports the notion that "there is a significant relationship between a state's share of the Defense Department's purchases of goods and a state's recent ability to generate new manufacturing jobs" (O'hUllachain 1987, 221). New defense-related manufacturing jobs, new civilian manufacturing jobs stimulated by defense R&D and goods purchases, and jobs created through the multiplier effects of defense spending were large and leading components of the Massachusetts Miracle. Although defense spending was significant to the state as a whole, its effects were especially concentrated in the Route 128 area surrounding Boston. Indeed, the high-tech defense industry is so concentrated in the Route 128 area that the economic boom associated with it would more accurately have been called the "Route 128 miracle" rather than the Massachusetts Miracle.

As detailed in chapter 3, Cambridge, Lexington, and Waltham are three of the most defense-dependent municipalities located in the Route 128 "golden semicircle." Firms engaged in defense contracting account for a significant number of jobs in each municipality. The defense contracts of these firms grew steadily from 1979 to 1985, with Cambridge firms peaking at $495 million in 1984–85, Lexington firms peaking at $387 million in 1984–85, and Waltham firms peaking at $262 million in 1982–83 (U.S. Department of Defense 1980–86). By 1985, total prime contracts represented an almost billion-dollar infusion into the economies of these three municipalities with a combined population of fewer than two hundred thousand people.

Although the employment implications of defense spending for the Cambridge, Lexington, and Waltham economies are considered in detail in chapter 3, it should be reiterated here that more than twenty-four thousand defense-related jobs were created in these three municipalities at their defense contracting peaks, and this estimate does not include the multiplier effects of defense workers' spending in the civilian economy. The obvious question then arises: Why has defense spending not been a significant topic in public discourse on the Massachusetts economy? When the patterns and flows of investment in the Massachusetts economy are examined, one is left with the inescapable conclusion that defense investment has been important to the economy. In many places, such as Colorado Springs, Colorado, Houston, Texas, and Las Vegas, Nevada (Markusen et al. 1991; Parker and Feagin 1992), defense spending is publicly discussed and promoted. Yet in Massachusetts it is downplayed. There is a clear divergence between material patterns of defense investment in the Massachusetts space-economy and public representations of that space. To understand this divergence we must consider the contradictions of Massachusetts politics.

Representation, Scale, and the Political Discourse of Defense Spending

Given Massachusetts's long history of economic hardship and its disproportionate defense dependency, one might expect—based solely on the economic interests of Massachusetts residents—that there would be strong public support in Massachusetts for defense spending. Yet this has not been the case. To understand the lack of clear public discussion on the role of defense spending in Massachusetts's economy, one must consider that Massachusetts politicians have had to attract support from both the state's liberal/pacifist voters and voters concerned with the growth of the state's defense-related high-tech industries.

Massachusetts's congressional delegation has long been one of the most liberal in the United States on defense issues; at the same time it has quietly supported funding for defense-related programs with significant economic implications for the state. The key to Massachusetts politicians' ability to "have it both ways" has been the way in which they have shaped public discourse to obscure the contradiction between a liberal foreign policy and economic dependency on defense spending.

The incorporation of liberal defense positions into the dominant political discourse of Massachusetts can be traced at least back to the ban the bomb movement of the early 1960s. The movement got a significant boost in Massachusetts when Harvard professor H. Stuart Hughes ran for the U.S. Senate against Edward Kennedy in 1962 on an explicitly pro-peace, anti-nuclear testing platform; although Hughes was defeated, his campaign is frequently credited with having raised Kennedy's sensitivity to peace issues, persuaded President John Kennedy to press for a Partial Nuclear Test Ban Treaty, and revitalized the Massachusetts peace movement. Anti–Vietnam War protests were particularly strong in Massachusetts later in the decade, and riding on the wave of that protest liberal Michael Harrington and anti-war activist Father Robert Drinan joined the Massachusetts congressional delegation in 1970. The Massachusetts congressional delegation, led by Senators Kennedy and Paul Tsongas and Speaker of the House Tip O'Neill, maintained one of the most liberal voting records on defense issues in the country from the late 1970s through the mid-1980s.

But there is another side to the liberal voting record of the Massachusetts congressional delegation. Although the Massachusetts delegation opposed the MX missile, antisatellite weapons, and numerous other weapons systems, it supported several weapons systems that brought jobs to Massachusetts. On the forefront of efforts to bring jobs to Massachusetts was Tip O'Neill—U.S. representative for his native Cambridge, Somerville, Waltham, and parts of Boston—who wielded enormous influence in his roles as House majority leader and later Speaker of the House.

O'Neill grew up in a poor, working-class neighborhood of Cambridge and throughout his political career built a reputation as a "one-man Welfare Department for Massachusetts," a "work and wages Democrat" who believed that "God's work starts with getting a fellow a job" (Nyhan 1994, 73). He learned the importance of actively supporting federal programs particularly beneficial to Massachusetts in the early 1960s when Cambridge lost the NASA mission control center to Houston—despite Cambridge's clear edge in relevant expertise over all other sites in the United States—as the result of the political maneuvering of Representative Albert Thomas (Texas), head of the Independent Agencies Subcommittee of the House Appropriations Committee (Warsh 1988). In the aftermath of the mission control center loss, the Massachusetts delegation stepped up its own maneuvering. Citing Don Price in *The Scientific Estate* (1965), Warsh argues that

> When O'Neill, in January 1963, declined a very favorable proposition from NASA to hire engineers for Washington jobs on a strictly nonpartisan basis, Price wrote, he was acting on the basis of a deep understanding of the relationship between political and economic power: "If he turned down Washington jobs on behalf of his constituents, it was because he was interested in a far more substantial form of patronage: contracts in Boston for industrial corporations and universities" [1965, 21]. The balance had decisively shifted away from standing armies to technological weapons and the experts who built them—wizards, in Churchill's phrase, or boffins, in the British slang of the war—and increasingly, the politicians realized it. (Warsh 1988, 326)

Massachusetts was well positioned to benefit from the increasing emphasis on sophisticated military technology, and Massachusetts politicians have worked to exploit this. Indeed, during Ronald Reagan's presidency O'Neill admonished the Democratic Party not to appear weak on defense, backed "compromise" budgets with large increases in military spending, and at one point was labeled "Ronald Reagan's secret weapon" by conservative columnist William Safire (Karp 1988). Yet, in Massachusetts, O'Neill developed a reputation as the "bravest resister to the Reaganomics tide," criticizing Reagan's budgets on "the fairness issue" (Nyhan 1994). Redistribution of federal spending to favor defense industries, however, was not part of the fairness critique.

Generally, members of the Massachusetts congressional delegation have opposed broad measures to boost defense spending and supported symbolic legislation to halt the arms race, such as the Freeze resolution. These are the votes that have been emphasized to voters back home, yet the same congressional representatives have supported defense programs that would benefit their districts or state. Leavitt (1986) sums up the behavior of the Massachusetts congressional delegation well:

> In Washington, a congressman *[sic]* can protest the military budget and/or specific military programs, while also supporting programs which provide

contracts and jobs in his home district. A number of Massachusetts congressmen follow just this path. The delegation's unanimous support for bringing the Surface Action Group to Boston Harbor is one example of the underside of the state's congressional liberalism. The efforts of Tip O'Neill and Nick Mavroules to maintain full funding for the Navy F/A-18 fighter plane, whose engines are manufactured by General Electric in Mavroules' district in Lynn, is another. Representative Chester Atkins, whose Fifth district includes defense industry strongholds like Andover, Bedford, Lowell, Wayland and Sudbury, provides the common congressional refrain in Massachusetts: "I fight against the MX, but as long as we are going to build fifty of them and put people to work in my district then I am going to help the people on the local level." (47)

The Massachusetts congressional delegation, in short, has adopted a very liberal stance on defense issues in general, while supporting those specific programs that are of particular benefit to the state. With political discussion of defense issues confined to particular projects—and even then with little fanfare—the broad significance of defense spending to the state has rarely entered into public discourse; as a consequence the congressional delegation has been able to promote a pro-peace image and defense-based economic stimulus simultaneously. Indeed, it would be extremely difficult for members of the congressional delegation to develop a liberal, pro-peace image at home without (1) *publicly representing defense spending, in general, as insignificant* (often by omission of the topic) and (2) *quietly working to promote local defense-based industry.* To do otherwise would be to raise the contradictions between support for a nonmilitaristic foreign policy and dependence on military spending for job growth. Although the direct actions of the congressional delegation have been important in promoting defense-based economic growth in Massachusetts, its indirect actions—such as the promotion of Massachusetts-based presidential science advisers—have also been significant. MIT and Harvard University–based scientists have long had a virtual lock on the position of presidential science adviser. They have included MIT's Vannevar Bush (Roosevelt), MIT's James Killian (Eisenhower), Harvard's George Kistiakowsky (Eisenhower), MIT's Jerome Wiesner (Kennedy), Harvard Ph.D. Don Hornig (Johnson), MIT Radiation Lab director Lee DuBridge (Nixon), MIT Ph.D. Edward David Jr. (Nixon), MIT's H. Guyford Stever (Nixon and Ford), and MIT's Frank Press (Carter). As Warsh (1988, 326) notes, "Ronald Reagan's science advisor, George Keyworth II, was the first man to hold the job who never went to school or taught in Boston— and he was born in Boston." Presidential science advisers have significantly influenced the priorities of the nation's scientific research in a variety of ways, not least of which being the selection of corporate advisory committees that determine the need for particular weapons programs benefiting particular firms and places (Adams 1986). Isolated from electoral scrutiny, MIT and Harvard University–based science advisers have been able to promote infusions of national defense-related R&D money into Massachusetts without making significant political waves. Again, the reality of defense-related economic development differs from its public representation—if it is publicly represented at all. The representation of Massachusetts as a state without significant defense-dependency also occurs at the scale of Massachusetts state politics. The economic turnaround known as the Massachusetts Miracle began under conservative, avidly pro-business Democratic governor Edward King. King's central—and virtually only—promise was to improve the Massachusetts business climate and in turn provide jobs. King strongly supported measures such as the Massachusetts High Technology Council/Citizens for Limited Taxation–backed Proposition 2½ (capping property taxes), the establishment of the Bay State Skills Corporation to subsidize the training of engineers and technicians for high-tech capital, and the start-up of the quasi-public Massachusetts Technology Park Corporation in an ill-fated attempt to get a Massachusetts semiconductor industry off the ground. Although all of these measures benefited Massachusetts's high-tech defense-related industries, none of them were linked to defense issues in public debate, most likely so as to not further alienate Massachusetts's traditionally liberal voters and the budding peace movement.

King won the strong support of business interests, but this proved insufficient against a rejuvenated Michael Dukakis in 1982. (Dukakis was turned out of office after his first term by King in 1978.) Dukakis defeated King after having rebuilt his liberal coalition and taken on a more business-friendly stance. Significantly, Dukakis strongly criticized the Reagan military buildup as wasteful and excessive. In April 1983 Dukakis assailed Reagan's defense policies as "leading us down the road to economic ruin and nuclear confrontation" (Mahoney 1983, 90). In 1985 he argued that the 1986 federal budget proposal "takes programs which invest in our people and the quality of their lives and which have already been cut substantially and cuts them even further. It takes a wasteful and bloated defense budget and increases it by 12%" (Commonwealth of Massachusetts 1985, i). Once again, opposition to the arms race was not portrayed as inimical to the economic recovery of the state. In this respect Dukakis's statements represented a mere continuation of those of his predecessor and of the Massachusetts congressional delegation: the contradictions between advocating a nonmilitaristic foreign policy and relying on defense-based stimulation of the Massachusetts economy were never raised. Dukakis's stance did differ from others' in an important respect, however: Dukakis did not merely downplay the connection between the defense buildup and Massachusetts's economic recovery, he argued that the buildup actually harmed the Massachusetts economy. Dukakis never acknowledged the role of the Carter/Reagan defense buildup in Massachusetts's economic recovery. While drawing attention to Massachusetts's loss of federal grants for state and local programs of a half billion dollars per year between 1981 and 1984, he did not publicly acknowledge that defense spending in Massachusetts increased by about two billion dollars per year during the same period (Leavitt 1986). Instead, the growth of high-tech industry, his own administration's economic development programs, and reduced taxes were purported to have brought about the state's economic recovery (ibid.).

It was in Dukakis's interest to argue that federal defense policy hurt the Massachusetts economy. Given the state's long history of economic hardship and Dukakis's own difficulties with various fractions of capital in the state, it was extremely important that his policies, not federal defense spending, be seen as having spurred the economic turnaround. Thus Dukakis, who genuinely opposed militarism, along with the Massachusetts congressional delegation and the academic/scientific policy elite from MIT and Harvard, contributed to the widely held but false notion that military spending was unrelated to the health of the Massachusetts economy. Indeed, in 1985, despite publicly available data showing defense contracting in Massachusetts at an all-time high and widespread recognition of the significance of defense spending among executives of defense-related high-tech industries, only 5 percent of Massachusetts residents believed that defense spending was related to the state's economic recovery (ibid.) and defense industry executives felt the need to explore ways of communicating the significance of the state's defense industry to the public (Knapp 1985).

Clearly, the public rhetoric adopted by Massachusetts politicians operating at both the federal and state levels served to obscure the significance of defense spending in Massachusetts and thus skew the electorate's view of its narrow (economic) material interests. By effectively representing defense spending in Massachusetts as insignificant, federal and state politicians unwittingly impeded the growth of movements that might have criticized the economic implications of peace politics. In the early 1980s this proved fortuitous for peace organizations promoting new representational spaces devoid of militarism (at local, state, and national scales), because such positions could be advocated without addressing their economic implications. But as the peace movement moved out of the realm of symbolism and began to propose measures that would have material effects, the disjuncture between the common public representation of the significance of defense spending and the material reality became a liability. Peace organizations were unprepared to address the economic implications of their proposals when those implications were finally raised.

New Representations and Scale: The Politics of Peace

In Massachusetts in the early 1980s, the escalation of the arms race and the turnaround of the Massachusetts economy were generally perceived as two separate processes. Peace organizers in this period were quite successful, in no small measure, because of their strategy of mobilizing public opinion behind local *nonbinding* referenda that allowed voters to express opposition to the arms race without having to seriously consider the material, economic effects actual implementation of such measures could have on their local economies. Significantly, because nonbinding measures had no immediate or even likely long-term impact, actors whose economic well-being was linked to defense spending saw little reason to mount significant counter-campaigns. Instead, they preferred to maintain a low profile as long as their federal defense funding remained assured.

The effectiveness of the nonbinding referenda strategy was first demonstrated in western Massachusetts on election day 1980. With wording modeled on the emerging Freeze movement's call for "an immediate, verifiable, mutual halt to the production, testing, and deployment of new nuclear weapons and their delivery systems" (Solo 1988, 19), nonbinding referenda were passed in fifty-nine of the sixty-two western Massachusetts towns where they were on the ballot and received 59 percent of the overall vote. Reagan carried thirty-three of these sixty-two towns in the same election, indicating that support for Reagan could not be equated with support for escalation of the arms race. Following the western Massachusetts example, the national Freeze movement adopted a strategy in which local Freeze chapters would utilize, among other tools, local referenda, city council resolutions, petitions, and endorsements from local community leaders to mobilize public opinion against the arms race. The national Freeze's long-term, five-year plan called for (1) demonstrating the Freeze's potential to stop the arms race; (2) building broad and visible public support; (3) directing public opinion to pressure national legislative and administrative policymakers; and (4) adopting the Freeze as national policy (McCrea and Markle 1989, 124). Notably absent from the Freeze's strategy was the development of alternative economic policies to offset economic displacement brought about by the loss of defense spending. This is not to suggest that Freeze organizers were unaware or insensitive to economic issues. Indeed, the author of *Call to Halt the Nuclear Arms Race,* Randall Forsberg, linked the Freeze to federal budget issues such as school lunches, infant nutrition, and black unemployment (Meyer 1990, 187), but Freeze education was divorced from Freeze political policy and strategy. As Pam Solo observed, "Keeping education separate from strategy was like giving the movement a lobotomy" (cited in ibid., 191).

Over the next several years the Freeze movement went forward as a series of local and state campaigns. The activities of local Freeze chapters in Cambridge, Lexington, and Waltham, Massachusetts, were representative of such campaigns. As detailed in chapters 3 and 4, these three municipalities differ significantly in terms of socioeconomic composition, local state political opportunity structures, and available organizational resources, but in all three municipalities activists were able to mobilize public opinion behind nonbinding Freeze referenda. Although important place-specific differences in recruitment strategies, target populations, and framing existed (chapter 4), there were certain commonalities in approach, in part owing to the fact that broad strategies were mapped out by state and national Freeze organizers, in part due to the fact that local Freeze chapter leaders interacted through congressional district and statewide Freeze meetings, and in part due to the participation of local Freeze organizers in events cosponsored with other Freeze and non-Freeze organizations. Working with local churches, schools, social movement organizations, and prominent citizens, Freeze organizers opened up channels of communication throughout their communities. Participation in a variety of activities such as sponsoring films and discussions, marching in parades and demonstrations, staffing information tables, participating in Hiroshima Day vigils, writing and meeting with congresspersons, canvassing neighborhoods, collecting petition signatures, running newspaper ads, and informing local media of Freeze activities all served to educate the public about the dangers of nuclear war and mobilize public opinion behind a freeze of the arms race.

As discussed in chapter 4, the 1981 townwide petition drive of the Lexington Committee for a Nuclear Weapons Freeze was instrumental not only in mobilizing resources and opinion locally, but also in convincing key congressional figures of the political merits of the Freeze campaign. Similar tactics were employed elsewhere, but due to different place-specific circumstances, with more modest results. Waltham Concerned Citizens attempted to demonstrate support for the Freeze to local officials in 1982 by conducting a door-to-door petition drive in the city's first ward. Bonny Saulnier of WCC explained that the first ward was chosen because "it includes a cross-section of the Waltham population and because Ward 1 city councilor, Peter Tromb-ley, is also a Massachusetts state representative" who would be voting on whether to place the Freeze referendum on the 1982 state ballot (*Middlesex News* 1982a). According to Marianne Lynnworth, WCC recognized that "Waltham is a different city. We have to educate other people first. We [peace activists] are a minority. We should face it. We have much to do before we approach City Council" (*Waltham News Tribune* 1982a). Accordingly, WCC distributed leaflets explaining the Freeze before any attempt was made to gather petition signatures. When petition signatures were collected, 635 of the approximately 800 people who were approached signed (79 percent). But despite WCC's strong backing, the Waltham City Council—unlike the Cambridge City Council or the Lexington Town Meeting—was reluctant to pass a Freeze resolution. The majority felt "the City Council was not the ap-propriate body from which to pass foreign policy resolutions" (*Waltham News Tribune* 1982b) and voted 8–6 to shelve it. However, a week later, after WCC argued that shelving the resolution infringed upon citizens' rights to petition governmental bodies, a city councillor argued that Waltham's de-fense industries were prime targets in the event of nuclear war (*Middlesex News* 1982b), and prominent church and School Committee members ex-pressed their support for the resolution, the city council reversed itself and approved the resolution 9–6.

The issue of local targeting was an important part of many local Freeze organizations' representational strategies. In early 1982 the city of Cam-bridge released its booklet *Cambridge and Nuclear Weapons: Is There a Place to Hide?* in response to the Federal Emergency Management Administration's 1981 nuclear war planning directive. The booklet included a map showing Cambridge as a nuclear target and discussed the destruction a nuclear attack would wreak. Also included was a list of fifteen different peace organizations citizens could join, as well as encouragement to voice concern to congress-persons and the president. At the behest of the Cambridge City Council, the booklet was widely disseminated—to more than 120 cities nationwide—and the representational strategy copied by many local Freeze chapters. The booklets and maps usually focused on nuclear destruction but rarely made any critical connection to local economic interests in the defense economy. Waltham Concerned Citizens produced a flier with Waltham represented as a nuclear target (figure 17; also produced in Spanish) and connected the arms race to economic issues, but without mentioning Waltham's vested in-terest in the defense economy. In essence, local Freeze chapters unwittingly suppressed discussion of fundamental economic issues in much the same manner as state and national politicians.

What one nuclear
weapon would do to
Cambridge.

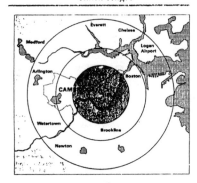

 If You Were Further Away
(1.7 to 2.7 miles from the bomb)
Suppose you were away from Cambridge – doing
errands, visiting a friend at work – outside this
circle of complete and immediate devastation. Imagine that you were
one of a group of 10 persons, in Watertown (or Brookline or
downtown Boston). Half would die and four of five of you would be
injured. Of the survivors of the blast of the explosion as many as half
might ultimately die from burns. Others would die, sooner or later,
from exposure to radiation. If it were downtown Boston, tall buildings
would collapse and fill the streets with debris. Most automobiles,
police cars, buses and firetrucks would be destroyed.

 If You Were Still Further Away
(2.7 to 4.7 miles from the bomb)
Imagine instead that you were fortunate to be
further away from Cambridge, working in Revere,
Everett, or Forest Hills. Even at that distance half the people would be
killed or injured. Most of the planes and hangars at Logan Airport
would be destroyed. Factories would be severely damaged. Buildings
would lose their windows and frames and interior partitions. The
contents of upper floors would be blown out and walls would crack.
Debris in the streets would prevent vehicular traffic. Fires would spread
throughout much of the area and burn for at least a day, destroying at
least half the buildings. Under certain circumstances a vast "firestorm"
might occur, burning out of control at temperatures of thousands of
degrees. Where this happened so much air would be sucked up that
thousands of people would die from lack of oxygen.

If You Were Even Further Away
For up to hundreds of miles away, depending upon
wind patterns, the nature of the bomb, and other
factors, radiation would kill thousands more. The
radiation would be spread by tons and tons of particles of
contaminated soil and debris floating and drifting away from the blast
area. The deaths would be rapid or slow and would include unborn
generations due to the effect of radiation on genetic characteristics.
For many of those who survived, the recovery would be long and
painful, perhaps with permanent disability.

If You Were In Cambridge
(0.0 to 1.7 miles from the bomb)
Suppose a one-megaton bomb were dropped near
ground level over Cambridge City Hall. Almost all
Cambridge citizens would be killed. City Hall, the Central Square Post
Office, and the YMCA and YWCA — all would disappear into a crater
about 20 stories deep. A rim of deadly radioactive soil would be
thrown up twice as far as where the Police Station, the City Hall
Annex and the Manning Apartments for the elderly had been. Nothing
recognizable would remain from the riverfront to the rest of the City. Little
of significance would be left standing in the rest of the City. This "end
of the world" as we know it would occur within seconds.

Figure 15. Cambridge as a nuclear target. Source: City of Cambridge.

Nonetheless, the Freeze strategy was extremely effective, to a degree.
The Freeze was clearly successful in promoting representations of an arms
race–free world. It did this quite literally by suggesting that an expanding hi-
erarchy of spatial scales—municipalities, states, and eventually the entire
country—should not be subject to imperatives of the cold war in which the
central state was engaged. More than 70 percent of the voters in Cambridge,
Lexington, and Waltham approved the statewide nonbinding Freeze referendum of 1982. Support was widespread: the referendum passed by a comfort-
able margin in every precinct in each of these municipalities. The Cambridge
and Waltham city councils and the Lexington Town Meeting also passed
nonbinding resolutions supporting the Freeze. Nationwide, 370 city councils, 71 county boards, 446 town meetings, and 23 state legislatures passed
nonbinding Freeze referenda (McCrea and Markle 1989). When asked for
their opinion or vote, citizens overwhelmingly approved the new representational spaces of the Freeze. Indeed, an April 1982 ABC News/ *Washington
Post* poll showed 81 percent of Americans favoring the Freeze (Solo 1988).
On June 12, 1982, the largest demonstration in U.S. history occurred when
more than one million people rallied in favor of the Freeze in New York's
Central Park (Leavitt 1983b; Solo 1988; McCrea and Markle 1989). In the

There are also concerned groups and organizations which you can contact:

American Friends Service Committee
2161 Massachusetts Avenue
Cambridge, Massachusetts 02140
661-6130

The Catholic Connection
27 Isabella Street
Boston, Massachusetts 02117
482-6295

Council for a Livable World
11 Beacon Street
Boston, Massachusetts 02108
742-9395

Council for a Nuclear Weapons Freeze
2161 Massachusetts Avenue
Cambridge, Massachusetts 02140
491-7809

Educators for Social Responsibility
25 Kennard Street
Brookline, Massachusetts 02146
734-1111 ext. 335

Institute for Defense and Disarmament Studies
251 Harvard Street
Brookline, Massachusetts 02146
734-4216

Jobs With Peace
10 West Street
Boston, Massachusetts
451-3389

Lawyers Alliance for Nuclear Arms Control
P. O. Box 9171
Boston, Massachusetts 02114
227-0118

Mobilization for Survival
13 Sellers Street
Cambridge, Massachusetts 02139
354-0008

Physicians for Social Responsibility
23 Main Street, P. O. Box 144
Watertown, Massachusetts 02171
924-3468

Science for the People
897 Main Street
Cambridge, Massachusetts 02139
547-0370

Union of Concerned Scientists
1384 Massachusetts Avenue
Cambridge, Massachusetts 02138
547-5552

University Christian Movement
11 Garden Street
Cambridge, Massachusetts 02138
354-6583

U. S. Peace Council
P. O. Box 426, Astor Station
Boston, Massachusetts 02123
969-5571

Women's Party for Survival
56 North Beacon Street
Watertown, Massachusetts 02172
923-9542

Draw your own conclusion. Take action.

You may or may not agree with the City Council, but try and reach your own conclusion. Do not assume that someone else can be smarter than you are about this. Tell your City Council and School Committee members what else you think they should do. Tell President Reagan, Congressman O'Neill, and Senators Kennedy and Tsongas what you think they should do.

Figure 16. Peace organizations working to halt the arms race. Source: City of Cambridge.

same month, 2.3 million signatures collected on Freeze petitions were delivered to the U.S. and Soviet United Nations missions (Solo 1988).

The new representational spaces of the Freeze, however, only partially connected with the material spatial practices of defense-based investment. The material dangers that such spending posed were widely acknowledged, but the economic benefits wrought by military Keynesianism were ignored. As long as Freeze referenda were nonbinding and strictly symbolic, such contradictions were of little practical significance for the Freeze campaign. But such contradictions could not be ignored forever.

The first clear evidence of the problems caused by the disjuncture between the new representational spaces of the Freeze and the material spatial practices of defense investment arose as the Freeze movement turned to the central state. The Freeze resolution introduced in the U.S. House of Representatives by Representatives Markey (Massachusetts), Conte (Massachusetts), and Bingham (New York) and in the U.S. Senate by Senators Kennedy (Massachusetts) and Hatfield (Oregon) effectively constituted a shift in the Freeze movement from a multiplicity of local campaigns that had no material effect on defense spending to one directed at the central state that controls defense spending. Although the decentralized Freeze movement had been very successful in mobilizing public opinion behind a new representational

Figure 17. Waltham as a nuclear target. Source: Waltham Concerned Citizens.

space—a world free of the arms race—it did so without addressing relevant material spatial practices, that is, the infusion of substantial defense spending in local economies across the country.

The disjuncture between defense-based material practices and the new representational spaces became clear in the central state legislative arena. Congresspersons, aware of the importance of defense jobs in their districts (unlike many voters in Massachusetts and elsewhere), were hesitant to approve the Freeze resolution in its original form, which called for an end to the production, testing, and deployment of new nuclear weapons. Nonetheless, many wished to be viewed as publicly supporting the very popular Freeze. To do this, Congress essentially borrowed the strategy the Freeze itself had deployed: the Freeze resolution was amended to the point of becoming nonbinding and meaningless. Congress had been asked to choose between the new representational space of the Freeze and the material spatial practice of defense-based economic investment; it responded by deflecting attention from the contradiction between the two. Ultimately, however, it had to choose the old material practice or a new one; continued escalation of defense spending won out. The House passed the amended, nonbinding Freeze resolution on May 4, 1983 (with unanimous support from the Massachusetts congressional delegation); later in the same year the House approved the largest defense budget in U.S. history (through 1983) (Solo 1988).

At the local scale, the contradictions between the new representational spaces of the peace movement and the material spatial practice of defense investment continued to play out after the historic House votes. In Cambridge, Massachusetts, in particular, activists became increasingly frustrated with the inability of the Freeze movement to bring about material change in the defense policies of the central state. Peace activists had successfully used Nuclear Free Zone (NFZ) referenda in Massachusetts municipalities and elsewhere to challenge the nuclear arms policies of the president and Congress. But all of these challenges were symbolic; no existing NFZ was binding. In 1982 a group of Cambridge peace activists began to organize the Nuclear Free Cambridge (NFC) campaign—a campaign that would attempt, for the first time, to pass a binding referendum to halt all nuclear weapons–related activities in a defense-dependent municipality.

The NFC campaign, though initially favored by a majority of Cambridge residents, was defeated by a 60–40 margin in the November 1983 election by a coalition of economic actors that believed they would be negatively affected by the referendum. Although many factors contributed to the defeat of NFC (discussed in detail in chapter 6), a crucial factor was the neglect of the referendum's economic implications. Draper Laboratory, Cambridge's largest weapons contractor, along with numerous weapons contractors nation-wide, led the countermovement—Citizens Against Research Bans (CARB)—to NFC. Although the opposition of weapons contractors and the local chamber of commerce—which labeled the referendum "antibusiness"—was predictable, the opposition of labor and academics was not. CARB success-fully recruited prominent local labor and academic figures into the counter-movement and made the case that NFC would cause local business to lose revenue, local labor to lose jobs, and the academic community to lose aca-demic freedom (and jobs as well, through restrictions on research). During and after the campaign, NFC organizers were widely criticized for being ar-rogant, naive, and insensitive to the effect of the referendum on jobs (Brugman 1989).

The NFC campaign brought into sharp view the contradiction between the new representational spaces envisioned, at various scales, by the peace movement and the material spatial practices supported by central state de-fense spending. The binding NFC referendum did not allow politicians and voters to choose both. Confronted with the choice of a Cambridge free of nuclear weapons–related activities and a Cambridge receiving substantial weapons-related economic stimulus, voters chose the latter. Anticipation of just such an outcome precluded the introduction of similar referenda in Lexington, Waltham, and elsewhere. As one Lexington peace organizer sum-marized, "Raytheon [the largest Lexington defense contractor] . . . produces a lot of jobs . . . it's difficult for us to come to grips with that" (Tiffany 1990). Similarly, activists in Waltham recognized that "working class [de-fense workers] don't have very many other options [if they lose their jobs]" (Kricker 1990b). Clearly, peace organizers became aware of the economic significance of the measures they advocated after the experience of NFC. Indeed, after the NFC referendum, the Cambridge Peace Commission for-mulated a policy document addressing the conversion of defense industries to serve civilian markets; by focusing on conversion, explicit emphasis was paid to preserving local jobs. New peace organizations with an emphasis on job growth in a civilian economy, such as Jobs with Peace, were also founded. The new representational spaces of the peace movement and the material spatial practices of defense investment began in part, at least, to connect.

Summary and Implications

As the politics of peace and defense investment in Massachusetts illustrate, there is no necessary relationship among material spatial practices, repre-sentations of those practices, and new counterrepresentational spaces. The successes of the peace movement were based in large part on its ability to mobilize public opinion behind new representational spaces free of nuclear weapons or, at a minimum, free of participation in the escalation of the arms race. These spaces were formulated at a variety of scales—local, state, and national. Yet the scales of new representational spaces of peace rarely coincided with that of the material spatial practice of defense-based investment.

In Massachusetts, the ongoing disjuncture between new municipal and state representational spaces of peace and the nationally driven material spatial practice of defense-based investment was facilitated in two ways. First, Massachusetts politicians represented the revival of the Massachusetts economy as stemming from the actions of Massachusetts actors, not federal defense spending. Second, the peace movement built on these representations by mobilizing public opinion behind purely symbolic, nonbinding referenda that had no impact on the material practice of defense-based investment. These rhetorical strategies allowed the almost complete disjuncture between new representational spaces and material spatial practice to continue virtually unchallenged, until the binding NFC referendum forced voters to consider both simultaneously.

Had NFC organizers explicitly accounted for the material spatial practice of defense-based economic stimulus—and proposed alternatives to it—NFC likely would have fared better at the polls. However, even if NFC had been successful, it would have had little impact on the arms race.

The arms race was clearly driven by decisions made at the level of the central state, yet the only binding referendum offered in opposition was at the level of a local state. This is not to suggest that new representational spaces should only be proposed at the scale of the processes their proponents seek to alter. On the contrary, often the most effective strategy for garnering support for new representational spaces is to propose them in the places and at the scales at which they are likely to receive the most favorable reception—in other words, where political opportunity structures are favorable. But ultimately, new representational spaces must directly address the material practices they aim to replace, and they must do so at the scale of those practices. Accordingly, it is to issues of political opportunity structures and scale that we next turn.

6

Local and Central State Political Opportunity Structures: Material Interests and the Shifting Scale of Struggle

> The scale of struggle and the struggle over scale are two sides of the same coin. (Smith 1992, 74)

Although NSMs such as the peace movement differ from older movements in their emphasis on "the personal as political," they do not shrink from political battles in state arenas. Indeed, to the extent that these movements address oppression and domination stemming from systemic power relations institutionalized within and legitimized by the state, they must strive for a measure of state power. The primary distinction between NSMs and older social movements, instead, revolves around the form of justice they seek: empowerment rather than economic redistribution.

Any understanding of the strategies and empowerment potential of NSMs must be contextual. Social movements, for instance, operate within a variety of political structures, which vary from place to place and by geographic scale. Moreover, these structures are dynamic; the opportunities they afford shift geographically and temporally as power relations within local states and the central state change. Such geographic and temporal shifts have important implications for the success or failure of social movement campaigns. These shifts, however, do not predetermine the outcome of social movement campaigns. Rather, they suggest that the mobilization strategies chosen by social movements must be sensitive to changing geographic and historical conditions.

For the peace movement, empowerment has often meant gaining a meaningful voice in the decision-making processes of local states as well as the central state. The Cambridge, Massachusetts, peace movement—in particular its antinuclear weapons branch in the early 1980s—provides an especially clear example of the manner in which the changing political opportunities of the local and central states affect the nature, geographic scale, and efficacy of social movement mobilization. Cambridge peace movement campaigns have, at times, been directed at the central state; at other times the movement has directed its efforts toward, and even captured, the local state. Mobilization, moreover, has passed through major "cycles" of protest, at times influencing local, national, and/or international political stages, at other times fading into obscurity.

Analysis of the dynamics of the peace movement requires an approach that is both historical and sensitive to what Herod (1991) calls the dialectics of geographic scale. Such an approach necessitates attention to three interrelated questions: (1) Given that peace movement campaigns are frequently directed at local states, to what extent does capturing the local state represent real empowerment, that is, how much autonomy from both the central state and the interests of capital does the local state possess? (2) What structural conditions are likely to affect the inclusion or exclusion of peace groups from the decision-making processes of both the local and central states? (3) How do political and economic processes operating at different geographic scales articulate and influence the outcome of peace campaigns?

Accordingly, the first section of this chapter reviews some of the principal positions taken on local state autonomy and proposes that the local state possesses greater autonomy from the central state than from capital. The second section, drawing on Tarrow's (1983, 1989) work on political opportunity structures, offers a framework for understanding participation in and control of both the local and central states. The remainder of the chapter focuses on two Cambridge-based peace organizations during the most recent cycle of protest, emphasizing organizational capacities and mobilization strategies within the context of changing local and central state political opportunity structures. Of central interest is the relationship between two major anti–nuclear weapons campaigns, one ultimately directed at the central state (the Nuclear Freeze), and one directed at the local state (the Nuclear Free Cambridge campaign). These examples serve to illustrate the dialectical relationship between political structures and the agency of social movement organizations, as well as between local- and national-scale processes. Moreover, they provide lessons in both the potential for and limitations to political empowerment through the local state.

Conceptions of Local State Autonomy

There is considerable disagreement over how much autonomy should be attributed to local states. Several local state theorists (e.g., Saunders 1981,

1985; Cooke 1983; Duncan and Goodwin 1988; Duncan, Goodwin, and Halford 1988) grant the local state a large degree of political autonomy from the central state. Duncan, Goodwin, and Halford (1988) argue that the local state cannot be reduced to an agent of the central state; local state policies can vary considerably from those of the central state, within limits. Greer (1987, 526) goes so far as to argue that local states can essentially become independent states within a state, "highly immune from external political or bureaucratic pressures, responsive to local interests."

Other theorists (e.g., Cockburn 1977; Clark and Dear 1984) argue that the local state is merely the lower tier in a hierarchical state system: although its functions differ from those of the central state, it is subservient to and dependent on the central state. Cockburn views the local state as a sphere of class struggle over the reproduction of capitalist social relations, yet at the same time it is an agent for the central state that must, in turn, serve the needs of capital. Similarly, Clark and Dear consider the local state to be an apparatus of the central state, heavily dependent on the latter's financial resources, laws, and institutions. They, as well as Fincher (1987b), view the local state as a functional crisis-avoidance mechanism for the central state.

Comparison of the differing positions on the autonomy of the local state reveals very different foci of analysis: those who attribute a relatively high degree of autonomy to the local state generally focus on decision-making processes in local state and central state political institutions; those who grant the local state little autonomy take economic relations as the analytic point of departure. Yet politics and economics are deeply intertwined. States, both local and central, must maintain capital accumulation both to finance their own activities and to maintain a level of public support sufficient to keep governments in power.

Peterson (1981) goes so far as to argue that the necessity of competing with other cities for capital investment forces local states to adopt pro-growth policies, thereby making local politics largely irrelevant. Peterson's economic determinism, however, has met with considerable resistance. Mollenkopf (1983) and Stone (1987) emphasize multiple imperatives—both economic and political—facing the local state. The ways in which local officials respond to these imperatives are "shaped by the composition of the political coalitions they depend on for support and the structure of political organizations and institutions in their city" (Shefter 1985, 220).

Commenting on this literature, Cox (1993, 436) argues that "Local governments necessarily have an autonomy. They have it by virtue of constitutionally given powers and could not otherwise propound and implement policies. What seems to be at issue, therefore, is less the autonomy of cities—or of local governments as their representatives—than the effectiveness of those policies in achieving certain ends." The effectiveness of state policies is especially precarious when they threaten capital accumulation. Threats to capital accumulation can bring on economic disciplining (Harvey 1985b) in the form of capital strikes, capital flight, and/or support for opposing political groups. As we shall see, economic disciplining has extremely important implications for the empowerment of social movements, even those that are not economic in focus. When social movements are able to gain a voice in shaping public policy, their policies often have significant, though indirect, economic implications. These implications can provoke reactions from capital leading to the dismantling of programs backed by newly empowered groups and even the exclusion of such groups' voices from the state arena.

The ability of capital to discipline its opponents—and, by implication, the degree of state autonomy from capital—is not constant. "Depending on circumstances of time and place, capital or state will have some leverage . . . [L]ocally dependent businesses will be more subject to the demands of the state than those which are not locally dependent" (Cox 1991, 305). The crucial question for the potential of social movements, then, is not whether the political is autonomous from the economic, but rather *how the relationship between them is affected by the scale of dependence of local capitals.*

Although locally dependent capitals—those dependent on nonsubstitutable local social relations—have less leverage with the local state than highly mobile capitals, they are, by the same token, more likely to mobilize for local political battles because relocation is not an attractive option. Similarly, the local dependence of people makes them sensitive to local decisions that threaten the material foundations of their daily lives (Cox and Mair 1988). More locally dependent firms and people have greater stakes in the decisions of the local state, which, other things being equal, increases the likelihood that they will actively challenge local state policies that threaten their interests. Often overlooked in the local-dependence argument is the role extralocal allies may play. Local dependence viewed in isolation from extralocal relationships suggests relative powerlessness due to the inability to opt out of local conflicts. Yet it can, when organizational links are strong, promote solidarity and increase power through the assistance of extralocal allies. Low levels of local dependence tend to foster geographical mobility and individual action in response to conflict; high levels of local dependence tend to foster coalition building, often with extralocal allies who potentially face similar conflicts. Local power and vulnerability to economic or political disciplining, then, cannot realistically be viewed in isolation from the degree of local dependence and the strength of extralocal relationships.

The autonomy of the local state, in sum, is contingent. Policies of the local state are the outcome of complex struggles that are largely determined by the relative power of the contestants. The local state can serve as a vehicle—a collective agent—for intervention in social, political, and economic relations. Structures of access to state power, accordingly, bear heavily on the meaningful empowerment of social movements. Many groups and classes are actively excluded from participation in the local state. Others do not mobilize around their interests, for a variety of reasons. Understanding local mobilization processes and the structural conditions that affect political inclusion is crucial if we are to understand how the local state can be used as a vehicle to effect broader-scale social change. To this end, we turn to Tarrow's political process model.

Tarrow's Political Process Model

In analyzing the mobilization of political movements, Tarrow (1983, 1989) considers both the internal organizational capacities of social movement organizations and the external structure of political opportunities they face. His political process model represents an alternative to both structuralist models, which see politics as derivative of macro-scale structural change, and resource mobilization theory (RMT), which traces political mobilization almost exclusively to social movement organizations' resources and agency. Central to Tarrow's model is the notion of shifting structures of political opportunity that are not derived from economic conditions. Tarrow argues that both organizational resources and a favorable political opportunity structure are necessary for political success. Changes in political opportunity structures account for waves of political activism, or what he terms "cycles of protest."

As explained in chapter 3, political opportunity structures can be defined in terms of four characteristics that affect protest: (1) the openness or closure of formal political access—for example, whether councilpersons are elected by wards or at large, the ease of placing initiatives on the ballot—as well as the role of the dominant political coalitions in allowing nongoverning groups access to state power; (2) the stability of alignments within the political system—instability leading to a greater tolerance of protest; (3) the presence or absence of allies and support groups that can supply resources and raise expectations of success; and (4) divisions among the elite that can form openings for the formation of new coalitions (Tarrow 1989, 34).

In strategic terms, greater political opportunities lower the costs perceived by potential participants in social movements; this perception of lower costs may lead to a wave of mobilization that strengthens the political position of the movement and may create further political opportunities.

Although Tarrow's work provides a framework for understanding the dynamics of political mobilization that can influence or dictate the policies of the state, it suffers form a number of shortcomings. There are three critical difficulties in Tarrow's work stemming from relationships he does not identify: (1) the relationship between the economic and the political, discussed previously; (2) the sources and impacts of grievances; and (3) the dialectics of scale, particularly the relationship between local state and central state–focused mobilization.

Tarrow acknowledges the importance of dynamic social processes and events that may intensify or constitute new grievances for particular social groups and classes, and the role of social movement organizations in framing and defining those grievances. Nonetheless, he curiously downplays the importance of changed grievances as he concentrates on explaining social movement mobilization in terms of the interaction between internal organizational factors and political opportunity structures. In the process, political opportunity structures and grievances become conflated and the effects of the severity of potential movement participants' grievances are neglected.

Tarrow's other significant omission stems from his single-state analytic framework. Such a framework denies the reality of a geographically differentiated state system with a central state and multiple local states, each local state possessing a limited degree of autonomy. Even though coalitions of groups and classes controlling local states do not affect central state policy directly, they can affect political mobilization aimed at the central state. Conversely, central state politics and actions, which may or may not directly affect local state policy, can nevertheless impact upon local political mobilization, for example, by producing new grievances. Interactions among local states, moreover, may play a significant role in the diffusion of locally focused political mobilizations.

By recognizing a geographically differentiated state system and the analytic distinction between grievances and political opportunity structures, we can begin to understand that political mobilization need not be aimed at the state—central or local—whose actions produce grievances. Rather, if political opportunity structures differ significantly among central and local states, political mobilization may be directed at the state with the most open political structure. When political opportunity structures at the central state are relatively closed, resistance to central state policies may take root at the local state. Local states may, moreover, promote the broad diffusion of protest. In most cases protest, in and of itself, provokes little serious reaction from the central state or fractions of capital. When protests threaten significant economic interests, however, threatened fractions of capital can be expected to discipline the movement that would use state power—central or local—against them. The Cambridge, Massachusetts, anti–nuclear weapons movement provides an exemplary case study of these dynamics.

Conditions Favoring Political Mobilization in Cambridge, Massachusetts: Resources and Local State Structures

Very few cities in the United States could provide social movements with richer grounds for the development of organizational resources than Cambridge, Massachusetts. This rich base for organizational development, combined with an extremely open local state, created conditions that were near ideal for social movement mobilization in the early 1980s.

As the home of Harvard University, the Massachusetts Institute of Technology (MIT), and numerous other institutions of higher learning, Cambridge has long boasted a highly educated population. As detailed in chapter 3, in 1980 55 percent of residents age twenty-five and older had completed some college education; 43 percent had completed four or more years of college (U.S. Bureau of the Census 1983a). Cambridge residents were also relatively well-off: mean household income was $33,186 and median household income was $25,584 (1979 data converted to 1990 dollars) (ibid.; U.S. Bureau of Labor Statistics 1991). The educational and economic resources of Cambridge have provided social movements with a strong base from which to draw skilled organizers and financial support, as well as a well-informed and critical population. Cambridge, however, also has a strongly bifurcated class structure. Mean household income in 1980 was inflated by a minority of wealthy households and, while 40 percent of employed Cambridge residents worked in managerial and professional specialty occupations, the remainder worked in less secure and less well paid technical, sales, and administrative support (31 percent), manual labor (16 percent), and service (13 percent) occupations (U.S. Bureau of the Census 1983a).

Under most local state forms, the plurality of wealthy, highly educated residents would dominate the affairs of the local state. In Cambridge, however, the diverse socioeconomic composition of the city has been reflected in local politics since 1940, when Cambridge adopted a council-manager form of government with proportional representation. Under this extremely open local state form the city manager serves at the pleasure of the city council, and the mayor, who has no veto power, is appointed by the city council. This gives councilpersons a strong voice. More significantly, councilpersons are elected by proportional representation (P.R.), a method that is extremely rare in the United States.

Under P.R., voters rank candidates who are elected on the basis of their standing in the citywide rankings. This system differs considerably from "first past the post," district by district, winner-take-all systems, as well as from straight unranked citywide plurality systems (see chapter 3 for a detailed explanation). The adoption of P.R. is widely credited with "mobilizing previously paralyzed minorities" in Cambridge (Cambridge Editorial Research, Inc. 1965, 34). These previously excluded political minorities have combined to form the majority block in Cambridge City Council. Cambridge also promotes citizen involvement in the affairs of the local state by making it easy to place initiatives on the ballot. Nonbinding referenda can be placed on the ballot if the city council approves a petition signed by ten registered voters or if the petition is signed by 10 percent of all registered Cambridge voters. Binding referenda can be placed on the ballot with the signatures of 8 percent of all registered voters. In sum, the extremely open structural features of the Cambridge local state create a political opportunity structure that ranges in degrees of favorableness for particular political organizations and movements, but can rarely be considered rigidly closed. The Cambridge system, in combination with its diverse social structure, usually produces a 5 to 4 split among liberal Cambridge Civic Association councilpersons and moderate to conservative Independents, with coalitions shifting around specific issues. According to Cambridge Editorial Research, Inc. (1965, 34–35), "[g]overnment by coalition appears to stimulate more citizen participation than government by unilateral majority, partisan or nonpartisan. [A]n unusual number of Cambridge citizens participate in Cambridge affairs."

Cambridge residents have exploited the exceptional circumstances of their city to create a wide array of activist civic organizations. Although most of these organizations are concerned with local issues and have local constituencies, others channel local experiences of political efficacy toward broader, extralocal issues. Prominent among the latter are peace organizations. By the early 1980s, more than seventy peace movement organizations were located in Cambridge. In many cases, these organizations were started as local responses to national concerns. The Freeze was, of course, the most prominent among the Cambridge peace organizations of early 1980s.

The Nuclear Freeze Campaign

With the election of Jimmy Carter in 1976 the United States had a president who opposed the B-1 bomber, advocated cutting defense spending, favored arms control negotiations, and supported a comprehensive test ban treaty. The Congress was also relatively liberal. According to Tarrow's model, this relatively favorable political opportunity structure should have produced a wave of peace activism. Instead, without clear grievances over central state policy, very little peace mobilization was generated. This, according to Schrag (1987), was one reason the comprehensive test ban negotiations of 1978 failed; without a vocal and visible constituency supporting the negotiations, the modest opposition forces could not be overcome.

It was not until the middle of the Carter presidency, when the United States's foreign policy turned hawkish, that stirrings began within the peace movement. With the revolutions in Nicaragua and Iran and the need to have the SALT II treaty ratified by an increasingly conservative Senate, Carter changed his position in 1978 to advocate an arms buildup. With the taking of hostages in Iran and the Soviet invasion of Afghanistan, Carter became increasingly aggressive. He withdrew the SALT II treaty from consideration by the Senate in December of 1979 when the Soviet invasion of Afghanistan precluded any chance of its passage (Leavitt 1983a; Solo 1988; McCrea and Markle 1989). It was against this background of a hawkish turn in central state military policy and a dramatically unfavorable shift in the national political opportunity structure that the Nuclear Freeze campaign developed.

By the end of the Carter administration the peace movement no longer had any clear influence in Washington. However, as its access to and influence with the president and the Democratic Congress became increasingly circumscribed, the public once again became concerned with the arms race and peace mobilization began. It was in this new political climate that Randall Forsberg, who had studied military policy and arms control at MIT, issued her Nuclear Freeze proposal: *Call to Halt the Nuclear Arms Race.*

Forsberg was not the first to propose a nuclear weapons freeze. Richard Barnet, of the Institute for Policy Studies, first proposed a freeze in the spring 1979 issue of *Foreign Affairs,* and in June of the same year Senator Mark Hatfield offered an amendment to the SALT II treaty calling for a freeze on the deployment of strategic nuclear weapons (Leavitt 1983a; Solo 1988). Both of these proposals, however, were made before grievances over central state arms policy had increased dramatically. (The SALT II talks were still progressing; Afghanistan had not yet been invaded and accommodation with the Soviets still appeared possible.) The Barnet and Hatfield proposals, moreover, were not addressed to a network of organizations capable of generating political pressure. Forsberg's proposal, on the other hand, was presented after fears of a runaway arms race had become widespread; it was also presented to organizations with the resources to generate a large-scale political movement (Leavitt 1983a; Solo 1988; McCrea and Markle 1989).

Forsberg made her proposal in December 1979 to the annual convention of the umbrella activist organization Mobilization for Survival. The proposal called on the United States and the Soviet Union to "initiate an immediate, verifiable, mutual halt to the production, testing, and deployment of new nuclear weapons and their delivery systems" (Solo 1988, 19). Support for the Freeze spread rapidly through a well-developed network of peace, feminist, environmental, and religious organizations. Despite Carter's pro-arms buildup stance and the last-minute nature of organizing efforts at the Democratic National Convention, the Freeze resolution was endorsed by 40 percent of the convention delegates (Leavitt 1983a; Solo 1988). Building on a strategy paper drafted by Forsberg and George Sommaripa, Freeze activists planned a national Freeze conference for the spring of 1981 to refine the campaign strategy (ibid.).

With Reagan's clear victory in the 1980 election, one might have expected the Freeze campaign to fade. The national political opportunity structure had closed off drastically: Reagan, and the ultraconservative Congress that took office with him, precluded any possibility of a successful arms-control campaign aimed at the central state. Without the support of political elites at the national level, opportunities to form political alliances that could influence federal policy virtually disappeared. Yet—contrary to the predictions of Tarrow's model—the Freeze flourished. Reagan's bellicose rhetoric and actions (e.g., statements that referred to nuclear war as "winnable" and rejection of arms control) made the danger of an uncontrolled arms race and even nuclear war extremely clear; grievances over central state military policy spread through many sectors of the American public and reached levels of intensity not seen in the United States since the Vietnam War.

The Freeze campaign needed a strategy that would not focus on the central state and the certain defeat that awaited there. A decentralized strategy operating within a more favorable set of local political opportunity structures would seem to avoid the barriers of the central state. Indeed, the viability of such a strategy was proven on the same day Reagan was elected.

A series of referenda held in western Massachusetts on election day 1980 demonstrated that Reagan's electoral victory could not be equated with support for his military policies. A series of nonbinding referenda calling for measures very similar to the Freeze passed in fifty-nine of the sixty-two towns where they were on the ballot and received a 59 percent to 41 percent endorsement overall. Reagan carried a majority of these towns (Leavitt 1983a; Solo 1988; McCrea and Markle 1989). Following the western Massachusetts example, the Freeze adopted a decentralized public education strategy in which local chapters promoted the Freeze through local referenda, city council resolutions, petitions, endorsements from local community leaders, and other nonbinding local measures. Freeze strategists saw this as an important initial stage in a broader strategy of public opinion mobilization that would eventually lead to federal Freeze legislation (see chapter 5). Behind this strategy, however, lay a pluralistic, nonstructural conception of politics. Freeze strategists presumed that, "in a democracy, a proposal becomes politically viable when it has sufficient public support" (Nuclear Weapons Freeze Campaign 1981, 5).

The Freeze's local, decentralized strategy to garner public support was complemented by an appeal to middle-class, mainstream values. In the early years of the campaign, a variety of peace groups attempted to shape the Freeze to reflect their own ideals and interests. Radical groups wanting to challenge social, economic, and military institutions fundamental to American society were especially vocal. Forsberg, however, was adamant about maintaining a centrist base for the campaign. As she told Leavitt:

> I was concerned that the idea should not be co-opted and . . . diminished by the more radical peace groups with whom I was working and relying on, by their expressing the Freeze in language that reflected all these other values— the sort of pacifist-vegetarian anti-corporate value system—and by limiting the actions made in its name to direct action/civil disobedience kinds of things. I was very anxious that the language be very political, and therefore very middle class, very within-the-system, working with the system rather than alienating it [sic] from the system and giving up on it. (1983a, 23)

Forsberg's middle-class, decentralized strategy was astoundingly successful in mobilizing broad public support. Although conservative groups began to counterattack, their efforts were dwarfed by the success of the Freeze. By April 1982, 81 percent of American adults favored the Freeze, according to an ABC News/ *Washington Post* poll (Solo 1988). Altogether, several hundred city councils, county boards, town meetings, and state legislatures passed Freeze resolutions, more than two million signatures on Freeze petitions were presented to United States and Soviet Union United Nations missions, and the largest demonstration in the history of the United States was held in support of the Freeze (see chapter 5).

Following the massive mobilization of public support for the Freeze, Senators Kennedy and Hatfield and Representatives Markey, Conte, and Bingham moved the Freeze into the legislative arena of the central state in March 1982. The introduction of a resolution in the Senate and the House of Representatives calling for a mutually verifiable halt to the nuclear arms race constituted a "jump" in the scale of the Freeze campaign. Instead of a multiplicity of local campaigns that could have no binding effect on military policy, the Freeze was redirected at the central state that controls military policy. The new scale of the campaign, however, was not nearly as favorable as supporters thought.

Although the decentralized Freeze strategy had successfully mobilized public opinion in support of the Freeze, little had changed in the central state political opportunity structure. The Reagan administration and the conservative Congress remained firmly entrenched; the possibility of forming alliances remained limited to the relatively weak minority of liberal Congress members. Moreover, when the focus of the Freeze shifted to the central state, Freeze activists lost control of the movement. Lacking the skills and organizational resources to compete as power brokers in Congress, factions of the Democratic Party took control. As discussed in chapter 5, many members of the Democratic Party, as well as the Republican Party, were more concerned with safeguarding defense jobs in their districts than in halting the arms race. Few members of Congress were willing to support the Freeze in its original form, which called for an end to the production, testing, and deployment of all nuclear weapons. In order to simultaneously undermine the Freeze and be perceived as supporting it, a majority of members of Congress amended the resolution to the point of becoming meaningless, and then passed it. The Freeze was effectively co-opted and destroyed. Although a very weak version of the Freeze resolution was passed by the House on May 4, 1983, appropriations for the MX missile were approved that same month and the largest defense budget in U.S. history (through 1983) was approved later that year (Solo 1988).

The Nuclear Free Cambridge Campaign

Reacting to the frustrations of campaigns to change national military policy, peace activists in Cambridge began to search for ways to carry forward the cause of disarmament through measures that were significant, realizable, and local. The nuclear-free zone approach appeared to be an ideal tactic for avoiding the highly unfavorable central state political opportunity structure. As a Nuclear-Free America pamphlet argued:

> NFZ (nuclear free zone) campaigns can sustain and build upon the tremendous grass-roots experience, momentum, and political base established by the Freeze campaign. . . . NFZ is a local action that is not dependent upon the support or approval of Congress or the President . . . [it] forces citizens to debate and decide their own role and that of their communities in the nuclear arms race. (Cited in Minter 1984, 29)

Cambridge activists had good cause to believe they could be successful with such an approach. Political conditions in Cambridge had long been favorable to peace activism. Cambridge activists had repeatedly demonstrated their ability to use the very open local state to promote the cause of peace. The Cambridge City Council passed numerous peace-related resolutions, including a resolution calling for an end to the Vietnam War and one supporting the Freeze. But perhaps most significant was the city council's reaction to the Federal Emergency Management Administration's (FEMA) nuclear war plans.

In February 1981 FEMA released its Crisis Relocation Planning document. This civil defense document called on Cambridge to develop a plan to help its citizens survive nuclear war. Cambridge City Councilpersons were outraged that local governments were to be responsible for protecting the lives of Americans while the Reagan administration escalated the nuclear arms race and considered scenarios of "winnable" nuclear war. The city council responded by voting unanimously to refuse to participate in the FEMA program (Brugman 1987). Instead, the city council allocated the federal funds designated for nuclear war evacuation planning to a newly formed Cambridge Citizens' group, the Cambridge Peace Education Project (CPEP), to produce Cambridge's alternative civil defense booklet, *Cambridge and Nuclear Weapons: No Place to Hide*. When the booklet was completed, a massive outreach project was begun that eventually led more than 120 cities to reject FEMA's nuclear war defense planning (Brugman 1987). The success of the effort eventually led the council to create a permanent commission on nuclear disarmament and peace education in 1982—the Cambridge Peace Commission—as part of the local state.

The Cambridge local state not only favored peace activism; peace activism, and therefore opposition to central state military policy, had become institutionalized within the local state. The powerful political allies that were needed to enact significant local measures seemed to be available. It was against the backdrop of this highly favorable local political opportunity structure, an unfavorable national political opportunity structure, substantial organizational resources developed through decades of activism, and strongly felt grievances that the Nuclear Free Cambridge (NFC) campaign was conceived.

Although the nonbinding NFZ referendum that Cambridge voters overwhelmingly approved in 1981 represented an important expression of public opposition to central state military policy—74 percent voted in favor of the referendum (Hirschon 1983)—it produced no material effects. In 1982, NFC organizers decided that a binding referendum to halt all nuclear weapons–related activities in Cambridge should be placed on the ballot. For the first time, a city that had nuclear weapons firms representing a significant portion of the local economy (see chapter 3) would attempt to ban them. In contrast to the Freeze and nonbinding NFZ campaigns, NFC clearly had a radical agenda. NFC activists were prepared to change the economic structure of Cambridge in the process of contesting "the political processes, values, institutions, and norms which promote militarism . . . [and exposing] how militarism functions ideologically" (Levene 1985, 10).

A countermovement to NFC was quick to form. Draper Laboratory, Cambridge's largest weapons contractor, with military contracts in some years approaching a half-billion dollars (U.S. Department of Defense 1980–86), contested the legality of the referendum in the courts, and, when it lost, organized to fight the referendum in the public arena. The Chamber of Commerce issued an alert about the "antibusiness" ballot proposal and soon thereafter Citizens Against Research Bans (CARB) was formed. Local capital initially bankrolled CARB; Draper Laboratory and the Badger Corporation, a subsidiary of Raytheon (the largest military contractor in Massachusetts), each contributed $25,000 to the effort to defeat NFC. Defense contractors nationwide recognized the significance of the NFC campaign and were quick to follow suit; in the course of the campaign CARB received more than $500,000 in defense industry contributions from across the United States (Clendinen 1983; Wiegand 1983; Minter 1984; Levene 1985).

NFC activists focused on nuclear weapons isssues while downplaying the potential impacts of the NFC referendum on different classes and groups in Cambridge. In contrast, CARB conducted extensive research to identify potential class sensitivities and exploit them. Although CARB was spearheaded by Draper Laboratory and supported by weapons contractors nationwide, Draper and the other contractors maintained a very low profile so that CARB could be identified as a citizens', rather than a defense industry, organization (Minter 1984). With its substantial financial backing, CARB was able to hire experienced national opinion research and campaign consultants who helped it devise a multipronged strategy to defeat NFC. CARB argued that the NFC proposal would cause local business to lose revenue, local labor to lose jobs, and the academic community to lose academic freedom (Blodgett 1983; Clendinen 1983; Wiegand 1983; Levene 1985).

Local business's support of CARB was never in doubt. Considerably less certain, however, was the support of the working-class and academic sectors of Cambridge. Indeed, a poll conducted in September 1983 showed Cambridge residents favoring NFC by a 56 percent to 44 percent margin (Minter 1984). CARB, however, was able to recruit prominent figures from all three target groups (business, labor, and academia) and, utilizing an extensive and group-targeted media campaign, change public opinion. Widely publicized statements from local figures played a central role. According to a 1983 CARB advertisement, Ed Sullivan, business manager of Service Employees International Union Local 254, argued at a press conference that "The one unpardonable sin any working people can do to another is to take a man's livelihood away from him! And that's what this referendum proposes to do!" Even more significant, however, were endorsements by leading academic figures. Harvard president Derek Bok and MIT president Paul Gray spoke out against NFC, arguing that it would set a dangerous precedent in restricting academic freedom (in particular nuclear weapons research), and prominent arms control academics such as Kostas Tsipis and George Rathjens argued that local measures were inappropriate for addressing national issues (Blodgett 1983; Clendinen 1983; Wiegand 1983; Levene 1985). As CARB spokesman Richard Glaub framed the conflict, "the election did not concern nuclear war or a continuation of the arms race; no one wants either. Instead, the initiative, if passed, would be a unilateral decision by Cambridge in a matter that is the whole country's to decide" (Wiegand 1983, 11).

Shifting the geographic scale of the political struggle would clearly have worked to the advantage of nuclear weapons contractors, given the national political opportunity structure. Unable to force such a shift, CARB succeeded in delegitimizing the local NFC campaign by promoting an ideology according to which defense issues should only be addressed at a national scale. Ironically, CARB had to mask the fact that it received backing from weapons contractors across the nation. Had either the national scope of the organization or the fact that it was primarily a defense industry organization been widely known, its own legitimacy in the local political arena would have been seriously compromised.

The seriousness with which all parties approached the NFC campaign can be traced directly to the fact that significant material interests were at stake and that threats to those interests could not be escaped easily through relocation. As a nuclear weapons R & D firm dependent on a highly specialized local labor force, Draper's stakes in the NFC referendum were extremely high—as would be those of other nuclear weapons R & D firms in other cities if faced with a similar referendum. The precarious position of locally dependent defense contractors was evidenced in a plea contained in a fundraising letter circulated nationally for CARB by the Raytheon Corporation: "Let's make this campaign the last one of its type that we have to battle rather than the first of many" (cited in Levene 1985, 12).

An important part of CARB's campaign strategy was to convince particular classes and groups in Cambridge that their own material well-being was threatened by NFC. CARB predicted that both direct and indirect job loss (in the form of restrictions on academic freedom) would occur if the NFC referendum were passed. CARB's claims were clearly exaggerated; only Draper Laboratory was likely to be directly affected. (Additional jobs would have been lost due to lost multiplier effects.)

In short, while arguing that local state involvement in central state military policy was inappropriate, CARB actively solicited support from military capital outside of Cambridge. As NFC spokesman Dan Petegorsky summarized, "They outspent us 20 to 1 at least . . . We were not just fighting Draper Lab, we were fighting the Sperrys and the Raytheons, the entire national defense industry" (Blodgett 1983, 21). CARB ultimately defeated NFC by a 60 percent to 40 percent margin in the November 1983 election. CARB spent more than $17.50 per vote to defeat NFC—making the election one of the most costly in U.S. history (Levene 1985)—and temporarily left the Cambridge peace movement in disarray.

Summary and Implications

The Nuclear Freeze campaign and the Nuclear Free Cambridge campaign illustrate the critical implications that both geographic shifts in political opportunity structures and consensus around grievances can have for social movements striving for empowerment. As table 16 illustrates, both political opportunity structures and grievances underwent major changes during the most recent cycle of protest. Comparison of the political landscapes of Cambridge and the United States more generally shows that the peace movement was able to mobilize only when provocative central state actions produced openings for consensus building around strongly felt grievances. Contrary to Tarrow's model, favorable political opportunity structures were not associated with high levels of activism. Differences between political opportunity structures at the local and national scales, however, were decisive influences on the geographic strategies of political actors. Both the peace movement and defense fractions of capital followed scale-specific strategies, attempting to force struggle to the geographic scale at which political opportunity structures seemed most favorable to them at the time.

An unfavorable central state political opportunity structure and more favorable local political opportunity structures led the peace movement to stress a decentralized, locally oriented approach. Utilizing favorable local state political opportunity structures, the Freeze was highly successful in mobilizing public opinion against central state military policy. However, changing public opinion was only an interim goal of the peace movement. Its ultimate goal was to directly and materially alter central state military policy and defense-based economic structures; on these counts it met with defeat at both the central and local levels.

At the central state, congresspersons, many fearing the loss of defense-related jobs in their districts, amended the Freeze resolution to the point that it had no practical effect. In Cambridge, the NFC referendum that would have eliminated nuclear weapons contracting was defeated by CARB, an organization backed by a nationwide coalition of locally dependent defense firms. CARB defeated NFC by arguing that it intervened inappropriately in central state military policy and would result in job losses. Both the Freeze and the NFC campaigns demonstrate that new social movements, which nominally avoid issues of economic redistribution, can indeed have very significant economic implications. Although the local state may indeed possess the political autonomy to defy central state policy, attempts to materially affect those policies may, as Harvey suggests, meet with disciplining, if not through capital strikes or capital flight, then (as in the case of NFC) by powerful countermovements led by locally dependent fractions of capital.

This is not to argue that movements that challenge central state policy or the interests of particular fractions of capital can never gain meaningful empowerment. It does, however, indicate the inadequacy of pluralistic notions of politics: success on the level of symbolism—for example, the mobilization of public opinion—is a necessary, but often insufficient precondition for meaningful empowerment. In addition to mobilizing public opinion, movements must locate or create favorable political opportunity structures within state institutions that have the capacity for meaningful action.

Comparison of the Freeze and NFC campaigns raises a number of strategic questions for social movements. The achievement of many social movement goals requires capturing or influencing the central state, but this is not to downplay the role of decentralized, locally focused campaigns. The question of the appropriate geographic scale for social movement activities cannot be answered ahistorically. As the Freeze and NFC campaigns illustrate, political opportunity structures vary considerably over time and space. Given that movements are more likely to be successful when they can accumulate small victories, and that they often demobilize when they suffer major defeats, it would seem advantageous for movements to focus their activities at the geographic scale that offers the most favorable political opportunity structure.

An unfavorable national political opportunity structure does not preclude an effective national campaign. What it does suggest, however, is the need for changes in the national political opportunity structure before attempting meaningful action at the level of the central state. A successful

Table 16. National and local political opportunity structures and grievances during the most recent cycle of protest

	United States	Cambridge
1976	Generally favorable POS	Generally favorable POS
	Carter elected—sympathetic to peace movement	Open local state with strong liberal component
	Minimal grievances	Minimal grievances
	(little peace movement activity)	
1978	Less favorable POS	Generally favorable POS
	Carter advocates defense buildup; more conservative Congress	Open local state with strong liberal component
	Somewhat greater grievances	Somewhat greater grievances
	(little peace movement activity)	
1979	Unfavorable POS	Generally favorable POS
	Soviets invade Afghanistan; Carter withdraws SALT II; defense buildup	Open local state with strong liberal component
	Grievances build	Grievances build
	(stirrings in the peace movement; Forsberg drafts call)	
1980	Highly unfavorable POS	Very favorable POS
	Reagan and conservative Congress elected; massive defense buildup	Open local state with strong liberal component
	Strongly felt grievances	Strongly felt grievances
	(decentralized Freeze campaign begins)	
1981	Highly unfavorable POS	Highly favorable POS
	Reagan and conservative Congress still dominant; FEMA war planning directive	Open, very liberal local state city council rejects FEMA directive; nonbinding nuclear-free zone referendum passed
	Very strong grievances	Very strong grievances
	(decentralized Freeze campaign highly successful)	(CPEP; Freeze campaign)
1982	Highly unfavorable POS	Highly favorable POS
	Although some elites support Freeze, Reagan and conservative Congress still dominant; Kennedy and others introduce Freeze legislation	Open, very liberal local state Cambridge Peace Commission founded
	Very strong grievances	Very strong grievances
	(opinion poll shows 81 percent support Freeze, campaign switches to central state focus)	(CPEP; Freeze/NFC campaigns)

Table 16. (continued)

	United States	Cambridge
1983	Highly unfavorable POS	Mixed POS
	Reagan and conservative Congress still dominant	Open local state, polarization over NFC
	Very strong grievances	Very strong grievances
	(Freeze legislation amended and co-opted, Freeze campaign begins decline)	(NFC defeated by massive defense industry countermovement, peace movement in disarray)

grassroots campaign can alter the national political opportunity structure. But beware: it is important not to equate the mobilization of public opinion with a favorable political opportunity structure.

Other strategic questions are informed by consideration of geographic differences in political opportunity structures. The merits of reformist versus radical social movement campaigns vary with geographic scale. Given the structural characteristics of the U.S. central state, which institutionalizes a centrist two-party system, radical efforts directed at the central state would seem to have little chance of success. Formal political access is often more restrictive at the central level than at the local.

Action at the level of the central state in the United States would seem to dictate a reformist approach. Indeed, effecting change through the central state implies "working within the system" rather than challenging its foundations. With regard to peace issues, cancellation of the B-1 bomber, stopping the MX missile, or, most ambitiously, halting the testing, production, and deployment of nuclear weapons would seem to define the limits of what was politically feasible within the structural confines of the central U.S. political system during the 1980s.

More radical organizations, however, play a significant role through grassroots, decentralized efforts to educate the public, mobilize opinion, and redefine the boundaries of what is politically acceptable. These boundaries vary geographically and historically due to external events, the unforeseen consequences of social processes, and the efforts of movements posing fundamental questions. Reform and radical empowerment movements are by no means mutually exclusive. Indeed, they are often synergistic. But the political and geographic ground they can occupy will vary with the characteristics of political opportunity structures.

Conclusion: The Difference Geography Makes

> The relationship between class structures, political institutions, and power configurations . . . [affects] the likelihood of protest. (Wallace and Jenkins 1995, 97)

> [P]lace involves a conception of "topological" space in which diverse scales are brought together through networks of "internal" and "external" ties in defining geographical variation in social phenomena. This geographical variation responds to changes in the interaction of the networks that inter-weave the internal and the external, i.e., locale and location. In other words, geographical variation cannot be "read off" from one geographical scale. It is the necessary concomitant of the inter-relation of social processes on different scales that "come together" or are mediated through the cultural practices of particular places. Geography, therefore, is implicated in social processes rather than being a "backdrop" or a "board" upon which social processes are inscribed. (Agnew 1993, 263–64)

> [I don't] buy the argument that the poor and minorities aren't concerned about nuclear war. Of course they are, but [we need to do a better job of making the] connection between local [social] program cuts and [what's happening] at the national and international levels. (Palomba [Boston Mobilization for Survival] 1989a)

Resource mobilization theory, with its foundations in neoclassical economics and the *homo economicus* model of human nature, takes the individual as the building block of analysis: how individuals come to join and act in organizations is the focus of research. Political process research primarily focuses on state structures and dynamics (usually assuming an undifferentiated state), although it frequently does this in conjunction with analysis of organizational processes. New social movements research stresses broad structural changes that give rise to new demands, identities, and grievances, but usually ignores the ways in which political structures can shape or frustrate movements, and the ways in which organizations attempt to mobilize resources and public opinion. These approaches are clearly complementary rather than contradictory, but their successful synthesis must begin with the recognition that they address processes that are geographically structured. Social movement processes, in other words, are constituted through space, place, and scale, and that constitution affects how they interact, articulate, and play out.

It would be difficult to imagine a compelling analysis of collective action that considered only one geographic scale. Looking at the world through a lens of only one geographic scale might well capture the processes that tend to exhibit variation at that scale, but would miss significant processes manifest at both larger and smaller scales. Although there have been significant attempts to move toward sophisticated syntheses of diverse bodies of social movements theory, much of the social movements research has focused on one scale to the relative or even absolute exclusion of others.

In the research presented here I have attempted to consider the interaction of different-scale processes, none of which alone is sufficient to explain the timing and geographic pattern of peace activism. Researchers working within the resource mobilization tradition, as well as many social movement activists, commonly look to the strategies adopted or not adopted by organizations (and the individuals within them) to explain movement success or failure. Yet even in Cambridge, where the concentration of political expertise and organizational resources is probably greater than anywhere else in United States, peace organizations have been unable to generate even modest levels of protest without provocative central state actions around which to mobilize. On the other hand, when central state actions have facilitated consensus building around strong and clear grievances, mobilization has not automatically and ubiquitously materialized. In some places activism levels have been very high, in some places more moderate, and in some places (not studied here) virtually nonexistent. Just as clearly as individuals and organizations cannot, regardless of context, generate social movements, social movements do not automatically arise from broad-scale social change and the grievances it may give rise to.

Broad-scale social change must be interpreted by individuals in the context of social and cultural institutions and organizations, individuals object-ing to such change must organize, organizations must find a basis for soli-darity and mobilize resources for campaigns, and all this must be done in the context of political opportunity structures that affect the costs and likeli-hood of success of political action. Political opportunity structures, potential organizational resources, social and cultural institutions, collective identi-ties, and the effects of broad-scale social change vary from place to place. In short, the characteristics of places affect the ability of organizations to mobi-lize and campaign effectively.

We can clearly see place-specific conditions shaping peace campaigns in Cambridge, Lexington, and Waltham. The class composition, political oppor-tunity structures, educational levels, bases for solidarity, economic histories, and histories of activism vary considerably among the three municipalities. Freeze organizations in each municipality developed place-specific strategies for mobilizing against the actions of the central state. Cambridge Freeze ac-tivists, responding to already widespread sympathies for peace in Cambridge and the city's class divisions, emphasized the lobbying of congressmen and senators and de-emphasized cross-class, citywide sociospatial recruitment and alliance building. Lexington Freeze activists, responding to the relative social homogeneity of their town and the strong political networks estab-lished through the town meeting system, built a strong organization reach-ing all neighborhoods of Lexington. They used their broad base of support and substantial organizational resources to lobby their congressional delega-tion. Waltham activists approached a situation that seemingly defied suc-cessful peace mobilization—a working-class rather than middle-class class composition; a long history of local industrial decline, making residents es-pecially sensitive to threats to the employment base; an unfavorable political opportunity structure; little history of peace activism; and a poorly devel-oped activist network—and developed their own place-specific strategy. Waltham Concerned Citizens adopted an inclusive sociospatial recruitment strategy, tapped into existing nonactivist networks (including churches and civic organizations), held a number of events of interest to persons not al-ready sympathetic to the Freeze (and did so in accessible public spaces), took up other issues (such as housing) with broader working-class appeal, and in general recognized the need to clearly make their case and not assume that most people would automatically agree. Although WCC did not achieve the nationally recognized success of the Cambridge and Lexington Freeze cam-paigns, and activism levels among WCC members have generally been lower than in Cambridge and Lexington, WCC developed into a strong organiza-tion that was (and is) reasonably representative of Waltham citizens, and that under far less favorable circumstances successfully rallied Waltham behind the Freeze.

The importance of the place-specific circumstances facing, as well as strategies adopted by, the Cambridge, Lexington, and Waltham Freeze organizations can perhaps best be illustrated by posing counterfactual situations. Although the Cambridge Freeze strategy was very effective in Cambridge, it would likely have failed in Waltham. Recruiting organizers rather than the general public, relying on the support of elites, and not adopting tactics to build support in working-class parts of the city would have produced very little backing indeed. Moreover, the unfavorable political opportunity structure would almost certainly have precluded the passage of several pro-peace local measures, if not their introduction. Likewise, the Waltham strategy would not have been the most effective one for Cambridge. Public education work was not as critical in Cambridge and time spent in such activity would likely not have been as persuasive to Tip O'Neill and other members of the Massachusetts congressional delegation as the more direct lobbying that was pursued. The Lexington strategy, rooted in the town meeting system and a relatively homogeneous class structure, would probably not have worked nearly as well in Cambridge, where class divisions, at a minimum, would have required different tactics and rhetorical strategies in working-class neighborhoods. Clearly, geographic variations in interests, resources, political opportunities, and even forms of collective identity (place-based and otherwise) shaped the prospects and strategies of local peace organizations. Indeed, the genius of the Freeze campaign was that it adopted a highly decentralized strategy that allowed local organizations to devise effective strategies suited to place-specific circumstances.

One can always speculate how the strategies of different Freeze organizations might have been more appropriately and effectively matched to their municipalities.[1] Cambridge SANE/Freeze could have altered the geography and rhetorical strategies of recruitment to attract working-class support. WCC might have worked to change the local political opportunity structure, either through changing the city charter to institute proportional representation or through electing their own council candidates. Such strategies, however, would have required several years of work. The Lexington Committee for a Nuclear Weapons Freeze seemingly adopted a near-ideal strategy for a middle-class, mainstream organization operating in a relatively homogeneous, upper-middle-class town with a highly democratic local state. It might have adopted a multi-issue strategy that would have allowed it to remain viable over the long run (it disbanded in 1992), yet its narrow single-issue focus allowed it to mobilize strong support across Lexington—support that would have been diluted if other more controversial issues had been taken on.

As a movement to mobilize public opinion, the Freeze was an undeniable success. Yet when it came to changing U.S. defense policy, the Freeze fell far short of its goals. It was precisely two fundamental assumptions behind the mainstream, within-the-system Freeze strategy (as well as the NFC strategy) that ultimately led to defeat: the assumption (usually implicit) that economic issues are, or should be made to appear, separate from peace issues; and the assumption that winning majority support will lead to the achievement of a movement's objectives.

As public opinion polls showed, the Freeze campaign successfully rallied a large majority of the American public behind it. Likewise, the NFC campaign garnered majority support in Cambridge, until the CARB counter-campaign swayed opinion in the last two months of that campaign. Both the Freeze and NFC stressed the immorality, waste, and dangers (often place-specific) of the nuclear arms race and nuclear war. Neither campaign, however, clearly articulated the link between the arms race and the employment of substantial numbers of people. Neither offered plausible plans for providing alternative employment to those who would suffer economic dislocation as a result of ending the arms race. Although a clear majority in the U.S. House of Representatives passed a Freeze referendum, it was a very weak version that allowed congresspersons to protect and add defense-related jobs in their districts. The NFC referendum was defeated at the ballot after CARB made an apparently persuasive case that NFC would harm the Cambridge employment base.[2] That neither campaign seriously considered the economic implications of its proposals can, at least in part, be attributed to the memberships of the organizations. In the Boston metropolitan area, many Freeze organizations, as well as the Cambridge membership of Boston Mobilization for Survival, had memberships that were highly skewed toward people insulated from the fluctuating fortunes of the private for-profit economy. More diverse and representative memberships might well have resulted in greater attention to general economic concerns. The unrepresentativeness of memberships, in turn, can be partly attributed to the sociospatial recruitment strategies pursued by the organizations.

The Freeze campaign also erred in adopting a pluralist model of politics when a structuralist model would have been far more illuminating. The Freeze campaign won the "cash register" battle of pluralist opinion making, but the political opportunity structure it faced at the central state did not change. Incorrectly assuming it could replicate its successes at the far more favorable local state level, the Freeze tried to push through a central state resolution that was at odds with the extant structural arrangements. In essence, it jumped scales prematurely. Key political battles are not always just within the structures of the state; sometimes they are over the structures of the state. The Freeze needed to alter the political opportunity structure of the central state before attempting to pass legislation there.

It is precisely the dynamics that brought down the Freeze and NFC that illustrate the utility of adopting a geographically sensitized Habermasian framework for the analysis of social movements. There is a tendency in the social movements literature to divide social movements into broad categories of "old" economically focused movements or "new" lifeworld-focused movements. Movements themselves often unwittingly adopt such dualisms, such as when the peace movement campaigns as though its agenda had no economic implications. Although social movement organizations may focus on either system or lifeworld issues, those organizations, and people generally, are located simultaneously in both the system and the lifeworld—or, more accurately, systems and lifeworlds. There are very few actions that can be taken in one sphere without repercussions in the other. As Habermas has argued, people live simultaneously in objective, social, and subjective worlds. Accordingly, material phenomena must be interpreted and understood through sociocultural systems of meaning and evaluated against the backdrop of personal experience.

Social movements bear upon systemic processes (involving the coordination of material production in the economy and the state) in almost all cases. In the case of the peace movement, the production of weapons of mass destruction and the jobs and profits associated with them come into play. Defense contracting clearly has a distinct geography, affecting material interests in different places differently. One need not strain to imagine how the NFC campaign, for instance, might have ended differently were there no major weapons firms in Cambridge. Political opportunity structures also have a distinct geography affecting the costs that activists incur in campaigns. One can imagine how much more might have been accomplished in Waltham if participation in the local state were determined by proportional representation. But neither the simple presence or absence of material phenomena, nor the barriers and opportunities presented by state structures, can, in themselves, explain social or political action.

Material phenomena must be made understandable through cultural (lifeworld) codes that endow material phenomena with meaning and guide action in the world. Different place and class-based cultures develop to make sense of the material circumstances people in those places and classes encounter. Mobilizing support behind a movement, then, involves not only addressing material interests, but addressing them in ways that resonate with existing cultural codes—what Snow and Benford mean by "frames of reference." Such frames are geographically constituted, posing clear implications for the rhetorical strategies social movement organizations adopt as they try to win the support of different groups in different places.

Unlike strong culturalists, however, I do not wish to argue that culture is the ultimate determinant of social action. Just as material phenomena must be given symbolic meaning, systems of meaning must provide plausible guideposts for action vis-à-vis the material world. Systems of meaning are called into question and reformulated—although certainly not in a deterministic way—when they no longer make sense of the material world. Similarly, political opportunity structures play a role in shaping culture—especially political culture—as people learn, through experience, the costs and efficacy of political action in the places where (and times when) they live and act. Culture, then, while extremely important in shaping social action, is not a black box containing some final and essential explanation for all sorts of social, political, and economic phenomena. Just as systemic processes are shaped in the context of the lifeworlds, lifeworld processes (including the production and reproduction of culture) are shaped in the context of the systems.

The importance of both cultural "frames of reference" and material interests is clear in the cases examined here. At a fundamental level, much of the success of the peace movement was due to the fact that its message resonated with mainstream, middle-class values and concerns over threats to the continued material existence of humanity. When it came to somewhat more mundane concerns such as employment and profits, however, many branches of the peace movement had little to say. As long as measures proposed by the peace movement stayed far removed from changing de facto economic policies that provided jobs and profits, they met with little resistance. When workers' jobs and capital's profits were threatened (as in the case of NFC), however, the case for halting the arms race became less compelling.

Indeed, the cases studied here tend to undermine common generalizations about the peace movement being an innately white, well-educated, middle- and upper-middle-class movement. Waltham Concerned Citizens has shown that an organization knowledgeable about and sensitive to working-class community values can rally that community behind an important, although purely symbolic, statement of opposition to the arms race. Conversely, the NFC campaign showed that even highly educated, economically well-off people in a city highly sympathetic to the peace movement would vote down a measure to slow the arms race when convinced that it would threaten their material interests. Support for the peace movement, then, appears to be less a matter of innate middle-class predilection than the use of appropriate place-sensitive rhetorical strategies and the promotion of policies that minimize threats to people's everyday material existence.

Economic, political, and cultural processes become thoroughly entwined in collective political action. To understand these processes, a variety of geographically sensitive mid-level theories dealing with topics such as political opportunity, resource mobilization, economic restructuring, representation, and identity construction come in very handy. Mid-level theories, however, address their topics in a compartmentalized way that demands integration. Metatheories such as Habermas's theory of communicative action and Lefebvre's production of space provide us with some good general road maps to the articulation of mid-level theories and processes. Exactly how processes articulate, however, cannot be answered aspatially or ahistorically. Both systemic and lifeworld processes have their own geographies and histories; those geographies and histories structure their articulation in particular places and times. Collective political action takes different forms and reaches different levels of intensity in different places and eras—and often for reasons that differ from place to place and time to time.

The geographic structuring of a social movement clearly cannot be reduced to the inclusion of a "space variable" in an otherwise aspatial analysis. Geography is not a separate force; neither is it the outcome of aspatial social forces. It is, rather, a fundamental dimension through which all social processes are constituted, much like time. Just as changing the temporal constitution of events and processes would likely affect how social processes play out, so too would altering the geographic constitution of those events and processes. No wonder social movements struggle (sometimes consciously, sometimes not) to alter space, place, and scale relations as they pursue their goals. Attention to the geographic structuring of social movements may seem to introduce an unwanted degree of complexity for those accustomed to explaining collective action in terms of context-free factors. But real-world processes are complex. Attention to geographic structuring helps us to understand that complexity and identify the geographically variable causes of social movement success and failure. Such understanding is likely to reward the social movement analyst and activist alike.

Notes

Introduction

1. See, for example, Leavitt 1983a; Solo 1988; McCrea and Markle 1989; Kleidman 1990; Meyer 1990.

2. For a very good overview of Mill's comparative method, see Ragin (1987).

3. It is important to note that the survey data paint a picture of the four peace movement organizations in 1990, whereas this research is primarily concerned with peace movement mobilization from the late 1970s through the mid-1980s. Some discrepancies between these data and the situation in the early 1980s may exist because of changes associated with membership turnover and evolving political agendas. Nonetheless, the alternative—surveying only those who were active in the early 1980s and asking them to recall specific information about that time—would be fraught with greater problems: distorted recall and memory loss; incomplete and unreliable sampling frames because of the lack of accurate membership lists from that time. Data could be limited to what could be collected from current peace organization members who were also active in the early 1980s, but that would bias data toward long-term members who are only a small portion of those constituting an organization's membership at any given time. Because of these problems, it was decided that the most accurate facsimile of peace movement organizational resources in the early 1980s would be provided through a survey of the organizations' 1990 membership. Membership lists in 1990 were accurate and up-to-date and included the full range of supporters, from key activists to those whose support was strictly financial. Moreover, the nature of the four organizations had changed very little since the early 1980s.

4. A few members of Boston Mobilization for Survival also belonged to

Cambridge SANE/Freeze, the Lexington Committee for a Nuclear Weapons Freeze, and Waltham Concerned Citizens. A survey question asking which organization respondents felt most strongly affiliated with served to rectify the problem of dual affiliation. Respondents' responses were assigned to the organization with which respondents considered themselves most strongly affiliated.

5. The response rate for Cambridge SANE/Freeze was lower than what is typically required for a high degree of confidence in the representativeness of the data, but, as already noted, the lack of a pattern of bias in follow-up telephone calls to nonrespondents suggests that the lower response rate is not a significant problem.

6. As multi-issue organizations, both Boston Mobilization for Survival and Waltham Concerned Citizens addressed U.S. intervention in Central America and the apartheid regime in South Africa, in addition to the nuclear arms race. Activities not related to the nuclear arms race, however, are beyond the scope of this work.

7. When discussing comparative case study methodology, positivist friends often raise the perfectly legitimate question of the representativeness of the cases selected. The perfectly legitimate response is that cases are selected not for their representativeness, but rather for their ability to allow the analyst to clearly trace the complex ways in which a variety of processes and events interact, that is, to provide an in-depth understanding of the processes in question. Sometimes unrepresentative cases can provide the most insight into complex interactions. Does this mean that knowledge based on comparative case study analysis must be considered idiosyncratic? No. The social sciences have long recognized two forms of inference, statistical (based on empirical regularity) and logical (based on in-depth understanding and theoretically informed reasoning). Although statistical inference may be more widely employed today, logical inference remains a sound basis for reasoning to cases beyond those directly under scrutiny. As Mitchell (1983, 198) explains, in case study analysis, "The inference about the *logical* relationship between . . . two characteristics is not based upon the representativeness of the sample and therefore its typicality, but rather upon the plausibility or upon the logicality of the nexus between the two characteristics."

1. Missing Geography

1. Throughout this book social movements are broadly defined as collective mobilizations of people seeking social change. Social change often entails forms of political change.

2. Discussions of social movement diffusion, for instance, exhibit both tendencies. Hedstrom's (1994) analysis, while illuminating, considers space only in terms of distance. Most of the social movement diffusion literature deals only with its cross-national dimension (e.g., McAdam and Rucht 1993; Kriesi et al. 1995a). Similarly, comparative analysis of social movements is all but equated with cross-national com-

parison (e.g., Tarrow 1991; Jenkins and Klandermans 1995; Kriesi et al. 1995b; McAdam, McCarthy, and Zald 1996). Comparative analysis at other geographic scales is virtually nonexistent.

3. See, for example, Bennett and Earle's (1983) analysis of the failure of socialism in the United States, which highlights geographical variations in wage and skill differentials and their attendant impact on class politics.

2. A Geographic Model of Social Movement Mobilization

1. It should be noted that although the shared understandings arrived at through communicative action form the foundation of the lifeworld, all forms of action (strategic and instrumental as well as communicative) occur in the lifeworld. Thus, individuals within a community can be expected to engage in strategic and instrumental as well as communicative action.

2. I do not deny the increasing significance of mass communications, which entail primarily one-way, nondialogic flows of information from a producer to receivers in diverse places. With the global reach and homogenizing tendencies of the media, it no longer can be unequivocally asserted that consciousness is constructed in place. To greater or lesser degrees, we are all exposed to a common popular culture, politics, and coverage of world events, regardless of place. Nonetheless, place still plays a crucial role in structuring daily lives and understandings. It is in the context of discrete geographical settings that information is received, opportunities for genuine dialogue arise, and interpretations are formed. For further discussion, see Calhoun (1986), Sack (1988, 1990), Kirby (1989), Meyrowitz (1989, 1990), and Thompson (1990), and Adams (1998).

4. Space, Place, and Mobilization

1. "Membership" is used here in a broad sense. One need not be a dues-paying "member" to be on an organization's mailing list. Primary mailing lists include those who are most active; being on such a list does not necessarily indicate financial contribution or any other specific act conveying "membership."

2. Recruitment strategies are considered broadly here. All activities of social movement organizations are potential means of recruiting members. The particular events and activities that were especially significant to the organizations considered here are discussed in the following chapter dealing with their mobilization histories.

3. "Activism scores" were constructed based on responses to the questions posed in the survey of Cambridge, Lexington, and Waltham peace activists. Points were assigned to the types of political activities in which respondents participated and summed. Political activities and their assigned points include making monetary contributions to social movement organizations (1); public speaking on political issues (3); distributing literature or collecting petition signatures (3); writing or speaking to

elected officials (3); writing articles or editorials for publication (6); participating in marches or demonstrations (3); participating in peace walks or runs (3); participating in peace vigils (3); engaging in civil disobedience (5); campaigning for a peace candidate (3); campaigning for a peace referendum (3); serving on the board of a peace organization (15); other (3). Points were assigned to each activity to represent the approximate time commitment (e.g., serving as a peace organization board member is heavily weighted) or risk (e.g., engaging in civil disobedience is weighted above average) involved. Based on "natural" breaks in the frequency distribution of the activism index, respondents were assigned to one of three categories: low activism (0 to 9 points); medium activism (10 to 30 points); high activism (31 to 54 points). These scores represent a general measure of the activity of individuals, but should not be considered in any sense absolute or precise. As with all indices, scores are in large part a function of the measures and weighting by which they were constructed.

4. Standardized scores are the percentage of respondents from each organization who say they were "most active" or "moderately active" in a given year, divided by the percentage of respondents who had become politically active by that year (so that later years do not appear as the years of greatest activism by virtue of the fact that greater numbers of respondents were politically active).

Conclusion

1. This is to in no way negate the very substantial achievements of each of these organizations; there are good reasons—relating to the availability of necessary time, skill, and financial resources—why such strategic adjustments were not pursued.

2. In the wake of the NFC defeat, certain branches of the peace movement began to address these relationships. In 1985, the Cambridge City Council voted to support a research and planning project of the Cambridge Peace Commission addressing economic diversification and conversion (converting defense industries to produce for civilian markets). The commission's report, "The Cambridge Case for Diversification Planning: Towards Stability in an R & D Economy," was released in 1986. In 1988, state representative David Cohen introduced an economic conversion bill in the Massachusetts legislature. Members of Cambridge Peace Action (formerly SANE/Freeze), particularly Shelagh Foreman, have been very active in economic conversion work, while newer organizations such as Jobs with Peace explicitly link economic and peace issues and advocate more "rational, non-military-based," economic policy.

References

Abelson, Olivia. 1990a. Cambridge SANE/Freeze board member, interview by author, author's notes, Cambridge, Massachusetts, July 19.

———. 1990b. Cambridge SANE/Freeze board member, interview by author, author's notes, Cambridge, Massachusetts, August 29.

———. 1991. Cambridge SANE/Freeze board member, interview by author, author's notes, Cambridge, Massachusetts, August 8.

Abler, Ronald, John S. Adams, and Peter Gould. 1971. *Spatial Organization: The Geographer's View of the World*. Englewood Cliffs, N.J.: Prentice Hall.

Adams, Gordon. 1986. *The Politics of Defense Contracting: The Iron Triangle*. New Brunswick, N.J.: Transaction Books.

Adams, John S. 1973. "The Geography of Riots and Civil Disorders in the 1960s." In Melvin Albaum, ed., *Geography and Contemporary Issues*, pp. 542–64. New York: John Wiley and Sons.

Adams, Paul. 1998. "Network Topologies and Virtual Place." *Annals of the Association of American Geographers* 88 (1): 88–106.

Agnew, John A. 1987. *Place and Politics*. Boston: Allen and Unwin.

———. 1989. "The Devaluation of Place in Social Science." In John A. Agnew and James S. Duncan, eds., *The Power of Place*, pp. 9–29. Boston: Unwin Hyman.

———. 1993. "Representing Space: Space, Scale and Culture in Social Science." In James Duncan and David Ley, eds., *Place/Culture/Representation*, pp. 251–71. New York: Routledge.

———. 1995. "The Hidden Geographies of Social Science and the Myth of the Geographical Turn." *Environment and Planning D: Society and Space* 13: 379–80.

———. 1996. "Mapping Politics: How Context Counts in Electoral Geography." *Political Geography* 15(2): 129–46.

Agnew, John, and James Duncan, eds. 1989. *The Power of Place*. Boston: Unwin Hyman.

Amin, Ash, ed. 1994. *Post-Fordism*. Malden, Mass.: Basil Blackwell.

Anderson, Benedict. 1983. *Imagined Communities: Reflections on the Origins and Spread of Nationalism*. London: Verso.

Angel, David. 1989. Assistant professor, School of Geography, Clark University, interview by author, author's notes, Worcester, Massachusetts, September 6.

Arches, Joan. 1990. Coordinating committee member, Waltham Concerned Citizens, interview by author, author's notes, Waltham, Massachusetts, August 28.

Arond, Lester. 1990. Board member, Lexington Committee for a Nuclear Weapons Freeze, interview by author, author's notes, Cambridge, Massachusetts, July 24.

Aveni, Adrian F. 1978. "Organizational Linkages and Resource Mobilization: The Significance of Linkage Strength and Breadth." *Sociological Quarterly* 19: 185–202.

Axelrod, Morris. 1956. "Urban Structure and Social Participation." *American Sociological Review* 21: 14–18.

Axelrod, Robert. 1984. *The Evolution of Cooperation*. New York: Basic Books.

Bakshi, P. M., M. Goodwin, J. Painter, and A. Southern. 1995. "Gender, Race, and Class in the Local Welfare State: Moving beyond Regulation Theory in Analysing the Transition from Fordism." *Environment and Planning A* 27: 1539–54.

Balbus, Isaac. 1983. *Marxism and Domination*. Princeton, N.J.: Princeton University Press.

Barff, Richard, and Prentice L. Knight III. 1988. "The Role of Federal Military Spending in the Timing of the New England Economic Turnaround." *Papers of the Regional Science Association* 65: 151–66.

Barnes, Trevor J. and Eric Sheppard. 1992. "Is There a Place for the Rational Actor? A Geographical Critique of the Rational Choice Paradigm." *Economic Geography* 68(1): 1–21.

Barry, Brian. 1978. *Sociologists, Economists, and Democracy*. Chicago: University of Chicago Press.

Benford, Robert D. 1993a. "Frame Disputes within the Nuclear Disarmament Movement." *Social Forces* 71(3): 677–701.

———. 1993b. "You Could Be the Hundredth Monkey: Collective Action Frames and Vocabularies of Motive within the Nuclear Disarmament Movement." *Sociological Quarterly* 34(2): 195–216.

Benhabib, Seyla. 1986. The Generalized and the Concrete Other: Toward a Feminist Critique of Substitutionalist Universalism. *Praxis International* 5: 402–24.

Benko, Georges, and Ulf Strohmayer. 1997. *Space and Social Theory.* Malden, Mass.: Basil Blackwell.

Bennett, Sari, and Carville Earle. 1983. "Socialism in America: A Geographical Interpretation of Its Failure." *Political Geography Quarterly* 2(1): 31–55.

Berger, Johannes. 1991. "The Linguistification of the Sacred and the Delinguistification of the Economy." In Axel Honneth and Hans Joas, eds., *Communicative Action,* pp. 165–80. Cambridge: MIT Press.

Bernstein, Richard J., ed. 1985. *Habermas and Modernity.* Cambridge: MIT Press.

Bhaskar, Roy. 1979. *The Possibility of Naturalism.* Atlantic Highlands, N.J.: Humanities Press.

Bird, Jon, Barry Curtis, Tim Putnam, George Robertson, and Lisa Tickner, eds. 1993. *Mapping the Futures: Local Cultures, Global Change.* New York: Routledge.

Blaikie, Pers. 1978. "The Theory of the Spatial Diffusion of Innovations: A Spacious Cul-de-sac." *Progress in Human Geography* 2: 268–95.

Blaut, James. 1977. "Two Views of Diffusion." *Annals of the Association of American Geographers* 67: 343–49.

Block, Fred. 1987. *Revising State Theory.* Philadelphia: Temple University Press.

Blodgett, Mindy. 1983. "No-Nuke Question Bombs." *Cambridge TAB,* November 23, pp. 1–21.

Bourdieu, Pierre. 1977. *Outline of a Theory of Practice,* New York: Cambridge University Press.

Bowles, Samuel, and Herbert Gintis. 1986. *Democracy and Capitalism: Property, Community, and the Contradictions of Modern Social Thought.* New York: Basic Books.

Boyte, Harry C., and Sarah M. Evans. 1984. "Strategies in Search of America: Cultural Radicalism, Populism, and Democratic Culture." *Socialist Review* 75/76: 73–100.

Brigham, Nancy, John Marcy, Mike Ryan, and Paul Solman. 1971a. "Cambridge Report I: Land Racketeers Unveiled." *Phoenix,* October 12, pp. 1–19.

———. 1971b. "Cambridge Report II: The Power Axis." *Phoenix,* October 17, pp. 1–22.

Broadbent, Jeffrey. 1988. "State as Process: The Effect of Party and Class on Citizen Participation in Japanese Local Government." *Social Problems* 35: 131–44.

Brown, Michael P. 1997a. "Radical Politics Out of Place? The Curious Case of ACT UP Vancouver." In Steve Pile and Michael Keith, eds., *Geographies of Resistance,* pp. 152–67. London and New York: Routledge.

———. 1997b. *RePlacing Citizenship: AIDS Activism and Radical Democracy.* New York: Guilford Press.

Browne, Lynne E. 1984. "The New England Economy and the Development of High Technology Industries." *New England Economic Indicators* (August): 3–6.

———. 1988a. "Defense Spending and High Technology Development: National and State Issues." *New England Economic Review* (September/October): 3–22.

———. 1988b. "High Technology and Business Services." In David R. Lampe, ed., *The Massachusetts Miracle,* pp. 201–24. Cambridge: MIT Press.

Brugman, Jeb. 1987. *The Cambridge Idea: Fifth Anniversary Report of the Cambridge Commission on Nuclear Disarmament and Peace Education.* Cambridge: Cambridge Peace Commission.

———. 1989. Former director, Cambridge Peace Commission, telephone interview by author, author's notes, Cambridge, Massachusetts, August 25.

Buechler, Steven M. 1995. "New Social Movement Theories." *Sociological Quarterly* 36(3): 441–64.

Buttimer, Annette. 1979. "Reason, Rationality, and Human Creativity." *Geografiska Annaler* 61B: 43–49.

Bylinsky, Gene. 1976. *The Innovation Millionaires: How They Succeed.* New York: Charles Scribner's Sons.

Calhoun, Craig. 1986. "Computer Technology, Large-Scale Social Integration, and the Local Community." *Urban Affairs Quarterly* 22: 329–49.

———. 1988. "The Radicalism of Tradition and the Question of Class Struggle." In Michael Taylor, ed., *Rationality and Revolution,* pp. 129–75. New York: Cambridge University Press.

Cambridge Editorial Research, Inc. 1965. *The Cambridge Book 1966.* Cambridge: Cambridge Civic Association.

Cambridge Magazine. 1972. "I Bet You Can't Explain P.R."

Cambridge Peace Commission. 1986. A report of the Economic Security Committee. "The Cambridge Case for Diversification Planning: Towards Stability in an R&D Economy." Cambridge, Massachusetts.

Campbell-Elliot, Elizabeth. 1990. Massachusetts SANE/Freeze, interview by author, author's notes, Cambridge, Massachusetts, August 23.

Carlstein, Tommy, Don Parkes, and Nigel Thrift, eds. 1978. *Timing Space and Spacing Time.* 3 vols. New York: John Wiley and Sons.

Castells, Manuel. 1983. *The City and the Grassroots.* Berkeley: University of California Press.

Caulfield, Jon. 1988. "Canadian Urban Reform and Local Conditions." *International Journal of Urban and Regional Research* 12(3): 477–84.

Charlesworth, Andrew, ed. 1983. *An Atlas of Rural Protest in Britain 1548–1900.* Philadelphia: University of Pennsylvania Press.

Chauchi, Dick. 1990. Executive director, Citizens for Participation in Political Action (CPPAX), interview by author, author's notes, Boston, August 29.

Citizens for Participation in Political Action. 1987. *The Hughes Campaign: 25 Years Later.* Boston: CPPAX.

————. ca. 1989. *Citizens for Participation in Political Action* (pamphlet). Boston: CPPAX.

City of Cambridge. 1982. *Cambridge and Nuclear Weapons: Is There a Place to Hide?* City of Cambridge, Massachusetts.

Clark, Gordon L., and Michael Dear. 1984. *State Apparatus.* Boston: Allen and Unwin.

Clark, Gordon L., J. McKay, G. Missen, and M. Webber. 1992. "Objections to Economic Restructuring and the Strategies of Coercion: An Analytical Evaluation of Policies and Practices in Australia and the United States." *Economic Geography* 68(1): 43–59.

Clark, Helene. 1993. "Sites of Resistance: Place, 'Race,' and Gender as Sources of Empowerment." In Peter Jackson and Jan Penrose, eds., *Constructions of Race, Place and Nation,* pp. 121–42. Minneapolis: University of Minnesota Press.

————. 1994. "Taking Up Space: Redefining Political Legitimacy in New York City." *Environment and Planning A* 26(6): 937–55.

Clendinen, Dudley. 1983. "With Money and Experts, Cambridge Lab Beats Research Ban." *New York Times,* November 12, p. 2A.

Cockburn, Cynthia. 1977. *The Local State.* London: Pluto Press.

Codrescu, Andrei. 1996. *The Dog with the Chip in His Neck.* New York: Picador.

Cohen, Jean. 1985. "Strategy or Identity: New Theoretical Paradigms and Contemporary Social Movements." *Social Research* 52: 663–716.

Coleman, James S. 1990. "Norm-Generating Structures." In Karen Cook and Margaret Levi, eds., *The Limits to Rationality,* pp. 250–73. Chicago: University of Chicago Press.

Commonwealth of Massachusetts. 1985. *Analysis Fiscal 1986 Federal Budget.* Boston: Office of Federal Relations.

Cooke, Philip. 1983. *Theories of Planning and Spatial Development.* London: Hutchinson.

————. 1985. "Radical Regions? Space, Time, and Gender Relations in Emilia, Provence, and South Wales." In Gareth Rees, ed., *Political Action and Social Identity: Class, Locality, and Culture,* pp. 17–41. London: Macmillan.

————, ed. 1989a. *Localities.* London: Unwin Hyman.

————. 1989b. "Locality-Theory and the Poverty of 'Spatial Variation.'" *Antipode* 21(3): 261–73.

Cope, Meghan. 1996. "Weaving the Everyday: Identity, Space, and Power in Lawrence, Massachusetts, 1920–1939." *Urban Geography* 17(2): 179–204.

Cosgrove, Dennis. 1986. "Sense of Place." In R. J. Johnston, D. Gregory, and D. M. Smith, eds., *Dictionary of Human Geography,* p. 425. Oxford: Basil Blackwell.

Cox, Kevin R. 1984. "Neighborhood Conflict and Urban Social Movements:

Questions of Historicity, Class, and Social Change." *Urban Geography* 5(4): 343–55.

———. 1986. "Urban Social Movements and Neighborhood Conflicts: Questions of Space." *Urban Geography* 7(6): 536–46.

———. 1988. "Urban Social Movements and Neighborhood Conflicts: Mobilization and Structuration." *Urban Geography* 8(4): 416–28.

———. 1989. "The Politics of Turf and the Question of Class." In Jennifer Wolch and Michael Dear, eds., *The Power of Geography: How Territory Shapes Social Life*, pp. 61–90. Winchester, Mass.: Unwin Hyman.

———. 1991. "Questions of Abstraction in Studies in the New Urban Politics." *Journal of Urban Affairs* 13(2): 267–80.

———. 1993. "The Local and the Global in the New Urban Politics: A Critical View." *Environment and Planning D: Society and Space* 11: 433–48.

Cox, Kevin R., and Andrew Mair. 1988. "Locality and Community in the Politics of Local Economic Development." *Annals of the Association of American Geographers* 78(2): 307–25.

———. 1989a. "Levels of Abstraction in Locality Studies." *Antipode* 21(2): 121–32.

———. 1989b. "Urban Growth Machines and the Politics of Local Economic Development." *International Journal of Urban and Regional Affairs* 13: 137–46.

———. 1991. "From Localised Social Structures to Localities as Agents." *Environment and Planning A* 23: 197–213.

Crenson, M. A. 1978. "Social Networks and Political Processes in Urban Neighborhoods." *American Journal of Political Science* 22(3): 578–94.

Cresswell, Tim. 1996. *In Place/Out of Place: Geography, Ideology, and Transgression.* Minneapolis: University of Minnesota Press.

Crist, John T. 1994. "Review of 'Terrains of Resistance: Nonviolent Social Movements and the Contestation of Place in India' by Paul Routledge." *Contemporary Sociology* 23(4): 544–45.

Cronin, Bruce. 1990. National coordinating committee member, Mobilization for Survival, telephone interview by author, author's notes, New York, August 30.

Crumm, Anne. 1990. Emerita board member, Cambridge Lobby for a Nuclear Weapons Freeze, telephone interview by author, author's notes, Martha's Vineyard, Massachusetts, August 20.

Cutter, Susan. 1988. "Geographers and Nuclear War: Why We Lack Influence on Public Policy." *Association of American Geographers* 78(1): 132–43.

Cutter, Susan, H. Briavel Holcomb, and Dianne Shatin. 1986. "Spatial Patterns of Support for a Nuclear Weapons Freeze." *Professional Geographer* 38(1): 42–52.

———. 1987. "From Grass Roots to Partisan Politics: Nuclear Freeze Referenda in New Jersey and South Dakota." *Political Geography Quarterly* 6(4): 287–300.

Dalton, Russell J. 1995. "Strategies of Partisan Influence: West European Environmental Groups." In J. Craig Jenkins and Bert Klandermans, eds., *The Politics of Social Protest: Comparative Perspectives on States and Social Movements,* pp. 296–323. Minneapolis: University of Minnesota Press.

Davis, Lester A. 1982. *Technology Intensity of U.S. Output and Trade.* Washington, D.C.: International Trade Administration, U.S. Department of Commerce.

Dawes, Robyn, Alphons van de Kragt, and John Orbell. 1990. "Cooperation for the Benefit of Us, Not Me or My Conscience." In Jane Mansbridge, ed., *Beyond Self-Interest,* pp. 97–110. Chicago: University of Chicago Press.

de Certeau, Michel. 1984. *The Practice of Everyday Life.* Trans. Steven Rendall. Berkeley: University of California Press.

Delaney, David, and Helga Leitner. 1997. "The Political Construction of Scale." *Political Geography* 16(2): 93–97.

Demko, George, Virginia Sharp, Jacque Harper, and Carl Youngmann. 1973. "Student Disturbances and Campus Unrest in the United States: 1964–1970." In Melvin Albaum, ed., *Geography and Contemporary Issues,* pp. 533–41. New York: John Wiley and Sons.

DeNardo, J. 1985. *Power in Numbers.* Princeton, N.J.: Princeton University Press.

Dennis, Christie. 1991. Cambridge SANE/Freeze board member, interview by author, author's notes, Cambridge, Massachusetts, September 2.

Dews, Peter, ed. 1986. *Habermas: Autonomy and Solidarity.* London: Verso.

Dillman, Donald. 1981. *Mail and Telephone Surveys: The Total Design Method.* New York: John Wiley and Sons.

Dorfman, Nancy S. 1988. "Route 128: The Development of a Regional High Technology Economy." In David R. Lampe, ed., *The Massachusetts Miracle,* pp. 240–74. Cambridge: MIT Press.

Duncan, James, and David Ley, eds. 1993. *Place/Culture/Representation.* New York: Routledge.

Duncan, Simon, and Michael Goodwin. 1982. "The Local State and Restructuring Social Relations." *International Journal of Urban and Regional Research* 6: 153–86.

———. 1988. *The Local State and Uneven Development.* London: Polity Press.

Duncan, Simon, Michael Goodwin, and Susan Halford. 1988. "Policy Variations in Local States: Uneven Development and Local Social Relations." *International Journal of Urban and Regional Research* 12(1): 107–28.

Dunleavy, Patrick. 1980. *Urban Political Analysis: The Politics of Collective Consumption.* London: Macmillan.

Eagleton, Terry. 1991. *Ideology.* New York: Verso.

Earle, Carville. 1993. "Divisions of Labor: The Splintered Geography of Labor

Markets and Movements in Industrializing America, 1790–1930." *International Review of Social History* 38: 5–37.

Eddy, Regina. 1989. Boston-area director, Jobs with Peace, interview by author, author's notes, Boston, August 23.

Eder, Klaus. 1985. "The New Social Movements: Moral Crusades, Political Pressure Groups, or Social Movements?" *Social Research* 52(4): 869–900.

———. 1993. *The New Politics of Class: Social Movements and Cultural Dynamics in Advanced Societies.* Newbury Park, Calif.: Sage.

Ehrenreich, John, and Barbara Ehrenreich. 1977. "The Professional-Managerial Class." *Radical America* 11: 7–31.

Eisinger, Peter. 1973. "The Conditions of Protest Behavior in American Cities." *American Political Science Review* 67: 11–28.

Ellis, Mark. 1995. "The Determinants of Regional Differences in Strike Rates in the U.S., 1971–77." *Annals of the Association of American Geographers* 82(1): 48–63.

Elster, Jon. 1989. *The Cement of Society.* Cambridge: Cambridge University Press.

Ennis, James, 1987. "Fields of Action: Structure in Movements' Tactical Repertoires." *Sociological Forum* 2(3): 520–33.

Ennis, James, and Richard Schreuer. 1987. "Mobilizing Weak Support for Social Movements: The Role of Grievance, Efficacy, and Cost." *Social Forces* 66(2): 390–409.

Entrikin, J. Nicholas. 1976. "Contemporary Humanism in Geography." *Annals of the Association of American Geographers* 66(4): 615–32.

———. 1991. *The Betweenness of Place.* Baltimore: Johns Hopkins University Press.

Epstein, Barbara. 1990. "Rethinking Social Movement Theory." *Socialist Review* 20: 35–65.

Escobar, Arturo, and Sonia E. Alvarez, eds. 1992. *The Making of Social Movements in Latin America.* Boulder, Colo.: Westview Press.

Esping-Anderson, Gösta, Roger Friedland, and Erik Olin Wright. 1976. "Modes of Class Struggle and the Capitalist State." *Kapitalistate* 4–5: 186–224.

Ferguson, Ronald, and Helen Ladd. 1986. *Economic Performance and Economic Development Policy in Massachusetts.* Discussion Paper D86–2, State, Local, and Intergovernmental Center, John F. Kennedy School of Government, Cambridge: Harvard University.

Ferree, Myra Marx. 1992. "The Political Context of Rationality: Rational Choice Theory and Resource Mobilization." In Aldon D. Morris and Carol McClurg Mueller, eds., *Frontiers in Social Movement Theory,* pp. 29–52. New Haven: Yale University Press.

Ferree, Myra Marx, and Frederick Miller. 1985. "Mobilization and Meaning: Toward an Integration of Social Movements." *Sociological Inquiry* 55: 38–51.

Fields, A. Belden. 1988. "In Defense of Political Economy and Systemic Analysis: A

Critique of Prevailing Theoretical Approaches to the New Social Movements." In Carey Nelson and Lawrence Grossberg, eds., *Marxism and the Interpretation of Culture,* pp. 141–56. Urbana and Chicago: University of Illinois Press.

Fincher, Ruth. 1987a. "Defining and Explaining Urban Social Movements." *Urban Geography* 8(2): 152–60.

———. 1987b. "Space, Class and Political Processes: The Social Relations of the Local State." *Progress in Human Geography* 11(4): 496–515.

Fincher, Ruth, and Jacinta McQuillen. 1989. "Women in Urban Social Movements." *Urban Geography* 10(6): 604–13.

Fireman, Bruce, and William Gamson. 1979. "Utilitarian Logic in the Resource Mobilization Perspective." In Mayer Zald and John McCarthy, eds., *The Dynamics of Social Movements,* pp. 8–45. Cambridge: Winthrop.

Foreman, Shelagh. 1990a. Board member, Cambridge SANE/Freeze, interview by author, author's notes, Cambridge, Massachusetts, July 26.

———. 1990b. Board member, Cambridge SANE/Freeze, interview by author, author's notes, Cambridge, Massachusetts, August 29.

———. 1990c. Board member, Cambridge SANE/Freeze, interview by author, author's notes, Cambridge, Massachusetts, August 30.

Forsberg, Randall. 1979. *Call to Halt the Nuclear Arms Race.* Brookline, Mass.: Institute for Defense and Disarmament Studies.

Fox, W. 1987. "Less Defense Spending Would Help Bay State, Says National Group." *Boston Globe,* April 23, p. 41.

Fraser, Nancy. 1987. "What's Critical about Critical Theory? The Case of Habermas and Gender." In Seyla Behabib and Drucilla Cornell, eds., *Feminism as Critique: Essays on the Politics of Gender in Late-Capitalist Societies.* Minneapolis: University of Minnesota Press.

Freeman, Jo. 1979. "Resource Mobilization and Strategy." In Mayer Zald and John McCarthy, eds., *The Dynamics of Social Movements,* pp. 167–89. Cambridge: Winthrop.

Friedland, Roger, and Deirdre Boden, eds. 1994. *Now Here: Space, Time and Modernity.* Berkeley: University of California Press.

Friedman, Debra, and Doug McAdam. 1992. "Collective Identity and Activism: Networks, Choices, and the Life of a Social Movement." In Aldon D. Morris and Carol McClurg Mueller, eds., *Frontiers in Social Movement Theory,* pp. 156–73. New Haven: Yale University Press.

Gamson, William. 1975. *The Strategy of Social Protest.* Homewood, Ill.: Dorsey Press.

———. 1990. *The Strategy of Social Protest.* 2d. ed. Belmont, Calif.: Wadsworth.

Gamson, William, and David Meyer. 1996. "Framing Political Opportunity." In Doug McAdam, John D. McCarthy, and Mayer N. Zald, eds., *Comparative*

Perspectives on Social Movements, pp. 275–90. New York: Cambridge University Press.

Geiser, Kenneth. 1989. Assistant professor, Department of Planning, Tufts University, interview by author, author's notes, Brighton, Massachusetts, September 8.

Gerlach, Luther P. 1983. "Movements of Revolutionary Change: Some Structural Characteristics." In J. Freeman, ed., *Social Movements of the Sixties and Seventies,* pp. 133–47. Longman.

Gerlach, Luther P., and Virginia M. Hine. 1970. *People, Power, Change: Movements of Social Transformation.* New York: Bobbs-Merrill.

Gerson, Joe. 1990. New England regional disarmament coordinator, American Friends Service Committee, interview by author, author's notes, Cambridge, Massachusetts, August 30.

Giddens, Anthony. 1979. *Central Problems in Social Theory.* Berkeley and Los Angeles: University of California Press.

———. 1981. *A Contemporary Critique of Historical Materialism.* Berkeley and Los Angeles: University of California Press.

———. 1984. *The Constitution of Society.* Berkeley and Los Angeles: University of California Press.

Gilligan, Carol. 1981. *In a Different Voice.* New York: Cambridge University Press.

Gitelman, Howard. 1967. "The Waltham System and the Coming of the Irish." *Labor History* 8: 227–53.

Goodwin, M., S. Duncan, and S. Halford. 1993. "Regulation Theory, the Local State, and the Transition of Urban Politics." *Environment and Planning D: Society and Space* 11: 67–88.

Gottdiener, Mark. 1985. *The Social Production of Urban Space.* Austin: University of Texas Press.

———. 1987. *The Decline of Urban Politics.* Beverly Hills, Calif.: Sage.

Gouldner, Alvin. 1979. *The Future of Intellectuals and the Rise of the New Class.* New York: Oxford University Press.

Grasek, Susan, and Phyllis Emigh. 1987. *Grassroots Peace Directory: New England.* Washington, D.C.: Congressional Quarterly Press.

Greer, James L. 1987. "The Political Economy of the Local State." *Politics and Society* 15(4): 513–38.

Gregory, Derek. 1985. "Suspended Animation: The Stasis of Diffusion Theory." In Derek Gregory and John Urry, eds., *Social Relations and Spatial Structures,* pp. 296–336. London: Macmillan.

———. 1986. "Realism." In Ronald J. Johnston, Derek Gregory, and David M. Smith, eds., *Dictionary of Human Geography,* pp. 387–90. Oxford: Basil Blackwell.

———. 1989a. "The Crisis of Modernity? Human Geography and Critical Social

Theory." In Richard Peet and Nigel Thrift, eds., *New Models in Geography*, vol. 2, pp. 348–85. Boston: Unwin Hyman.

———. 1989b. "Presences and Absences: Time-Space Relations and Structuration Theory." In David Held and John Thompson, eds., *Social Theory of the Modern Societies: Anthony Giddens and His Critics,* pp. 185–214. Cambridge: Cambridge University Press.

———. 1990. "Chinatown, Part Three? Soja and the Missing Spaces of Social Theory." *Strategies* 3: 40–104.

———. 1994a. *Geographical Imaginations.* Cambridge, Mass.: Basil Blackwell.

———. 1994b. "Spatiality." In Ronald J. Johnston, Derek Gregory, and David M. Smith, eds., *The Dictionary of Human Geography,* pp. 582–85. Cambridge, Mass.: Basil Blackwell.

Gregory Derek, and John Urry, eds. 1985. *Social Relations and Spatial Structures.* London: Macmillan.

Grossman, Jerome. 1987. "From Stuart Hughes to Robert Drinan." In *The Hughes Campaign: 25 Years Later,* pp. 21–22. Boston: CPPAX.

Habermas, Jürgen. 1981. "New Social Movements." *Telos* 49: 33–37.

———. 1982. "A Reply to My Critics." In John Thompson and David Held, eds., *Habermas: Critical Debates,* pp. 219–83. Cambridge: MIT Press.

———. 1984. *The Theory of Communicative Action.* Vol. 1. Boston: Beacon Press.

———. 1985. "Questions and Counterquestions." In Richard Bernstein, ed., *Habermas and Modernity,* pp. 192–216. Cambridge: MIT Press.

———. 1987. *The Theory of Communicative Action.* Vol. 2. Boston: Beacon Press.

———. 1989. "Towards a Communication Concept of Rational Collective Will Formation." *Ratio Juris* 2(2): 140–52.

———. 1991. "A Reply." In Axel Honneth and Hans Joas, eds., *Communicative Action,* pp. 214–64. Cambridge: MIT Press.

Hagerstrand, Torsten. 1968. *Innovation Diffusion as a Spatial Process.* Chicago: University of Chicago Press.

———. 1970. "What about People in Regional Science?" *Papers and Proceedings of the Regional Science Association* 24: 7–21.

———. 1975. "Space, Time, and Human Conditions." In Anders Karlqvist, Lars Lundqvist, and Folke Snickars, eds., *Dynamic Allocation of Urban Space,* pp. 3–14. Lexington, Mass.: Saxon House.

———. 1978. "Survival and Arena: On the Life-History of Individuals in Relation to Their Geographical Environment." In Tommy Carlstein, Don Parkes, and Nigel Thrift, eds., *Timing Space and Spacing Time,* vol. 2, pp. 122–45. New York: John Wiley and Sons.

———. 1982. "Diorama, Path and Project." *Tijdschrift voor Economische en sociale Geografie* 73: 323–39.

Haggett, Peter. 1990. *The Geographer's Art.* Cambridge, Mass.: Basil Blackwell.

Hall, George D. 1981a. *Directory of Massachusetts Manufacturers 1981–1982.* Boston: George D. Hall.

———. 1981b. *Massachusetts Service Directory 1981–1982.* Boston: George D. Hall.

———. 1985a. *Directory of Massachusetts Manufacturers 1985–1986.* Boston: George D. Hall.

———. 1985b. *Massachusetts Service Directory 1985–1986.* Boston: George D. Hall.

Hannigan, John A. 1985. "Alain Touraine, Manuel Castells and Social Movement Theory: A Critical Appraisal." *Sociological Quarterly* 26(4): 435–54.

———. 1988. *Democracy in Kingston: A Social Movement in Urban Politics, 1965–70.* Kingston and Montreal: McGill-Queen's University Press.

Harris, Richard. 1987. "A Social Movement in Urban Politics." *International Journal of Urban and Regional Research* 11(3): 363–77.

———. 1988. "The Interpretation of Canadian Urban Reform." *International Journal of Urban and Regional Research* 12(3): 485–89.

Harrison, Bennett. 1984. "Regional Restructuring and 'Good Business Climates': The Economic Transformation of New England since World War Two." In W. Sawers and W. Tabb, eds., *Sunbelt/Snowbelt: Urban Development and Regional Restructuring,* pp. 48–96. New York: Oxford University Press.

———. 1988. "The Economic Development of Massachusetts." In David R. Lampe, ed., *The Massachusetts Miracle,* pp. 74–88. Cambridge: MIT Press.

———. 1989. Professor, Department of Planning, MIT, telephone interview by author, author's notes, Cambridge, Massachusetts, September 8.

Harrison, Bennett, and Jean Kluver. 1989. "Re-assessing the 'Massachusetts Miracle': Reindustrialization and Balanced Growth, or Convergence to 'Manhattanization'?" *Environment and Planning A* 21: 771–801.

Hartsock, Nancy. 1990. "Foucault on Power: A Theory for Women?" In L. Nicholson, ed., *Feminism/Postmodernism,* pp. 157–75. New York: Routledge.

Harvey, David. 1982. *The Limits to Capital.* Chicago: University of Chicago Press.

———. 1985a. *Consciousness and the Urban Experience.* Baltimore: Johns Hopkins University Press.

———. 1985b. *The Urbanization of Capital.* Baltimore: Johns Hopkins University Press.

———. 1989. *The Condition of Postmodernity.* Cambridge, Mass.: Basil Blackwell.

———. 1996. *Justice, Nature, and the Geography of Difference.* Cambridge, Mass.: Basil Blackwell.

Heckman, John S. 1980a. "Can New England Hold onto Its High Technology Industry?" *New England Economic Review* (March/April): 35–44.

———. 1980b. "The Future of High Technology Industry in New England: A Case Study of Computers." *New England Economic Review* (January/February): 5–17.

Hedstrom, Peter. 1994. "Contagious Collectivities: On the Spatial Diffusion of Swedish Trade Unions, 1890–1940." *American Journal of Sociology* 99(5): 1157–79.

Heiman, Michael, ed. 1996. "Special Issue: Race, Waste and Class." *Antipode* 28 (2): 111–203.

Henry, David. 1983. "Defense Spending: A Growth Market for Industry." *U.S. Industrial Outlook 1983*: 39–47.

Herbert, Steve. 1996. "The Normative Ordering of Police Territoriality: Making and Marking Space with the Los Angeles Police Department." *Annals of the Association of American Geographers* 86(3): 567–82.

Herod, Andrew. 1991. "The Production of Scale in United States Labour Relations." *Area* 23(1): 82–88.

———. 1997. "Labor's Spatial Praxis and the Geography of Contract Bargaining in the U.S. East Coast Longshore Industry, 1953–89." *Political Geography* 16(2): 145–69.

Hirsch, Joachim. 1980. *Der Sicherheitsstaat.* Frankfurt: Evangelische Verlagsanstalt.

Hirschon, Paul. 1983. "Nuclear-Free City Proposed." *Boston Globe,* March 12, pp. 17–18.

Hoffman, Kathy. 1989. Cambridge Peace Commission director, interview by author, author's notes, Cambridge, Massachusetts, August 22.

Honneth, Axel, and Hans Joas, eds. 1991. *Communicative Action.* Cambridge: MIT Press.

hooks, bell. 1990. *Yearning: Race, Gender, and Cultural Politics.* Boston: South End Press.

Hoy, John C. 1988. "Higher Skills and the New England Economy." In David R. Lampe, ed., *The Massachusetts Miracle,* pp. 331–47. Cambridge: MIT Press.

Hudson, Ray, and David Sadler. 1986. "Contesting Work Closures in Western Europe's Old Industrial Regions: Defending Place or Betraying Class?" In Allen Scott and Michael Storper, eds., *Production, Work, Territory,* pp. 172–94. London: Allen and Unwin.

Hunter, Albert. 1974. *Symbolic Communities: The Persistence and Change of Chicago's Local Communities.* Chicago: University of Chicago Press.

Inglehart, Ronald. 1971. "The Silent Revolution in Europe: Intergenerational Change in Post-Industrial Societies." *American Political Science Review* 65: 991–1017.

———. 1977. *The Silent Revolution: Changing Values and Political Styles among Western Publics.* Princeton, N.J.: Princeton University Press.

Jameson, Fredric. 1984. "Postmodernism, or the Cultural Logic of Late Capitalism." *New Left Review* 146: 53–92.

Jencks, Christopher. 1979. "The Social Basis of Unselfishness." In H. Gans, N. Glazer,

J. Gusfield, and C. Jencks, eds., *On the Making of Americans,* pp. 63–86. Philadelphia: University of Pennsylvania Press.

Jenkins, J. Craig. 1983. "Resource Mobilization Theory and the Study of Social Movements." *Annual Review of Sociology* 9: 527–53.

———. 1995. "Social Movements, Political Representation, and the State: An Agenda and Comparative Framework." In J. Craig Jenkins and Bert Klandermans, eds., *The Politics of Social Protest: Comparative Perspectives on States and Social Movements,* pp. 14–35. Minneapolis: University of Minnesota Press.

Jenkins, J. Craig, and Bert Klandermans, eds. 1995. *The Politics of Social Protest: Comparative Perspectives on States and Social Movements.* Minneapolis: University of Minnesota Press.

Jenkins, J. Craig, and Charles Perrow. 1977. "Insurgency of the Powerless: Farm Worker Movements 1946–1972." *American Sociological Review* 42: 249–68.

Johnston, Hank, Enrique Laraña, and Joseph R. Gusfield. 1994. "Identities, Grievances, and New Social Movements." In Enrique Laraña, Hank Johnston, and Joseph R. Gusfield, eds., *New Social Movements: From Ideology to Identity,* pp. 3–35. Philadelphia: Temple University Press.

Johnston, Ronald. J. 1991. *A Question of Place.* Cambridge, Mass.: Basil Blackwell.

Jonas, Andrew. 1993. "A Place for Politics in Urban Theory: The Organization and Strategies of Urban Coalitions." *Urban Geography* 13(3): 280–90.

———. 1994. "The Scale Politics of Spatiality." *Environment and Planning D: Society and Space* 12: 257–64.

Jones, John Paul, III, and Pamela Moss. 1995. "Democracy, Identity, Space." *Environment and Planning D: Society and Space* 13: 253–57.

Jones, John Paul, III, Wolfgang Natter, and Theodore Schatzki, eds. 1993. *Postmodern Contentions: Epochs, Politics, Space.* New York: Guilford Press.

Kanter, Rosabeth M. 1972. *Commitment and Community: Communes and Utopias in Sociological Perspective.* Cambridge: Harvard University Press.

Karp, Walter. 1988. *Liberty under Siege: American Politics, 1976–1988.* New York: Holt.

Katznelson, Ira. 1976. "Class Capacity and Social Cohesion in American Cities." In Louis H. Masotti and Robert L. Lineberry, eds., *The Urban Politics,* pp. 19–35. Cambridge, Mass.: Ballinger.

———. 1981. *City Trenches: Urban Politics and the Patterning of Class in the United States.* Chicago: University of Chicago Press.

Keith, Michael, and Steve Pile, eds. 1993. *Place and the Politics of Identity.* New York: Routledge.

Kirby, Andrew. 1989. "A Sense of Place." *Critical Studies in Mass Communications* 3: 322–26.

Kitschelt, Herbert. 1986. "Political Opportunity Structures and Political Protest:

Anti-Nuclear Movements in Four Democracies." *American Sociological Review* 49: 770–83.

———. 1991. "Resource Mobilization Theory: A Critique." In Dieter Rucht, ed., *Research on Social Movements: The State of the Art in Western Europe and the USA,* pp. 323–47. Boulder, Colo.: Westview Press.

Klandermans, Bert. 1988. "The Formation and Mobilization of Consensus." In Bert Klandermans, Hanspeter Kriesi, and Sidney Tarrow, eds., *International Social Movement Research,* vol. 1, *From Structure to Action: Comparing Social Movement Research across Cultures,* pp. 173–96. Greenwich, Conn.: JAI Press.

Klandermans, Bert, Hanspeter Kriesi, and Sidney Tarrow, eds. 1988. *International Social Movement Research,* vol. 1, *From Structure to Action: Comparing Social Movement Research across Cultures.* Greenwich, Conn.: JAI Press.

Klandermans, Bert, and Sidney Tarrow. 1988. "Mobilizing into Social Movements: Synthesizing European and American Approaches." In Bert Klandermans, Hanspeter Kriesi, and Sidney Tarrow, eds., *International Social Movement Research,* vol. 1, *From Structure to Action: Comparing Social Movement Research across Cultures,* pp. 1–38. Greenwich, Conn.: JAI Press.

Kleidman, Robert. 1990. "Organization and Mobilization in Modern American Peace Campaigns." Doctoral dissertation, Ann Arbor: University Microfilms International.

Knapp, Caroline. 1985. "State Defense Contractors Pool Their Resources." *Boston Business Journal,* March 4–10.

Knight, Prentice, and Richard Barff. 1987. "Employment Growth and the Turnaround of the New England Economy." *Northeast Journal of Business and Economics* 14: 1–15.

Kricker, Dee. 1990a. Coordinating committee member, Waltham Concerned Citizens, interview by author, author's notes, Waltham, Massachusetts, June 19.

———. 1990b. Coordinating committee member, Waltham Concerned Citizens, interview by author, author's notes, Waltham, Massachusetts, July 27.

———. 1990c. Coordinating committee member, Waltham Concerned Citizens, interview by author, author's notes, Waltham, Massachusetts, August 28.

Kriesi, Hanspeter. 1988. "The Interdependence of Structure and Action: Some Reflections on the State of the Art." In Bert Klandermans, Hanspeter Kriesi, and Sidney Tarrow, eds., *International Social Movement Research,* vol. 1, *From Structure to Action: Comparing Social Movement Research across Cultures,* pp. 349–68. Greenwich, Conn.: JAI Press.

———. 1995. "The Political Opportunity Structure of New Social Movements: Its Impact on Their Mobilization." In J. Craig Jenkins and Bert Klandermans, eds., *The Politics of Social Protest: Comparative Perspectives on States and Social Movements,* pp. 167–98. Minneapolis: University of Minnesota Press.

Kriesi, Hanspeter, Ruud Koopmans, Jan Willem Duyvendak, and Marco G. Guigi. 1995a. "The Cross-National Diffusion of Protest." In Hanspeter Kriesi, Ruud Koopmans, Jan Willem Duyvendak, and Marco G. Guigi, *New Social Movements in Western Europe: A Comparative Analysis,* pp. 181–206. Minneapolis: University of Minnesota Press.

———. 1995b. "Outcomes of New Social Movements." In Hanspeter Kriesi, Ruud Koopmans, Jan Willem Duyvendak, and Marco G. Guigi, *New Social Movements in Western Europe: A Comparative Analysis,* pp. 207–37. Minneapolis: University of Minnesota Press.

Laclau, Ernesto, and Chantal Mouffe. 1985. *Hegemony and Socialist Strategy: Towards a Radical Democratic Politics.* London: Verso.

Laws, Glenda. 1994. "Oppression, Knowledge, and the Built Environment." *Political Geography* 13(1): 7–32.

League of Women Voters. 1980. *Waltham, MA.* Waltham, Mass.: League of Women Voters.

Leavitt, Robert. 1983a. *Freezing the Arms Race: The Genesis of a Mass Movement.* Cambridge: Harvard College.

———. 1983b. *Freezing the Arms Race (Sequel): The Debate.* Cambridge: Harvard College.

———. 1986. *By the Sword We Seek Peace: Military Spending and State Government in Massachusetts.* Boston: Leavitt.

———. 1989a. Institute for Defense and Disarmament Studies, interview by author, author's notes, Brookline, Massachusetts, August 24.

———. 1989b. Institute for Defense and Disarmament Studies, interview by author, author's notes, Brookline, Massachusetts, August 25.

Lefebvre, Henri. 1979. "Space: Social Product and Use Value." In J. W. Freiburg, ed., *Critical Sociology,* pp. 285–95. New York: Irvington.

———. 1991. *The Production of Space.* Trans. Donald Nicholson-Smith. Cambridge, Mass.: Basil Blackwell.

Leitner, Helga. 1990. "Cities in Pursuit of Economic Growth: The Local State as Entrepreneur." *Political Geography Quarterly* 9: 146–70.

———. 1997. "Reconfiguring the Spatiality of Power: The Construction of a Supranational Migration Framework for the European Union." *Political Geography* 16: 123–43.

Levene, Susan. 1985. "Civil Disobedience Begins at Home: The Nuclear Free Cambridge Campaign." *Radical America* 1: 6–22.

Ley, David. 1978. "Social Geography and Social Action." In David Ley and Marwyn Samuels, eds., *Humanistic Geography,* pp. 41–57. London: Croom Helm.

Lipietz, Alain. 1977. *Le capital et son espace.* Paris: Maspero.

Lipsky, Michael. 1968. "Protest as a Political Resource." *American Political Science Review* 621: 1144–58.

———. 1970. *Protest in City Politics.* Chicago: Rand McNally.

Lobao, L. 1994. "The Place of 'Place' in Current Sociological Research." *Environment and Planning A* 26: 665–68.

Local Growth Policy Committee. 1976. *Lexington: Local Growth Policy Statement.* Lexington, Mass.: Town of Lexington.

Mahoney, Frank. 1983. "Dukakis Attacks Arms Buildup." *Boston Globe,* April 17, p. 90.

Mair, Andrew. 1989. "Review: 'Place and Politics' by J. Agnew." *Annals of the Association of American Geographers* 79(3): 457–60.

Malecki, Edward J. 1981. "Government Funded R and D: Some Regional Economic Implications." *Professional Geographer* 33: 72–82.

———. 1982. "Federal R and D Spending in the United States of America: Some Impacts on Metropolitan Economies." *Regional Studies* 16: 19–35.

———. 1984. "Military Spending in the US Defense Industry: Regional Patterns of Military Contracts and Subcontracts." *Environment and Planning C: Government and Policy* 2: 31–44.

———. 1986. "Research and Development and the Geography of High Technology Complexes." In John Rees, ed., *Technology, Regions, and Policy,* pp. 51–74. Totowa, N.J.: Rowman and Littlefield.

Mansbridge, Jane. 1990. "On the Relation of Altruism and Self-Interest." In Jane Mansbridge, ed., *Beyond Self-Interest,* pp. 133–46. Chicago: University of Chicago Press.

Marden, Peter. 1997. "Geographies of Dissent: Globalization, Identity and the Nation." *Political Geography* 16(1): 37–64.

Markusen, Ann. 1985. *Profit Cycles, Oligopoly, and Regional Development.* Cambridge: MIT Press.

———. 1986. "Defense Spending and the Geography of High Tech Industries." In John Rees, ed., *Technology, Regions, and Policy,* pp. 94–119. Totowa, N.J.: Rowman and Littlefield.

———. 1987. *Regions.* Totowa, N.J.: Rowman and Littlefield.

———. 1988. Personal communication (letter in possession of author), November 28.

———. 1989. "Industrial Restructuring and Regional Politics." In Robert Beauregard, ed., *Economic Restructuring and Regional Politics,* pp. 115–48. Newbury Park, Calif.: Sage.

Markusen, Ann, and Robin Bloch. 1985. "Defensive Cities: Military Spending, High Technology, and Human Settlements." In Manuel Castells, ed., *High Technology, Space, and Society,* pp. 106–20. Beverly Hills, Calif.: Sage.

Markusen, Ann, Peter Hall, and Amy Glasmeier. 1986. *High Tech America: The What, How, Where and Why of the Sunrise Industries.* Boston: Allen and Unwin.

Markusen, Ann, Peter Hall, Scott Campbell, and Sabina Deitrick. 1991. *The Rise of the Gunbelt.* New York: Oxford University Press.

Marston, Sallie A. 1988. "Neighborhood and Politics: Irish Ethnicity in Nineteenth Century Lowell, Massachusetts." *Annals of the Association of American Geographers* 78: 414–32.

Marullo, Sam. 1996. "Frame Changes and Social Movement Contraction: U.S. Peace Movement Framing after the Cold War." *Sociological Inquiry* 66(1): 1–28.

Massachusetts High Technology Council. 1988. "A New Social Contract for Massachusetts." In David R. Lampe, ed., *The Massachusetts Miracle,* pp. 155–68. Cambridge: MIT Press.

Massey, Doreen. 1983. "Industrial Restructuring as Class Restructuring: Production, Decentralization and Local Uniqueness." *Regional Studies* 17: 73–89.

———. 1984a. "Introduction: Geography Matters." In Doreen Massey and John Allen, eds., *Geography Matters!* pp. 1–11. New York: Cambridge University Press.

———. 1984b. *Spatial Divisions of Labour.* London: Macmillan.

———. 1992. "Politics and Space/Time." *New Left Review* 196: 65–84.

———. 1994. *Space, Place, and Gender.* Minneapolis: University of Minnesota Press.

———. 1995. "Thinking Radical Democracy Spatially." *Environment and Planning D: Society and Space* 13: 283–88.

Massey, Doreen, and John Allen, eds. 1984. *Geography Matters!* New York: Cambridge University Press.

McAdam, Doug. 1982. *Political Process and the Development of Black Insurgency 1930–1970.* Chicago: University of Chicago Press.

———. 1988. *Freedom Summer.* New York: Oxford University Press.

———. 1996. "Conceptual Origins, Current Problems, Future Directions." In Doug McAdam, John D. McCarthy, and Mayer N. Zald, eds., *Comparative Perspectives on Social Movements,* pp. 23–40. New York: Cambridge University Press.

McAdam, Doug, John D. McCarthy, and Mayer N. Zald, eds. 1996. *Comparative Perspectives on Social Movements.* New York: Cambridge University Press.

McAdam, Doug, and Dieter Rucht. 1993. "The Cross-National Diffusion of Movement Ideas." *Annals of the American Academy of Political and Social Science* (July): 56–74.

McCarthy, John D., and Mayer N. Zald. 1973. *The Trend of Social Movements in America.* Morristown, N.J.: General Learning Press.

———. 1977. "Resource Mobilization and Social Movements: A Partial Theory." *American Journal of Sociology* 82: 1212–41.

McCrea, Frances B., and Gerald E. Markle. 1989. *Minutes to Midnight: Nuclear Weapons Protest in America.* Beverly Hills: Sage.

Melucci, Alberto. 1980. "The New Social Movements: A Theoretical Approach." *Social Science Information* 19(2): 199–226.

———. 1985. "The Symbolic Challenge of Contemporary Movements." *Social Research* 52(4): 789–816.

———. 1988. "Getting Involved: Identity and Mobilization in Social Movements." In Bert Klandermans, Hanspeter Kriesi, and Sidney Tarrow, eds., *International Social Movement Research,* vol. 1, *From Structure to Action: Comparing Social Movement Research across Cultures,* pp. 329–48. Greenwich, Conn.: JAI Press.

———. 1989. *Nomads of the Present: Social Movements and Individual Needs in Contemporary Society.* Philadelphia: Temple University Press.

———. 1994. "A Strange Kind of Newness: What's 'New' in New Social Movements?" In Enrique Laraña, Hank Johnston, and Joseph R. Gusfield, eds., *New Social Movements: From Ideology to Identity,* pp. 101–30. Philadelphia: Temple University Press.

Meyer, David S. 1990. *A Winter of Discontent: The Nuclear Freeze and American Politics.* New York: Praeger.

———. 1993a. "Institutionalizing Dissent: The United States Structure of Political Opportunity and the End of the Nuclear Freeze Movement." *Sociological Forum* 8(2): 157–79.

———. 1993b. "Peace Protest and Policy: Explaining the Rise and Decline of Antinuclear Movements in Postwar America." *Policy Studies Journal* 21(1): 35–51.

Meyrowitz, Joshua. 1989. "The Generalized Elsewhere." *Critical Studies in Mass Communications* 6: 326–34.

———. 1990. "On 'The Consumer's World: Place as Context' by Robert Sack." *Annals of the Association of American Geographers* 80: 1129–32.

Middlesex News. 1982a. "City Is Anti-Nuke, Survey Says." August 11, p. 1.

———. 1982b. "Council Changes Stance to Support Nuclear Freeze." October 26, p. 1.

Miller, Byron A. 1992. "Collective Action and Rational Choice: Place, Community, and the Limits to Individual Self-Interest." *Economic Geography* 68(1): 22–42.

———. 1994. "Political Empowerment, Local-Central State Relations, and Geographically Shifting Political Opportunity Structures: Strategies of the Cambridge, Massachusetts, Peace Movement." *Political Geography* 13(5): 393–406.

———. 1997. "Political Action and the Geography of Defense Investment: Geographical Scale and the Representation of the Massachusetts Miracle." *Political Geography* 16(2): 171–85.

Minter, Susan. 1984. "Organizing for Peace: The History of a Local Struggle within a Growing National Movement." Unpublished thesis, Harvard-Radcliffe College, Cambridge.

————. 1990. Former Nuclear Free Cambridge campaign coordinating committee member, telephone interview by author, author's notes, Boston, August 30.

Mitchell, J. Clyde. 1983. "Case and Situational Analysis." *Sociological Review* 31: 187–211.

Mollenkopf, John. 1983. *The Contested City.* Princeton, N.J.: Princeton University Press.

Moore, Barrington. 1966. *Social Origins of Dictatorship and Democracy.* Boston: Beacon Press.

Morris, Aldon D., and Carol McClurg Mueller, eds. 1992. *Frontiers in Social Movement Theory.* New Haven: Yale University Press.

Mouffe, Chantal. 1993. *The Return of the Political.* London: Verso.

————. 1995. "Post-Marxism: Democracy and Identity." *Environment and Planning D: Society and Space* 13: 259–65.

Nollert, Michael. 1995. "Neocorporatism and Political Protest in the Western Democracies: A Cross-National Analysis." In J. Craig Jenkins and Bert Klandermans, eds., *The Politics of Social Protest: Comparative Perspectives on States and Social Movements,* pp. 138–64. Minneapolis: University of Minnesota Press.

Nuclear Weapons Freeze Campaign. 1981. *Strategy for Stopping the Nuclear Arms Race.* Saint Louis: Nuclear Weapons Freeze Campaign.

Nyhan, David. 1994. "Who'll Sit at the Head of the Table?" *Boston Globe,* January 9, p. 73.

Oberschall, Anthony. 1973. *Social Conflict and Social Movements.* New York: Prentice Hall.

————. 1978. "The Decline of the 1960s Social Movements." In Louis Kriesberg, ed., *Research in Social Movements, Conflict, and Change,* vol. 1, pp. 257–89. Greenwich, Conn.: JAI Press.

————. 1980. "Loosely Structured Collective Conflict: A Theory and an Application." In Louis Kriesberg, ed., *Research in Social Movements, Conflict, and Change,* vol. 3, pp. 45–68. Greenwich, Conn.: JAI Press.

O'Connell, Kevin. 1990. State director, Massachusetts SANE/Freeze, interview by author, author's notes, Cambridge, Massachusetts, August 14.

Offe, Klaus. 1985. "New Social Movements: Challenging the Boundaries of Institutional Politics." *Social Research* 52(4): 817–68.

O'hUallachain, Breandan. 1987. "Regional and Technological Implications of the Recent Buildup in American Defense Spending." *Annals of the Association of American Geographers* 77(2): 208–23.

Oliver, Pamela. 1984. "If You Don't Do It, Nobody Else Will: Active and Token Contributors to Local Collective Action." *American Sociological Review* 49: 601–10.

Oliver, Pamela, and Gerald Marwell. 1992. "Mobilizing Technologies for Collective Action." In Aldon D. Morris and Carol McClurg Mueller, eds., *Frontiers in Social Movement Theory*, pp. 251–72. New Haven: Yale University Press.

Olson, Mancur. 1965. *The Logic of Collective Action.* Cambridge: Harvard University Press.

O'Neill, Tip. 1987. *Man of the House: The Life and Political Memoirs of Speaker Tip O'Neill.* New York: Random House.

———. 1994. *All Politics Is Local and Other Rules of the Game.* New York: Random House.

Opp, Karl-Dieter. 1988. "Community Integration and Incentives for Political Protest." In Bert Klandermans, Hanspeter Kriesi, and Sidney Tarrow, eds., *International Social Movement Research*, vol. 1, *From Structure to Action: Comparing Social Movement Research across Cultures*, pp. 83–102. Greenwich, Conn.: JAI Press.

Opp, Karl-Dieter, Steven Finkel, Edward Muller, Gadi Wolfsfeld, Henry Dietz, and Jerrold Green. 1995. "Left-Right Ideology and Collective Political Action: A Comparative Analysis of Germany, Israel, and Peru." In J. Craig Jenkins and Bert Klandermans, eds., *The Politics of Social Protest: Comparative Perspectives on States and Social Movements*, pp. 63–95. Minneapolis: University of Minnesota Press.

Ó Tuathail, Gearóid. 1995. "Political Geography 1: Theorizing History, Gender and World Order amidst Crises of Global Governance." *Progress in Human Geography* 19(2): 260–72.

Palomba, Tony. 1989a. Coordinating committee member, Boston Mobilization for Survival, and aide to Boston City Councilwoman Rosaria Salerno, interview by author, author's notes, Boston, August 26.

———. 1989b. Coordinating committee member, Boston Mobilization for Survival, and aide to Boston City Councilwoman Rosaria Salerno, interview by author, author's notes, Cambridge, Massachusetts, August 30.

———. 1990a. Coordinating committee member, Boston Mobilization for Survival, and aide to Boston City Councilwoman Rosaria Salerno, interview by author, author's notes, Boston, June 19.

———. 1990b. Coordinating committee member, Boston Mobilization for Survival, and aide to Boston City Councilwoman Rosaria Salerno, interview by author, author's notes, Boston, August 18.

———. 1990c. Coordinating committee member, Boston Mobilization for

Survival, and aide to Boston City Councilwoman Rosaria Salerno, interview by author, author's notes, Boston, August 25.

Parker, Richard, and Joe Feagin. 1992. "Military Spending in Free Enterprise Cities: The Military-Industrial Complex in Houston and Las Vegas." In Andrew Kirby, ed., *The Pentagon and the Cities,* pp. 100–125. Newbury Park, Calif.: Sage.

Peck, Jamie. 1996. *Work-Place: The Social Regulation of Labor Markets.* New York: Guilford Press.

Peck, Jamie, and Adam Tickell. 1992. "Local Modes of Social Regulation? Regulation Theory, Thatcherism and Uneven Development." *Geoforum* 23(3): 347–63.

Peet, Richard. 1989. Professor, School of Geography, Clark University, interview by author, author's notes, Worcester, Massachusetts, September 6.

Peet, Richard, and Nigel Thrift, eds. 1989. *New Models in Geography.* 2 vols. Boston: Unwin Hyman.

Peterson, Paul. 1981. *City Limits.* Chicago: University of Chicago Press.

Pickvance, Chris G. 1985. "The Rise and Fall of Urban Movements and the Role of Comparative Analysis." *Environment and Planning D: Society and Space* 3: 31–53.

———. 1986. "Concepts, Contexts and Comparison in the Study of Urban Movements: A Reply to Manuel Castells." *Environment and Planning D: Society and Space* 4: 221–31.

Pile, Steve, and Michael Keith, eds. 1997. *Geographies of Resistance.* London and New York: Routledge.

Piven, Frances Fox, and Richard Cloward. 1979. *Poor People's Movements: Why They Succeed, How They Fail.* New York: Vintage.

Plotke, David. 1990. "What's So New about New Social Movements?" *Socialist Review* 20(1): 81–102.

Pred, Allan. 1983. "Structuration and Place: On the Becoming of Sense of Place and Structure of Feeling." *Journal for the Theory of Social Behavior* 13: 157–86.

———. 1984. "Place as Historically Contingent Process: Structuration and the Time-Geography of Becoming Places." *Annals of the Association of American Geographers* 74(2): 279–97.

———. 1986. *Place, Practice, and Structure.* Totowa, N.J.: Barnes and Noble Books.

Price, Don K. *The Scientific Estate.* Cambridge: Harvard University Press.

Probyn, Elspeth. 1996. *Outside Belongings.* New York: Routledge.

Pudup, Mary Beth. 1988. "Arguments within Regional Geography." *Progress in Human Geography* 12: 369–90.

Pulido, Laura. 1994. "Restructuring and the Contraction and Expansion of Environmental Rights in the United States." *Environment and Planning A* 26: 915–36.

————. 1996. *Environmentalism and Economic Justice: Two Chicano Struggles in the Southwest.* Tucson: University of Arizona Press.

Ragin, Charles. 1987. *The Comparative Method: Moving beyond Qualitative and Quantitative Strategies.* Berkeley: University of California Press.

Rees, Gareth. 1985. "Introduction: Class, Locality and Ideology." In Gareth Rees, ed., *Political Action and Social Identity: Class, Locality, and Culture,* pp. 1–16. London: Macmillan.

Relph, Edward. 1976. *Place and Placelessness.* London: Pion.

Reynolds, David R. 1994. "Political Geography: The Power of Place and the Spatiality of Politics." *Progress in Human Geography* 18(2): 234–47.

Rogers, Alisdair. 1990. "Towards a Geography of the Rainbow Coalition, 1983–89." *Environment and Planning D: Society and Space* 8(4): 409–26.

Rose, Gillian. 1993. *Feminism and Geography: The Limits of Geographical Knowledge.* Minneapolis: University of Minnesota Press.

Rose, Jennifer. 1990a. Coordinating committee member, Waltham Concerned Citizens, interview by author, author's notes, Waltham, Massachusetts, August 6.

————. 1990b. Coordinating committee member, Waltham Concerned Citizens, interview by author, author's notes, Waltham, Massachusetts, August 20.

Rosen, Sumner. 1987. "The Transformation of Politics in Massachusetts." In *The Hughes Campaign: 25 Years Later,* pp. 14–15. Boston: CPPAX.

Rosenblum, Rachel. 1990. Board member, Lexington Committee for a Nuclear Weapons Freeze, interview by author, author's notes, Cambridge, Massachusetts, August 24.

————. 1992. Board member, Lexington Committee for a Nuclear Weapons Freeze, personal communication (letter in possession of author), July 8.

Ross, Robert. 1989. Professor, Department of Sociology, Clark University, interview by author, author's notes, Worcester, Massachusetts, September 6.

Ross, Robert, and Kent Trachte 1990. *Global Capitalism: The New Leviathan.* Albany: State University of New York Press.

Routledge, Paul. 1993. *Terrains of Resistance: Nonviolent Social Movements and the Contestation of Place in India.* Westport, Conn.: Praeger.

————. 1994. "Backstreets, Barricades, and Blackouts: Urban Terrains of Resistance in Nepal." *Environment and Planning D: Society and Space* 12: 559–78.

————. 1997. "A Spatiality of Resistances: Theory and Practice in Nepal's Revolution of 1990." In Steve Pile and Michael Keith, eds., *Geographies of Resistance,* pp. 68–86. London and New York: Routledge.

Rucht, Dieter. 1988. "Themes, Logics, and Arenas of Social Movements: A Structural Approach." In Bert Klandermans, Hanspeter Kriesi, and Sidney Tarrow, eds., *International Social Movement Research,* vol. 1, *From Structure to*

Action: Comparing Social Movement Research across Cultures, pp. 305–28. Greenwich, Conn.: JAI Press.

———. 1996. "The Impact of National Contexts on Social Movement Structures: A Cross-Movement and Cross-National Comparison." In Doug McAdam, John D. McCarthy, and Mayer N. Zald, eds., *Comparative Perspectives on Social Movements,* pp. 185–204. New York: Cambridge University Press.

———, ed. 1991. *Research on Social Movements: The State of the Art in Western Europe and the USA.* Boulder, Colo.: Westview Press.

Ruddick, Susan. 1996. "Constructing Difference in Public Spaces: Race, Class, and Gender as Interlocking Systems." *Urban Geography* 17(2): 132–51.

Rudnick, Marc. 1990. Coordinating committee member, Waltham Concerned Citizens, interview by author, author's notes, Waltham, Massachusetts, August 17.

Rustin, Michael. 1987. "Place and Time in Socialist Theory." *Radical Philosophy* 47: 30–36.

Sack, Robert D. 1974. "The Spatial Separatist Theme in Geography." *Economic Geography* 50: 1–19.

———. 1980. *Conceptions of Space in Social Thought.* Minneapolis: University of Minnesota Press.

———. 1986. *Human Territoriality.* Cambridge and New York: Cambridge University Press.

———. 1988. "The Consumer's World: Place as Context." *Annals of the Association of American Geographers* 78: 642–64.

———. 1990. "Reply: Strangers and Places without Context." *Annals of the Association of American Geographers* 80: 133–35.

Sandel, Michael. 1982. *Liberalism and the Limits of Justice.* New York: Cambridge University Press.

Saunders, Peter. 1981. *Social Theory and the Urban Question.* New York: Holmes and Meier.

———. 1985. "Space, the City and Urban Sociology." In Derek Gregory and John Urry, eds., *Social Relations and Spatial Structures,* pp. 67–89. London: Macmillan.

Savage, Michael. 1987. *The Dynamics of Working-Class Politics: The Labor Movement in Preston 1880–1940.* Cambridge: Cambridge University Press.

Saxenian, Annalee. 1985. "Silicon Valley and Route 128: Regional Prototypes or Historic Exceptions?" In Manuel Castells, ed., *High Technology, Space, and Society,* pp. 81–105. Beverly Hills, Calif.: Sage.

Sayer, Andrew. 1984. *Method in Social Science.* London: Hutchinson.

Schrag, Peter. 1987. "Two Visits to the Executive Office Building." In *The Hughes Campaign: 25 Years Later,* pp. 7–10. Boston: CPPAX.

Segal, Eric. 1990. Former Nuclear Free Cambridge campaign coordinating committee member, interview by author, author's notes, Medford, Massachusetts, August 9.

Seidman, Steven, and David Wagner, eds. 1992. *Postmodernism and Social Theory.* Cambridge, Mass.: Basil Blackwell.

Sharp, Virginia. 1973. "The 1970 Postal Strikes: The Behavioral Element in Spatial Diffusion." In Melvin Albaum, ed., *Geography and Contemporary Issues,* pp. 523–32. New York: John Wiley and Sons.

Shefter, Martin. 1985. *Political Crisis/Fiscal Crisis.* New York: Basic Books.

Sheppard, Eric. 1994. "Review of 'Postmodernism and Social Theory' by Seidman and Wagner, Eds." *Environment and Planning D: Society and Space* 12: 776–77.

Shields, Rob. 1991. *Places on the Margin: Alternative Geographies of Modernity.* New York: Routledge.

Silber, Ilana Friedrich. 1995. "Space, Fields, Boundaries: The Rise of Spatial Metaphors in Contemporary Sociological Theory." *Social Research* 62(2): 323–55.

Skocpol, Theda, and Margaret Somers. 1980. "The Uses of Comparative History in Macrosocial Inquiry." *Comparative Studies in Society and History* 22: 174–97.

Smith, Neil. 1984. *Uneven Development: Nature, Capital, and the Production of Space.* Oxford: Basil Blackwell.

———. 1987. "Dangers of the Empirical Turn: The CURS Initiative." *Antipode* 19(1): 59–68.

———. 1992. "Geography, Difference, and the Politics of Scale." In Joe Doherty, Elspeth Graham, and Mo Malek, eds., *Postmodernism and the Social Sciences,* pp. 57–79. London: Macmillan.

———. 1993. "Homeless/Global: Scaling Places." In Jon Bird, Barry Curtis, Tim Putnam, George Robertson, and Lisa Tickner, eds., *Mapping the Futures: Local Cultures, Global Change,* pp. 87–119. New York: Routledge.

Smith, Neil, and Cindy Katz. 1993. "Grounding Metaphor: Towards a Spatialized Politics." In Michael Keith and Steve Pile, eds., *Place and the Politics of Identity,* pp. 67–83. New York: Routledge.

Smith, Rebecca L. 1984. "Creating Neighborhood Identity through Citizen Activism." *Urban Geography* 5(1): 49–70.

———. 1985. "Activism and Social Status as Determinants of Neighborhood Identity." *Professional Geographer* 37(4): 421–32.

Snow, David A., and Robert D. Benford. 1988. "Ideology, Frame Resonance and Participant Mobilization." In Bert Klandermans, Hanspeter Kriesi, and Sidney Tarrow, eds., *International Social Movement Research,* vol 1, *From Structure to Action: Comparing Social Movement Research across Cultures,* pp. 197–217. Greenwich, Conn.: JAI Press.

Snow, David A., E. Burke Rochford Jr., Steven K. Worden, and Robert D. Benford.

1986. "Frame Alignment Processes, Micromobilization, and Movement
Participation." *American Sociological Review* 51: 464–81.

Snow, David A., Louis A. Zurcher Jr., and Sheldon Ekland-Olson. 1980. "Social
Networks and Social Movements." *American Sociological Review* 45: 787–801.

———. 1992. "Master Frames and Cycles of Protest." In Aldon D. Morris and
Carol McClurg Mueller, eds., *Frontiers in Social Movement Theory*, pp. 133–55.
New Haven: Yale University Press.

Soja, Edward. 1989. *Postmodern Geographies.* New York: Verso.

Solo, Pam. 1988. *From Protest to Policy.* Cambridge: Ballinger.

Sommaripa, George. 1990. Director, Interstate Freeze Lobbying Network, telephone
interview by author, author's notes, Cambridge, Massachusetts, August 22.

Staeheli, Lynn A. 1994. "Restructuring Citizenship in Pueblo, Colorado."
Environment and Planning A 26: 849–71.

Staeheli, Lynn A., and Meghan Cope. 1994. "Empowering Women's Citizenship."
Political Geography 13(5): 443–60.

Stefano, Steve. 1993. Executive director, CPPAX, telephone interview by author,
author's notes, Boston, December 13.

Stoecker, Randy. 1995. "Community, Movement, Organization: The Problem of
Identity Convergence in Collective Action." *Sociological Quarterly* 36(1): 111–30.

Stone, Clarence. 1987. "The Study of the Politics of Urban Development." In
Clarence Stone and Heywood Sanders, eds., *The Politics of Uneven Development*,
pp. 2–22. Lawrence: University Press of Kansas.

———. 1991. "The Hedgehog, the Fox, and the New Urban Politics: Rejoinder to
Kevin Cox." *Journal of Urban Affairs* 13(3): 289–97.

Storper, Michael, and Allen Scott. 1989. "The Geographical Foundations and
Social Regulation of Flexible Production Complexes." In Jennifer Wolch and
Michael Dear, eds., *The Power of Geography: Territory Shapes Social Life*,
pp. 19–40. Boston: Unwin Hyman.

Swyngedouw, Erik. 1989. "The Heart of the Place: The Resurrection of Locality in
an Age of Hyperspace." *Geografiska Annaler* 71B: 31–42.

Tarrow, Sidney. 1983. *Struggling to Reform: Social Movements and Policy Change
during Cycles of Protest.* Western Societies Paper No. 15. Ithaca, N.Y.: Cornell
University.

———. 1988. "Old Movements in New Cycles of Protest: The Career of an Italian
Religious Community." In Bert Klandermans, Hanspeter Kriesi, and Sidney
Tarrow, eds., *International Social Movement Research*, vol. 1, *From Structure to
Action: Comparing Social Movement Research across Cultures*, pp. 281–304.
Greenwich, Conn.: JAI Press.

———. 1989. *Struggle, Politics, and Reform: Collective Action, Social Movements, and Cycles of Protest.* Western Societies Program Occasional Paper No. 21. Ithaca, N.Y.: Cornell University.

———. 1991. "Comparing Social Movement Participation in Western Europe and the United States: Problems, Uses, and a Proposal for Synthesis." In Dieter Rucht, ed., *Research on Social Movements: The State of the Art in Western Europe and the USA,* pp. 392–419. Boulder, Colo.: Westview Press.

———. 1996. "States and Opportunities: The Political Structuring of Social Movements." In Doug McAdam, John D. McCarthy, and Mayer N. Zald, eds., *Comparative Perspectives on Social Movements,* pp. 41–61. New York: Cambridge University Press.

Taylor, Charles. 1989. *Sources of the Self.* Cambridge: Harvard University Press.

Taylor, Michael. 1982. *Community, Anarchy, Liberty.* Cambridge and New York: Cambridge University Press.

———. 1987. *The Possibility of Cooperation.* Cambridge and New York: Cambridge University Press.

———. 1988. "Rationality and Revolution in Collective Action." In Michael Taylor, ed., *Rationality and Revolution,* pp. 63–97. Cambridge and New York: Cambridge University Press.

———. 1989. "Structure, Culture, and Action in the Explanation of Social Change." *Politics and Society* 17: 115–62.

———. 1990. "Cooperation and Rationality: Notes on the Collective Action Problem and Its Solution." In Karen Cook and Margaret Levi, eds., *The Limits to Rationality,* pp. 222–39. Chicago: University of Chicago Press.

Taylor, Verta, and Nancy E. Whittier. 1992. "Collective Identity in Social Movement Communities: Lesbian Feminist Mobilization." In Aldon D. Morris and Carol McCurg Mueller, eds., *Frontiers in Social Movement Theory,* pp. 104–29. New Haven: Yale University Press.

Thompson, John. 1983. "Rationality and Social Rationalization: An Assessment of Habermas's Theory of Communicative Action." *Sociology* 17: 278–94.

———. 1990. *Ideology and Modern Culture.* Stanford, Calif.: Stanford University Press.

Thompson, John, and David Held, eds. 1982. *Habermas: Critical Debates.* Cambridge: MIT Press.

Thrift, Nigel. 1983. "On Determination of Social Action in Space and Time." *Society and Space* 1: 23–57.

———. 1985. "Flies and Germs: A Geography of Knowledge." In Derek Gregory and John Urry, eds., *Social Relations and Spatial Structures,* pp. 366–403. London: Macmillan.

Thrift, Nigel, and P. Williams. 1987. "The Geography of Class Formation." In

Nigel Thrift and Peter Williams, eds., *Class and Space: The Making of Urban Society*, pp. 1–22. London and New York: Routledge and Kegan Paul.

Tiffany, Kay. 1990. Board member, Lexington Committee for a Nuclear Weapons Freeze, interview by author, author's notes, Lexington, Massachusetts, August 7.

Tilly, Charles. 1973. "Do Communities Act?" *Sociological Inquiry* 43: 209–40.

———. 1978. *From Mobilization to Revolution*. New York: Random House.

———. 1984. "Social Movements and National Politics." In Charles Bright and Susan Harding, eds., *Statemaking and Social Movements: Essays in History and Theory*, pp. 297–317. Ann Arbor: University of Michigan Press.

Tilly, Charles, and Louise Tilly. 1981. *Collective Action and Class Conflict*. Newbury Park, Calif.: Sage.

Touraine, Alain. 1981. *The Voice and the Eye: An Analysis of Social Movements*. Trans. Alan Duff. New York: Cambridge University Press.

———. 1985. "An Introduction to the Study of Social Movements." *Social Research* 52(4): 749–88.

———. 1992. "Beyond Social Movements." *Theory, Culture, and Society* 9: 125–45.

Tuan, Yi Fu. 1976. "Humanistic Geography." *Annals of the Association of American Geographers* 66(2): 266–76.

———. 1977. *Space and Place*. Minneapolis: University of Minnesota Press.

Unger, Roberto. 1975. *Knowledge and Politics*. New York: Free Press.

Urry, John. 1986. "Locality Research—the Case of Lancaster." *Regional Studies* 20(3): 233–42.

U.S. Bureau of the Census. 1983a. *1980 Census of Population and Housing: Massachusetts*. Washington, D.C.: U.S. Government Printing Office.

———. 1983b. *Current Industrial Reports: Shipments to Federal Government Agencies, 1983*. Washington, D.C.: U.S. Government Printing Office.

———. 1986. *Statistical Abstract of the United States*. Washington, D.C.: U.S. Government Printing Office.

U.S. Bureau of Labor Statistics. 1987. *Handbook of Labor Statistics*. Washington, D.C.: U.S. Government Printing Office.

———. 1991. *Consumer Price Index*. Washington, D.C.: Government Printing Office.

U.S. Department of Defense. 1980–86. *DOD Prime Contract Awards by State, City, and Contractor*. Washington, D.C.: Directorate for Information Operations and Reports.

Useem, Bert. 1980. "Solidarity Model, Breakdown Model, and the Boston Anti-Busing Movement." *American Sociological Review* 45: 357–69.

Wallace, Michael, and J. Craig Jenkins. 1995. "The New Class, Postindustrialism, and Neocorporatism: Three Images of Social Protest in the Western Democracies." In J. Craig Jenkins and Bert Klandermans, eds., *The Politics of Social*

Protest: Comparative Perspectives on States and Social Movements, pp. 96–137. Minneapolis: University of Minnesota Press.

Walsh, Edward. 1981. "Resource Mobilization and Citizen Protest in Communities around Three Mile Island." *Social Problems* 29: 1–21.

Waltham News Tribune. 1982a. "Anti-Nuke Group Takes a Grass-Roots Approach." January 7, p. B1.

———. 1982b. "Council to Consider Nuclear Freeze Vote." October 25, p. A1.

Warde, Alan. 1989. "Recipes for Pudding: A Comment on Locality." *Antipode* 21(3): 274–81.

Warsh, David. 1988. "War Stories: Defense Spending and the Growth of the Massachusetts Economy." In David R. Lampe, ed., *The Massachusetts Miracle,* pp. 314–30. Cambridge: MIT Press.

Webber, Melvin M. 1964. *Explorations into Urban Structure.* Philadelphia: University of Pennsylvania Press.

Wellman, Barry. 1979. "The Community Question." *American Journal of Sociology* 84: 1201–31.

Wiegand, David. 1983. "Cambridge Makes History at the Polls: 'Nuke Free' Trounced; Cable Passes, but Recount Seen." *Cambridge Chronicle,* November 17, pp. 1–11.

Wolch, Jennifer, and Michael Dear. 1989. *The Power of Geography: How Territory Shapes Lives.* Boston: Unwin Hyman.

Wright, Erik Olin. 1978. *Class, Crisis, and the State.* London: Verso.

Yapa, Lakshman S. 1977. "The Green Revolution: A Diffusion Model." *Annals of the Association of American Geographers* 67: 350–59.

Young, Iris. 1986. "Impartiality and the Civic Public: Some Implications of Feminist Critiques of Modern Political Theory." *Praxis International* 5: 381–401.

———. 1990. *Justice and the Politics of Difference.* Princeton, N. J.: Princeton University Press.

———. 1996. "Gender as Seriality: Thinking about Women as a Social Collective." In Ruth-Ellen B. Joeres and Barbara Laslett, eds., *The Second Signs Reader,* pp. 158–83. Chicago: University of Chicago Press.

Zald, Mayer, and John McCarthy. 1980. "Social Movement Industries." *Resources, Social Movements, Conflict and Change* 3: 1–20.

Zald, Mayer N., and Roberta Ash. 1966. "Social Movement Organizations: Growth, Decay and Change." *Social Forces* 44: 327–40.

Index

BYRON A. MILLER is assistant professor of geography at the University of Cincinnati. His research interests include the geographic structuring of social movements, state restructuring, sustainable development, and social theory. He is a board member of the Urban Geography specialty group of the Association of American Geographers.